★ REDWOOD COUNTRY ★

REDWOOD COUNTRY

The Lava Region
and The Redwoods

AMERICAN FOLKWAYS

Edited by Erskine Caldwell

In Preparation

AMERICAN
FOLKWAYS

EDITED BY ERSKINE CALDWELL

REDWOOD COUNTRY

The Lava Region and The Redwoods

BY ALFRED POWERS

DUELL, SLOAN & PEARCE · NEW YORK

CONTENTS

LAVA REGION

LAVA DESERT, by Joaquin Miller

viii   CONTENTS

FOREWORD

REDWOODS AND THE HALTING LAVA

Outside the Circle of Fire stood the sequoias and redwoods—no more sequoias than can be catalogued one by
one, but redwoods beyond individual enumeration by a
gang of timber cruisers in a single lifetime.

Elsewhere even the solid rocks melted, as they will melt
at twelve hundred degrees centigrade. Fluid and bubbling,
they lay upon the earth as water upon a lake bed. They
flowed in wide bands as water in a river channel. They
upheaved into ridges and ranges, into buttes and peaks;
and at a later period these peaks themselves, explosive
underneath their uncooled heat, retched out their stony
insides in crater eruptions.

In all this there was a redwoods sanctuary, untouched,
unburnt, uncovered. It consisted of a narrow fringe beside
the western ocean, no wider than you can drive a car across
in an hour, no longer than you can drive a car through in
a day.

The large area taken in a holocaust greater than John

in Patmos saw; this small area, densely columned with trees, entirely spared. One having to be resurrected from the dead. The other unchanged from its primeval creation, uninterrupted since the first planting, a relic of how fair the earth once was, a pattern for making it fair again.

Violence ceased. But the land had no drainage for the molten flow. It lay in vast plains, finally cold and black. It stretched in congealed streams—one in the region of the Upper Snake is a hundred miles wide, four hundred miles long, only one of many but in its single self larger than the whole redwoods sanctuary. Here underneath a blasted and forbidding surface, five hundred miles away from the nearest living redwood, the paleobotanists, the botanizers in stone, have come upon kinsmen of the redwoods—and sequoias too, companionably fossilized, though they live today mutually aloof, without a single instance of association, a redwood never being found in the dry Sierras, a sequoia never along the foggy coast.

Omnipotence is more prodigal even than the creature made in His image. But both deity and mortal are ceaseless rebuilders out of the desolation they bring. So Omnipotence caused the Snake River of today to flow over the outstretched corpse of that river of fire. He softened its barrenness with vegetation—bunch-grass, sage, and scraggly juniper. He gave it the animation of jackrabbits, coyotes, deer, antelope, and sleek panthers in silhouette upon the rimrock like carved ones at a temple entrance.

And man, on his part, made a national recreation ground out of the most recently exploding peak, so that it and all its ravaged territory became more profitable than if spread out in fields or green meadows. In a number of places he molded and cemented the pumice into bricks for buildings. He used the caves as livestock shelters when warm chinook winds failed to rout the blizzards from the rangelands. One cavern, then as now perpetually heaped with ice, furnished a pioneer saloon-keeper coolness by the wagonload for his drinks in the hot summer weather. Valleys once brimming with lava now grow bread for millions, in soil deep and inexhaustible.

As fencing, the lava saved stockmen miles of juniper posts and barbed wire, an inheritance most used by Pete French, the cattle king, who was forever filling in the gaps of the rimrock—'never saw a rimrock running along a line but what he rode it out with a fence idea in his mind.' He kept happily on till he had enclosed 120,000 acres.

It served to keep men's imaginations fresh and credulous, as in the case of O. M. Rosendale, a mining engineer, traveling alone on horseback in Harney County, Oregon:

> Cliffs of black basaltic formation, without a vestige of vegetation, rose abruptly from the desert and formed a narrow defile. After passing through the defile and leading my wornout horse, I proceeded to scale a hill for the purpose of getting my bearings, as I evidently had lost them for the last six hours. Turning on one point of the hillside, which was half-filled with sand-blown crevices, a strange sight was presented to me. There before me were about sixty-five cliff-dwellers' habitations, deserted of course, but in a fair state of preservation. The clear and unclouded sky was looking upon a picture of queer and very strangely formed small buildings, roofless, bound together with no material whatsoever, but hewn with all the skill of the ancient craftsmen.

The lava preserved gold in a hundred thousand vaults, each vault with more in it than in a national bank. From underneath the slag and scoria was taken out wealth in an amount to change the economy of nations, more than the Spaniards found in all the days of their wide searching. But the hunters of it put a wreckage upon the land itself second only to that of the inundating lava, through which they dug and tunneled to the blue lead where an acreage no bigger than a suburban chicken ranch might yield a million dollars. They left scars less extensive but more dis-

figuring than the ancient fires, which at least gave a
grandeur and a terrible harmony to their desolation.

For a long time it looked as if the redwoods country
would not be profaned by the ruinous hordes flocking into
California, as if they were held back by the same vigilance
that had held back the fires. It was saved from the earliest
exploiters, the fur hunters, because there were no beaver
streams flowing between the colossal boles, and indeed what
beaver could have gnawed a redwood down? The otherwise omnipresent Hudson's Bay Company did not operate
in these umbrageous precincts. There were only otters for
the Russians, but these were out in the harm-proof sea.
Gold likewise glistened only along the ocean, in black sand
upon short segments of non-stony beaches. The absence of
these lures to greedy men guarded this second Eden like
a flaming sword and cherubims.

Humboldt Bay, though known to the old Spanish navigators, was seventy-five years in being rediscovered. Then
this redwoods harbor and the great redwoods river, the
Klamath, were a disappointment and a reproach, for they
were not navigable back into the aurific lava country. The
grandest forest upon the globe did not transfer greed from
gold to itself. Up to this point the eternal protectorate was
still in force.

But the harbor had been found, not leading back into
the rich Trinity Hills, yet opening into an ocean that
washed a thousand shores. Eureka started out to be a second
San Francisco. Hither came ships in ever-larger numbers.
Hence they sailed, and the cargoes they carried then, and
have carried for nearly a hundred years, were the big trees.

The devouring lumbermen had come. The guardianship
that had lasted since the far beginning, had surely ended
now.

But it hadn't. The redwood, though it lives long as if
life were a precious, unrenewable thing, is almost incom-

parable among trees in its self-regeneration. Along the southern highway leading from Route 101 to the Mendocino coast you pass tracts which were logged off in the seventies. You know, because you can read about it in the old magazines of that period. And you can see the stumps by the hundred as you drive along, but you see them amidst another great forest, already with big and lofty columns, phoenix-like.

For more than half a century this remarkable self-restoration quality of the trees themselves was their only important safeguard. Axmen and sawyers found no sanctity to dispute them.

Then, before it was too late, the tourists came, as saviors, not as destroyers. Some of them only bought a few hamburger sandwiches, only stayed one night in an auto camp, only needed a few gallons of gas, but because of their multitudes they left behind an impressive revenue. A standing tree began to have as much value as a sawed-down one; let it stand another three hundred years, as it would probably do if let alone, and the profit on it as something to be looked at would be immeasurably greater than as something to be made into lumber. The tourist's primary interest was in beholding them alive, many of them together in groves, whole congregations of them rising far up toward the white and fretted clouds. He wished his spirit to feel the awe of such venerable age, the refreshment and reassurance of finding them look so young withal—the symbol of man's own utmost search: perpetual life with perpetual youth. This endless procession became a powerful agent of the changed times in the age-old decree of preservation.

Saved from the lava fires. Then for centuries free from the trespass of civilized man, for centuries inhabited by improvident Indians for whom a dozen great trees a year would suffice for all their needs. No beavers, no gold. Intrinsic resurrection. The tourists. All these on the saving side; all these over against the lumberman. Has there been indeed some ordination for not letting perish all this mystery, all this majesty?

In this Folkways volume the redwoods have been given the main place, but they are quite properly followed by substantial attention to the big surrounding lava region, under which no telling how many redwood forests are buried, and with which the redwood country is connected in modern life in a thousand ways.

From a little north of the California line, the main redwood belt of today, in forest density or frequent groves, extends as the crow flies through three degrees of latitude or roughly, as man travels and by their own winding contour, about two hundred and fifty miles and hardly ever being more than thirty-five miles wide. It goes on, archipelago-like, to Mt. Tamalpais, Cahill Ridge, and Santa Cruz.

The original range was pushed back and back when the adobe Spaniards were succeeded by the United States choppers and sawyers and splitters. The southernmost redwood grew twelve miles south of Punta Gorda; the northernmost on the Chetco River of Oregon. In these utmost reaches the redwood belt was five hundred miles long.

The standing timber today is mostly in the three northern California coast counties—Mendocino, Humboldt, Del Norte—and edging over grudgingly into Curry County of Oregon. South of these, Sonoma County is still to be counted in redwoods territory, but not importantly so any more.

This seems to be a pretty large area when you are traveling in it and actually experiencing its distances, but it is small in comparison with the lava region, which, as covered in this volume, includes approximately the northern third of California and the southern third of Oregon, the northern half of Nevada, and the southern half of Idaho.

Altogether, the volume's immense locale extends south

and north along the coast—Route 101—from Russian River
to the Siuslaw River. It goes up the interior valleys along
Route 99, from Yuba City and Marysville to the Calapooya
Mountains south of Cottage Grove. Along the arid thoroughfare east of the Sierras and Cascades—Route 395—it reaches
from Carson City to Burns. From the Nevada capital east,
its southern border lies along Route 50 to the Utah line.
From Burns its northern border runs east to Ontario, Weiser,
Boise, and Idaho Falls, and far out there in Idaho the
smooth, broad pavement of Route 30 may have deep under
it fossil remains of ancestral redwoods.

A NOTE ON SOURCES

———

With avoidance, it is believed, both of postulates and a cumbersome supererogation of credit, in quoting short matter flavoringly rather than documentarily, the narrative has not been impeded by acknowledgments in the text or adventitiously vexed by footnotes or appended references.

Sources of the longer and substantive quotations are indicated, though not always with formal bibliographical fullness.

The whole region covered in this Folkways volume has not previously had a book about it. Parts of it have been put in much paper-bound miscellany; in state, local, and topical works; and most importantly in county histories—thick and heavy quartos teeming with biographies, vanity tomes of another day. But in their bigness is a great deal that is nowhere else and, minus the easily recognizable refrain of eulogy, they are splendidly accurate. A few volumes and large numbers of pamphlets and articles make up the redwood literature, prevailingly of botanical character.

Periodical files have yielded abundantly: *Overland Monthly* (still good for a long time after Bret Harte's departure, with the notable Northern California Indian series by Stephen Powers, and the Big Blue obituary) ; *Hutching's Illustrated California Magazine* and *Sunset* in San Francisco; the *West Shore, Pacific Monthly,* and *Timberman* in Portland; the state historical quarterlies, particularly California's; and a considerable assortment of lesser publications which went along gravely or gaily for a while and then, in the lighthearted necrological parlance of the times, winked out.

Continuous and broken runs of several dozen newspapers which can still be found, are storage bins of first-hand accounts of the area. At Yreka, county-seat of Siskiyou County, is a remarkable archives set-up, where is the largest depository of what was contemporaneously written about Captain Jack and the Modoc War. Its early newspaper files have been preserved to an unusual extent, in wide coverage of northern California and southern Oregon. These, dating back to the 'Fifties, are not kept by the present newspaper, the county historical society, or the city library, but in the county clerk's office in the courthouse, where the accustomed alert courtesies to Siskiyou citizens are equally the writing stranger's. It is a researcher's paradise.

The record of the present and recent has come from travel in most of the region and residence in parts of it; from the Redwood Empire Association, the California Redwood Association, and Save-the-Redwoods League; from local, state, and national government officials; from fifty counties reporting on their kingdom-sized provinces; and from numerous helpful individuals, who also have importantly filled in older gaps and obscurities. Of special assistance were Ella Hendricks, Red Bluff librarian, with data on John Brown's widow; Alfred A. Monner of Portland with the basic version of the Rogue River rolling stone; Emil R. Peterson of Coos Bay with information on ocean log rafts; and Thomas E. Riley of Portland, field work companion over some thousands of miles of redwood and lava country.

REDWOOD COUNTRY

The Lava Region
and The Redwoods

REDWOODS

SONG OF THE REDWOOD TREE

by

Walt Whitman

. . . A murmuring, fateful, giant voice, out of the earth and sky,
Voice of a mighty dying tree in the Redwood forest dense.

Farewell, my brethren,
Farewell, O earth and sky—farewell, ye neighboring waters;
My time has ended, my term has come.

Along the northern coast,
Just back from the rock-bound shore, and the caves,
In the saline air from the sea, in the Mendocino country,
With the surge for bass and accompaniment low and hoarse,
With crackling blows of axes, sounding musically, driven by strong
    arms,
Riven deep by the sharp tongues of the axes—there in the Redwood
    forest dense,
I heard the mighty tree its death-chant chanting.

The choppers heard not—the camp shanties echoed not;
The quick-ear'd teamsters, and chain and jack-screw men, heard not,
As the wood-spirits came from their haunts of a thousand years, to join
    the refrain;
But in my soul I plainly heard.

Murmuring out of its myriad leaves,
Down from its lofty top, rising two hundred feet high,
Out of its stalwart trunk and limbs—out of its foot-thick bark,
That chant of the seasons and time—chant, not of the past only, but
    the future.

You untold life of me,
And all you venerable and innocent joys,
Perennial, hardy life of me, with joys, 'mid rain, and many a summer
    sun,

I

And the white snows, and night, and the wild winds; . . .
Joys of the life befitting me and brothers mine,
Our time, our term has come.

Nor yield we mournfully, majestic brothers,
We who have grandly fill'd our time . . .

Thus, on the northern coast,
In the echo of teamsters' calls, and the clinking chains, and the music
    of choppers' axes,
The falling trunk and limbs, the crash, the muffled shriek, the groan,
Such words combined from the Redwood-tree—as of wood-spirits' voices
    ecstatic, ancient and rustling,
The century-lasting, unseen dryads, singing, withdrawing . . .
The chorus and indications, the vistas of coming humanity—the settle-
    ments, features all,
In the Mendocino woods I caught.

1

THE QUICK AND THE DEAD

DAWN REDWOODS

Dawn Redwoods have been found alive, with green foliage and flowing sap. They were thought to have become extinct in the fifth geological age back, a duration to which the rise and fall of Rome are but a whisper in the dark. To scientific diggers they have been familiar as fossils in the ancient chalks and clays coeval with the remains of forty-foot lizard beasts and great fliers having wings membraneous like a bat's. Such fossil relics have been particularly noted in Japan and Manchuria.

Americans learned in 1948, from the field work of one of their own scholars, of the continuing existence of some Dawn Redwood groves. T. Wang, a Chinese forester, had found the first tree in 1944—standing alone with a temple under it. Despite his work in the woods, his laboratory hours in herbariums, his study of forestry volumes, this tree resembled nothing in his knowledge or in his experience. By the standards to which he was accustomed in his land, it seemed to him of enormous size; it was a hundred feet high.

Two smaller specimens were in the vicinity, near the village of Mo-tao-chi, and that was all.

Fortunate that he was a trained man and carried more away with him than his wonder. He took along some twigs and needles and cones when he went back to Nanking. Forestry Professor W. C. Cheng examined them and studied them. He determined that these in genus and species did not belong to any known tree in the forests of China. But to pronounce something new is sometimes only a disclosure of the frailty of the pronouncer's learning, so an appeal was made to the eminent Dr. H. H. Hu at Peiping.

It wasn't as easy as identifying a man by his finger prints but it was a little like it. Already it had been competently settled that the twigs and needles and cones had no counterpart in herbarium specimens from trees growing anywhere in China. It remained to compare them with extinct specimens. And there they were, as like as two peas. The fossil impressions of twigs and needles and cones in the ancient clays from Manchuria and Japan were as if they had been made by these pluckings so recently brought from the temple tree at Mo-tao-chi. As Dr. Ralph W. Chaney said, "Here was a fossil come to life in the unexplored interior of China."

The Chinese are serene. Scholars are serene. In the double serenity of race and learning, did these men fail to cry out at the tremendous revelation? It is not known, but such a finding of such a continuity of life is recognized among other scholars as one of the most dramatic scientific discoveries of modern times.

Who named the tree? Chinese are not only serene but they are polite. Neither Professor Cheng nor the eminent Dr. Hu thought otherwise than to let humble Forester Wang, the true discoverer, call it what he wanted to. Dawn Redwood is the name he gave it.

The tree also received, and with it the misnamed fossils, a new generic name, *Metasequoia*. Previously all the redwood fossils were accredited to *Sequoia*, for these were considered to be almost exactly like the living redwoods in California. But these Japanese and Manchurian fossils, and the temple tree, have an *opposite* arrangement of twigs and cones, while on *Sequoia sempervirens* it is *spiral*. Another difference is that in the former the cones are attached to the end of naked stalks; in the latter, to needle-bearing twigs.

Such a discovery of another *Sequoia* sanctuary in remote Central China would naturally be of special interest to California. Dr. Chaney, professor of paleontology at Berkeley, organized an expedition to make further searches and investigations of these trees supposedly not existing since man himself existed. He was accompanied by Dr. Milton Silverman, scientific writer for the San Francisco *Chronicle*.

They went by air from San Francisco to Chunking, and thence, after being joined by Chinese scientists, by boat up the Yangtze Kiang to Wan-Hsien. There they left the great river and went south, using sedan chairs and baggage porters. After seventy miles of travel they came to the temple tree which Forester Wang had discovered. When the latter reported it as an enormous tree he was right by almost any standards of judgment, not only by those of wood-poor China. Dr. Chaney found it to be five feet, eight inches through above the buttress, and very close to the hundred-foot height which Wang had claimed. Its branches extended upward instead of downward, as they are familiarly known to do on the California redwoods. In addition, this *Metasequoia* is deciduous; in the winter it sheds its leaves. But it has the characteristic redness of bark, though not in the same degree its characteristic thickness. Any observer who had spent some time in a Mendocino or Humboldt grove could have quickly noted their similarity. Their cones and wood are much the same.

Thirty-five miles of rough traveling brought the party into the Valley of the Tiger and to a grove of over a hundred

Dawn Redwoods, none as big as the temple tree. Dr. Chaney and Dr. Silverman were the first foreigners ever to be seen at the village closest to these trees, so far is this sanctuary off the beaten track.

Dr. Hu and Forester Wang have since sent out search parties, with the result that a tree still bigger than the temple one has been reported, as well as a small grove at a twenty-four-hundred-foot elevation, the other groves being at the four-thousand-foot level.

Rainfall in this Chinese redwoods region is about the same as that at Eureka and Crescent City: fifty inches a year. In its mild, moist climate, and in the mild, moist climate of California, are the earth's only forests of naturally growing redwoods.

The individual Chinese trees were estimated not to be old in comparison with the California redwoods, perhaps five or six hundred years, but they are tremendously important as being a generation of the uninterruptedly oldest race of trees whereof man has knowledge.

The San Francisco *Chronicle* made a grand story of the expedition. The embellishing artwork showed how the Dawn Redwoods must have looked with dinosaurs all about on the ground and with the great batwinged pterodactyls flying overhead.

Dr. Chaney brought back with him four seedlings, ranging from six to sixteen inches high. Some reports have indicated that these were 'deluged with vitamins,' but Dr. Chaney says no chemical treatment has been or will be given the soil, over and above a mulch of conifer leafmold. The seedlings were potted and kept in a lath house on the University of California campus, not to be permanently planted for a year or perhaps two years.

Dr. Chaney also brought back to Berkeley a quantity of seeds and planted them. By the beginning of 1949 he had several hundred seedlings almost as large as the four carried from China, though in all cases with stems less heavy.

(Things Chinese seem to have great power of adjustment. When twenty-six of their pheasants were liberated in Oregon in 1881, they made themselves so immediately at home and multiplied so rapidly that in a dozen years there were more Chinese pheasants in Oregon than in China. The Chinese themselves have survived the vicissitudes of prejudice on the Pacific Coast.)

The *Sequoia sempervirens* in the main lends itself poorly to alien distribution. It has done very well in some sections of Europe and has migrated most successfully of all to New Zealand, where it has forested large tracts to produce a volume comparable to what it does in its native habitat. It dies or becomes an ignobly stunted thing in northern climates. Though flourishing satisfactorily in other parts of California and elsewhere as an ornamental tree, it has not been commercially transferred to other sections of the United States as a lumber tree.

Maybe it will be different with the Dawn Redwood, notwithstanding its limitation to a typical redwood climate in China. At least there is a chance that the several hundred seedlings, beginning so well at Berkeley, might start another great commercial tree in America just as the twenty-six Chinese pheasants in 1881 started one of the nation's principal gamebirds.

FOSSILS UNDER THE LAVA

At the base of Mt. Shasta, the ancient rocks underneath the lava deposits have been found imprinted with redwood cones and leaves. The redwoods' edge is now seventy miles west, but across them to the sea still falls the mountain's sunrise shadow.

To the north across the Siskiyous, around Ashland, fossil branchlets of *Sequoia langsdorfii* have been found in three places. More than a hundred miles still farther north, on the western slope of the Cascades where the lava flow was a thousand feet thick, paleontologists have discovered the *Sequoia angustifolia,* which also has been identified far across the Nevada desert at Elko.

In the Snake River region in southern Idaho, the shales so extensively contain leaves of *Sequoia angustifolia* as to make them seem a characteristic fossil of this Payette formation. Near Hailey, congealed lava spreads out like a black mantle over the level plains. At the base of the flow, in thin beds of tuffs and clays, this characteristic redwood occurs in well-preserved leaves. On the west side of the Owyhee range, but still in the Payette formation, are ancient strata of pure white sandstone and brownish clay. Both hold fossils of the type of *Sequoia gigantea,* but the one in the white sandstone is not the same as the one in the brown clay, which also holds the *Sequoia angustifolia.*

All told, more than two dozen fossil species of *Sequoia* have been identified and named, vestiges of a wide distribution in North America, such as *Sequoia brevifolia* from Alaska, *Sequoia ambigua* from Mexico, and *Sequoia condita* from Kansas.

Two foreign commercial trees—deservedly, because of the color of their lumber—bear the name of redwood: Redwood *Amazonias* and Andaman Redwood. The former has a light-red heartwood, with an orange tinge, and grows in Brazil. The latter has a rich red or crimson wood, streaked with red, and grows in Burma and the Andaman Islands. But neither is botanically related to the *Sequoias.*

PETRIFIED REDWOOD FOREST

In Sonoma County, five miles west of Calistoga and seventy miles north of San Francisco, is the most notable fossil exhibit. It was considered interesting enough by

Robert Louis Stevenson and Benjamin F. Taylor for each of them to put a chapter about it in a book. It hadn't yet been discovered when Bayard Taylor was in the neighborhood in 1859. An old historian, who was writing a very thick volume and couldn't linger, Flaubert-like, over his adjectives, called it 'a curious freak of nature.'

Redwoods, after being felled by the lumbermen, sometimes lie unused for a year or several years, but here they waited for untold centuries to be yarded, waited until quarrymen and not loggers would be the ones to do it if it were finally to be done. Over thirteen million acres of the public domain were homesteaded under the Timber and Stone Act, and of them all what tract was so doubly suitable as this claim taken up by an old Swede sailor?

It is a recumbent forest of stone, of huge down-timber turned to adamant, of petrified redwoods still enormous in their transformation—about a twenty-acre graveyard with upward of three hundred trees 'struck with a rocky immortality.' No top was found silicified, and only a few roots. But old scorchings were preserved upon the boles and whole blocks of charcoal were included in the flinty paralysis. Lumps of the thick bark were left clinging in perpetuated attachment. Altogether, the veins of quartz worked a marvelous verisimilitude. (Although redwoods today are little affected by pests and borers, imbedded in this stony wood have been found several specimens of petrified worms.)

The 'Queen of the Forest' lies in segments, the total of its vertebrae amounting to eighty feet. They are in truth huge cylinders of stone, being four yards through. The 'Monarch' is intact, prostrate upon the hillside for a distance of a hundred and twenty-five feet, with an average diameter of eight feet and with a ring count to show it was a thousand years old when it fell.

If after being covered up they had remained as timber, and rotted away at the rate of an inch-thick sheathing a century, would any of these trees be left now? Even their underground durability had to be given the permanence of rock to endure through all the time they have been there. Yet a visitor in the summer of 1881 declared that he saw marks of an ax upon the stony boles. He believed the chopping had taken place previous to petrification. What made him think so was that the cuts appeared 'at different angles to the grain of the wood.' To him the marks signified that man had dwelt in this California glen before erupting Mount St. Helena devastated the forest, felling the trees in its violence so that all the stony logs point away from it, none toward it. (These strokes of a prehistoric ax were not mentioned by Stevenson a year before, or by Taylor three years before.)

Benjamin F. Taylor, whose poem *The Isle of Long Ago* was a school-reader favorite, and Robert Louis Stevenson are the most famous chroniclers of the Petrified Forest. Taylor's account is the better of the two, both as a job of reporting and of literature.

Taylor's visit was in 1878, Stevenson's in 1880. Both were very much taken with the owner and excavator of the place. 'Petrified Charley,' Taylor called him, 'a tough old sailor aforetime.' He was equipped like Robinson Crusoe, except for a man Friday. He had a dog 'Rascal,' and a 'venerable, inquisitive and aggressive goat "Billy."' He said the logs were the old man's breadwinners: 'He pinches in an affectionate way the corrugated bark of these tumbled monoliths. . . . He picks up a few little stone chips and gives you [them], but he is prudent, for he sees thousands like yourself who will come for more chips.'

Stevenson put in some dialogue:

' "Who first found the forest?"

' "The first? I was that man," said he. "I was cleaning up the pasture for my beasts, when I found *this*"—kicking a great redwood, seven feet in diameter.

' "Were you surprised?"

' "Surprised? No! What would I be surprised about? What did I know about petrifactions—following the sea? I thought it was a stone; so would you, if you was cleaning up a pasture." '

Charley had a sign like an inn's. It said: *The Petrified Forest. Proprietor: C. Evans.* He sold petrifactions and photographs, and charged a half-dollar admission fee. An 1881 visitor found that Petrified Charley had just died.

'Altogether,' said Taylor, 'to a thoughtful man, the Petrified Trees are the most impressive things in California. They overwhelm your vanity with gray cairns of what once danced in the rain, whispered in the wind, blossomed in the sun. . . . What a rocking of the cradle there must have been when the earth quaked, and lava put these trees in flinty armor, and transfused their veins with dumbness.'

Stevenson found the old ex-sailor unearther of the trees more interesting than the trees themselves, and gave him more wordage than the latter. 'And the forest itself?' he rhetorically asked. 'There lie scattered thickly various lengths of petrified trunk. It is very curious, of course, and ancient enough, if that were all. Doubtless, the heart of the geologist beats quicker at the sight; but, for my part, I was mightily unmoved.'

There is now a movement to place the Petrified Forest in the keeping of the public as one of the California state parks. Of it Dr. Chaney says, 'This is the only known area where large numbers of fossil Coast Redwoods occur in immediate association with living redwoods.'

Meanwhile the gigantic corpses are privately owned, as they were by Charley Evans.

2

HEE-LI—DISCOVERER OF AMERICA

———————

GET READY for the year 1983.
You don't recall being drilled upon any important date '83
in school? Anyway, better get ready for it. In that year out
will go Columbus, out of the text books and out of national
observances. Out will go Leif Ericsson, the Norseman. We've
been honoring them for something they didn't do. In 1983
we'll celebrate the 2200th anniversary of the original discovery of America.

And the true discoverer will come into his own—Hee-li
of China.

This old celestial landed upon the California shore, and
if he didn't anchor in front of a grove of big trees, he un-
doubtedly saw a good deal of the redwoods in the three
months he was curiously and energetically poking about. He
ran head-on into the American continent between the thirty-
sixth and thirty-seventh degrees north latitude, probably in
Monterey Bay.

Padre Juan Crespi, on the Portola expedition in the fall
of 1769, traveled through a forest of reddish-colored trees
along the banks of the Pajaro River, near modern Watson-
ville. He called them *Palo colorado,* which means he called

them in his Spanish tongue 'redwood.' Fremont in 1846 is said to have made his headquarters in the capacious hollow of one of the Santa Cruz big trees. Here Archibald Menzies, the botanist with Captain George Vancouver, collected in 1792 the first scientific redwood specimen; it may still be seen in the herbarium of the British Museum. Then there is the Big Basin Redwood State Park, with the 'Mother of the Forest' three hundred and twenty feet high.

So Hee-li landed right among the redwoods. The time was June—precisely the tenth of that month—in 217 B. C.

Perhaps the best way to establish the date in terms of familiar history is to point out that while Hee-li was coming to the redwood coast of California, Hannibal was invading Rome in the Second Punic War, having come across the Alps the year before with his elephants. Think of Hee-li as a contemporary of Hannibal.

Hee-li and his pigtailed crew of ten men stayed in America for three months, from June tenth to the early part of September. He went south fifty miles and north a hundred. He bartered with the natives. He explored San Francisco Bay, to which he gave the name *Hong-Tsi,* meaning 'Great Bay.' In his own personal narrative of the voyage he extolled California's glorious climate (its perfection being thus recognized by the first civilized man to experience it).

Please don't picture Hee-li as trim and neat in sailor's clothes. He was a mariner, as any observing person would have noticed, having a sea-grown look and being definitely a tarry old Chinaman, but he wore 'blue cotton trousers baggy at the knees, a trifle wider than his jacket sleeves.' Withal, he was imperious as became a sea-captain, and it would have been better for him, as will duly appear, if he had been less so.

Now how did he get across the Pacific Ocean from China to the redwoods coast? Did he find himself in a rudderless junk that drifted along the well-known current in the way that caused other prehistoric visits from the Orient to the west coast of America?

Nothing of the kind. He sailed with definite intent, though he had no notion of discovering anything. He was trying to get home. You see, there was a little mistake.

It was the compass. Hee-li owned and was the captain of a small coast-trade junk. In the winter of 217 B. C. apparently in February, a terrible storm assailed his vessel and he was driven far out to sea amidst waves that rose up like the ridges of mountains. But the junk was a sturdy craft and weathered the gale. When the winds ceased, Hee-li headed for home, or thought he did. China, of course, was west. It was a simple matter of steering in that direction. He set his course by the compass.

But the China shores did not come in sight. Day after day they sailed and there was nothing except the wide-spreading surface of the sea. The great storm must have driven them a long distance in a short time.

You probably have known persons who banked absolutely on science and listened to nothing contrary to its evidence. Hee-li was such a one. He would not for a moment doubt the compass. That instrument represented infallible truth. Human observation was too often mere illusion.

What Hee-li didn't know was that something dreadful had happened to the compass. He was aware that his junk was infested with *yangi-si* bugs, something like our cockroaches. What junk wasn't? But he hadn't the least idea that one of these insects during the storm had got into the compass and utterly demoralized its magnetic pointings. The beetle, finding itself in that scientific imprisonment, lost all presence of mind and rushed about frantically over the face of the compass. The needle, of course, followed this animated loadstone. There was only one needle in the ancient Chinese compass: This always pointed south, the other directions being determinable from it. It was known as the 'South

Pointing Chariot.' Well, this single needle followed the bewildered bug all around the circle until the insect finally gave up the ghost. The needle that hovered over him pointed north when this happened. And the dead bug's corpse got wedged under the needle, which therefore stayed over him at north and never went back to south where it belonged and where Hee-li thought it was, for the *yangi-si* cockroach was completely concealed so as not to be detected by the slanting eyes of Hee-li or the slanting ones of the steersman.

Since the needle pointed north and Hee-li thought it was south, he was actually sailing east when all the time he imagined he was headed west toward home. No wonder he didn't come in sight of the China shore.

But day after day the sailors noticed something decidedly at odds with nature. According to the way they were sailing, the sun rose in the west and set in the east, quite contrary to the well-known habits of that great orb. They faced it every morning; it was at their back every afternoon.

After they had been voyaging twenty-five days one of the sailors screwed up enough courage to go to Hee-li. This before-the-mast fellow was Hi-thino.

He made a respectful obeisance and said, "Most Honorable and Worthy Captain, your humble servant asks permission to speak of something he has observed."

"Speak, Hi-thino," said the captain, "but express it within short length."

"The sun, Honorable and Worthy Master, have you not noticed it?"

"Not particularly. What of it?"

"Will my Greatly Respected Overseer look at it now?"

Hee-li's gaze was brief; quickly it became a questioning and intimidating stare fastened upon the sailor, who inquired, "Isn't it morning now, Illustrious Commander?"

"Cease your inane questions, Hi-thino. Has your mind

become diseased? Of course it is morning. I have just had my breakfast."

"You sail east, Benignant Sir; it is morning, yet you face the sun. Is it natural for this to rise differently from what it does in China? Worthy and Honorable Captain, permit your servant who bows before you in respect, permit him to ask if the compass might not tell us just the opposite of what is true and we are sailing east?"

"Impudent one, fit for dragon's food," cried Hee-li, "you come here brazenly to tell your captain in what direction to navigate his ship? Do you see this compass? Haven't we always sailed by it? Hasn't it always guided us right? Haven't my ancestors used it since the dynasty of the grandfather of our All Powerful Emperor Ching-Wa Wang? Dog of a sailor, for all this disrespect you will die."

Whereupon the captain picked up Hi-thino and tossed him overboard.

The other ten sailors looked in one another's faces and thereafter in silence accepted the direction, notwithstanding it remained contradictory to what was said by the sun in their eyes. After ninety-five more days, one hundred and twenty in all, they saw an unmistakable blur of land. So the captain had been right after all. Hi-thino had deserved to be sunk in the sea.

But when they came ashore they found a peculiar country. It was a gracious region, with perfect weather, and with those great trees. But assuredly they had never before visited this particular section of the China coast.

Two days after reaching Monterey Bay one of the sailors was put to work polishing the compass. This man discovered the dead *yang-si* bug. He respectfully summoned the captain. Upon the latter's orders, he removed the corpse, and lo, the needle swung to the opposite direction from where it had been, trembled, and stayed there.

"Hi-thino," said Hee-li contritely to that one's undersea ghost, "too short with you was your master's patience."

The captain knew then that this wasn't China and that they had sailed four months east, four months away from home. They prepared for the long trip back. Meanwhile they looked further into this delightful country, remarking they wouldn't mind settling here if it weren't so far from civilization. They spent a very pleasant three months with the friendly natives and in the transcendent weather.

Hee-li may not have kept a regular log, but he wrote an account of his voyage. This got filed away in the archives of Si-Ngan-Foo, and became forgotten, as has been the fate of many old manuscripts in such depositories. Besides, while from an American point of view it was an important document, the Chinese looked at it as just another reminiscence of a junk captain. He hadn't made special mention of the big trees he had seen, so his report was not valuable industrially for starting lumber import; besides, China had similar trees, as shown by the recent discovery of the Dawn Redwoods. The Chinese ones were less giant-like but the wood was the same, and the ancient cabinetmaker apparently didn't care, anymore than the modern one does, whether his lumber is from a big tree or a little one as long as a plank is large enough to serve his purpose.

To be sure, the *yangi-si* bug's corpse playing havoc with compass directions was an amusing incident, no doubt repeated by pigtailed idlers around Si-Ngan-Foo for a while, but humor is not a lasting thing, gathering reproach the older it gets. So Hee-li joined his ancestors in six feet of precious Chinese soil, and passed out of the memories of men. And what was in the archives was not a matter of curiosity. But a good thing about archives is that documents are added but never taken away; they are not recurrently cleaned out to the grief of history, as are the green and neatly upstanding depositories in a modern office.

So, while nobody ever looked at Hee-li's chronicle, it stayed there very safely through twenty-one long centuries, becoming in all conscience a dusty record.

It was not found till Benjamin Harrison was president.

Si-Ngan-Foo stands on the Hoang-ho in the province of Shen-see. There in 1890 went Dr. Shaw, the eminent missionary to China, who had strong predilections for research. Whether, after all, there had persisted some word-of-mouth tradition about Hee-li or whether the good doctor had just counted on happening upon a thing or two of interest, he headed for the archives. The nearby mission station of Ta-Koo furnished a converted native as his assistant.

The two zealous rummagers found the manuscript of Hee-li, telling of his voyage to California and the redwoods two and a half times as many years before Leif Ericsson as Leif was before Columbus. It was a discovery of the first order, and apparently Dr. Shaw was not troubled by any prospect of public doubt, for, after all, he was a reverend gentleman whose word was used to being accepted.

And, in the days of Benjamin Harrison, the world was not such a know-it-all place as it was to become with radio and airplanes. Dr. Shaw had his account published in a great New York newspaper; the editor in printing it did not put a bracketed piece in small type at the head warning the readers to believe it at their own risk.

It seems to have created little or no stir one away or the other, either of incredulity or of propaganda to replace Ericsson and Columbus with Hee-li in the schoolbooks.

In time, however, some scholars were to insist that Hee-li's voyage is quite apocryphal. One of them explained that the Chinese did not make use of compasses at sea until 600 A. D. Another has patronizingly remarked, 'The Hee-li narrative is an amusing example of unfounded fact masquerading as history.'

Mostly the old celestial navigator's trip has been ignored.

No specific Chinese voyage of antiquity has ever been accepted, but the probability of such voyages in general has been extensively admitted by historians. In the eighteenth and nineteenth centuries, as authentic records show, at least sixty Oriental crafts were driven across the Pacific Ocean. One responsible investigator said: 'There exist Chinese remains proving almost conclusively that the Chinese had appeared on our coast sometime in the dim reaches of the past. A large number of Chinese implements and coins have been found while excavating.'

But this evidence does not apply concretely to Hee-li. Nothing has been found in the redwoods that might have been left by him and his crew. If he was not an individual actuality, he still stands as a symbol of the thirty or so junk captains who may reasonably have drifted across the Pacific each century before recorded history, at the same rate as they definitely did in the last two centuries.

But before too summarily and cavalierly dismissing Hee-li and his sponsor, Dr. Shaw, who may have had his tongue in his cheek as even reverend gentlemen sometimes do, it is at least proper to ask why a doubting scholar has seemingly never gone to Si-Ngan-Foo to check up on Hee-li's log. Presumably if it stayed there from 217 B. C. to 1890 A. D. it would have remained from 1890 to now, even amidst the Chinese turmoil.

If the manuscript is there, and its contents are substantially as reported, then let the Scandinavian elements in behalf of Leif Ericsson and the Latin elements in behalf of Columbus be quiet, while a big nick is put in the glory of those two. Let the 2200th anniversary of Hee-li's discovery of America be observed throughout the nation in 1983, with a very special series of commemorative events in the redwoods country. The Chinese for the celebrations will have to be largely imported from San Francisco, for the redwoods have never been much of a Chinese stronghold.

3

KINGDOM OF QUIVIRA

———————

TWENTY-THREE miles south of the Coquille River, in the Oregon region of Port Orford cedar and myrtlewood, along the ocean on the Coast Highway—Route 101—you cross the small stream of Sixes River. A mile farther on, a side road leads to the right for five and a half miles to Cape Blanco, which juts far out toward where the sun goes down. You continue south through Port Orford, Gold Beach, and Brookings (on the Chetco River, northernmost reach of the redwoods, here six miles from the California line but farther from it inland where the trees grow). Soon on Route 101 you drive in among them, instantly getting and sharply losing the sense of their presence as almost at once you emerge, in a passage no longer than in and out of a highway tunnel, for these first ones are but a clump which have survived a terrible fire. On through Crescent City, up from its flatness onto the heights, winding among the big columns to the broad Klamath; through Trinidad, drowsy in its antiquity, through Arcata smelling of fresh sawdust and the fresh sea. Then through Eureka and out of it fifteen miles to a turn-off, thirty-five miles in all, to another far out-thrusting headland—Cape Mendocino.

You have been traveling—probably without knowing it —along the ocean edge of the fabulous Kingdom of Quivira. It includes all the redwood country except the most southern groves.

Old maps, made before the Pilgrims came to Plymouth Rock, located this kingdom in the region now occupied by northern California and southern Oregon. For two centuries it was put down on charts, atlases, and globes by renowned cosmographers on the strength of voyages which were never made, and of their own exuberant fancies. It was boldly set forth on Mercator's map in 1569. It appeared with remarkable persistence on others in 1570 (Ortelius), 1582 (Lok), 1587 (Hakluyt), 1592 (Plancius), 1597 (Wytfliet-Ptolemy), 1600 (Hondius), 1630 (Teixeira), 1637 (D'Avity), 1671 (Ogilby), 1750 (Delisle). Thus the widely-respected cartographers of various nations dwelt in factual terms with a myth, keeping the redwoods twice as long in the realm of Quivira as they have been in Del Norte, Humboldt, and Mendocino counties of California.

Quivira, the capital city, was located on the coast, usually in the neighborhood of Cape Mendocino. It was on a bay at the mouth of a big river. Far up this river was another important city, called Tuchano. South of Quivira, on the coast, was Cicuic, and south of it was Tiguex.

In addition to the maps, we have some quaint records, including one by Richard Hakluyt, who wrote as follows three-hundred-sixty years ago:

> ... and Francis Vasquez went to Tiguex, which standeth on the banke of a great river. There they had newes of Axa and Quivira. There they sayde was a King whose name was Tatarrax, with a long beard, horie headed. . . . They determined to goe thither, with intention to winter in so rich a countrey as that was reported to bee. . . .
>
> Quivira is in fortie degrees: it is a temperate countrey, and hath very good waters, and much grasse, plummes, mulberries, nuts, melons and grapes. . . . They apparell

themselves with oxe-hides and deeres skinnes. They sawe shippes on the sea coast, which bare Alcatrarzes or Pellicanes of golde and silver in their prows, and were laden with marchandises, and they thought them to be of Cathaya, and China, because they shewed our men by signes that they had sayled thirtie dayes.

This city of Quivira on the coast of northern California and southern Oregon was the same town you may perhaps have read about in United States history books in school. Originally it was located far in the interior, northeast of Santa Fe, possibly in southern Kansas. You will recall that Coronado went north from Mexico in 1540. He found that the Seven Cities of Cibola didn't amount to much, and that Quivira was an ordinary Indian wigwam village, not grand, not rich. The old mapmakers moved it over to the coast, and kept it there for two centuries, and the old chroniclers glorified it and wove mysteries about it and excited the imaginations of men.

Maldonada, one of these old liars, said that in 1588 he had gone a large number of leagues through the Strait of Anian: 'We concluded that continuing we might soon reach Quivira and Cape Mendocino.'

Torquemado said of Martin d'Aguilar that he ran before the wind and anchored near Cape Mendocino, and later discovered a rapid and abundant river which the strong current kept him from entering: 'It is supposed that this river is the one leading to a great city . . . and that the city called Quivira is in these parts.'

Truthful Coronado, in a letter to the Mexican viceroy in the summer of 1540, speaks of a map he had made. Cabrillo, who sailed up the coast in 1542, must also have made one. Yet the cartographers, without the sobering use of these maps, indulged in a great deal of pure fancy.

Gomara, in a book published in 1552, was the first one to move Quivira from the Great Plains to the coast of northern California in the redwoods country.

Quivira was created in an age as daringly mendacious as it was daringly alive—in the flood tide of men's spirits overflowing all the new real discoveries into endlessly imagined marvels. The actual voyaging of the *Golden Hind* did not lay the myth; Edward Wright's 1598 map named Drake as one of the sources; yet Quivira was still there in its old location near Mendocino, and New Albion was north of it.

Drake indeed stimulated a notable piece of invention, Lord Bacon's philosophical romance *New Atlantis,* one of the celebrated Utopias, with its Bensalem probably located in the redwoods country. (In this work published in 1629 is an Iron Curtain curiously familiar three and a quarter centuries later. Bensalem knew all about the rest of the world, which knew nothing about Bensalem. At regular intervals Bensalemites were sent out for observation sojourns in other nations, but during nineteen centuries only thirteen foreign visitors went back home with reports on Bensalem, and the Bensalemite authorities unworriedly figured these reports would not be believed anyhow.)

As late as 1603 the king of Spain and the viceroy of Mexico sent a navigator up the coast to find Quivira. Cabrillo was the one dispatched, with two ships and carrying secret instructions to that effect. Padre Ascension claims to have known about these confidential orders. Said he:

> Philip III found among his father's secret papers a sworn declaration that some foreigners had given him in which it is stated that they had seen and discovered some notable things, on passing through the Strait of Anian, where they were driven in a ship by the great force of continual winds. In this they relate how they passed from the North Sea to the South Sea by this strait, and that, while searching for shelter from the storm, they entered a copious river, on which they came in sight of a populous and rich city named Quivira, well filled with civilized, courteous and very literate people wearing clothes, and well fortified and surrounded by a wall. It was in the latitude of 40°, almost

on the same parallel and in the same neighborhood as *Cobo* Mendocino, which the ships came to sight in sailing from the Philippines to New Spain. Other particulars were contained in this declaration worth finding out and even investigating. All this moved his Majesty to make every effort to find out about such a famous city and discover its situation.

In the general latitude of Cape Mendocino the good padre reported that, notwithstanding every effort, no trace could be found of the rich capital. He declared:

> No news nor signs of the City of Quivira could be had during the whole course of the exploration . . . although some have thought that this Rio de Santa Inez [probably Mad River] is the one that reaches that city.

Cape Mendocino, approximate locality of the kingdom's capital, was pictured by the padre as no less than a place distilling death in its fogs and winds. The Philippine galleons on their return to Acapulco hit the coast in this region. Sight of land after all the leagues across the Pacific ought to have made the mariners glad. But when their eyes beheld Cape Mendocino, or some place in that latitude, a terrible sickness seized them. A man's whole body grew at once so sore 'that there was no relief except cries and groans.' Next came purple spots larger than great mustard seeds. Then bands two fingers wide appeared at the joints, hardening like stone to make the legs and thighs stiff and straight and setting them inflexibly in the position they were when attacked. There was no consolation except to ask God to help him or take him mercifully away from such an afflicted life. Sailor after sailor suddenly died, even while talking.

From this Cape Mendocino pestilence, solemnly declared the padre, resulted nearly all the deaths that took place in the crossing from the Philippines. The disease struck down more than forty men of Cabrillo's own fleet.

The report, in the digest of it here, is much less vivid than in the fullness of the friar's telling. These strange and destructive miasmas of Cape Mendocino increased the mystery of Quivira, whereof hoaryheaded Tatarrax was king.

The moderns who live in the vicinity of that northern California headland, especially Eureka—the present-day city of Quivira—will no doubt be surprised to hear their climate was once as noxious as the good padre reported it, when it is so salubrious now.

Actually, however, Cape Mendocino is almost startling as a dividing point. This great headland, making a change in the direction of the coastline, affects the character of the winds, the swell, the temperature. In January of 1886 a southwester registered a velocity of one hundred forty-four miles an hour. The great Pacific swell in heavy southerly weather causes the sea to break in nine fathoms. The water is nearly the same temperature as it is many leagues to the north at the Strait of Juan de Fuca, whence sometimes a vessel will carry clear weather all the way till running into dense fogs at Cape Mendocino and having them on into San Francisco.

So, after all, Cape Mendocino is rather a peculiar place, and the Spaniards three centuries ago in the simplicity of their living would have noticed things in nature concealed from our sophisticated awareness—and a little superstition, stimulated by the real singularity of this great promontory, could have made it into a suitable region for such a kingdom as Quivira.

For the long period of two hundred years the mythical realm remained upon the maps. So persistent is the hold of fable that down to about 1750 some men still believed that the Kingdom of Quivira—*Quivira Regnum*—actually existed. Today the territory of that long-imagined dominion is the Redwood Empire, exciting now with its forests, as it once did with its mystery, the imaginations of men.

4

TRINIDAD ADVENTURERS

THE YEAR was 1775. On the other side of the continent the settlers were getting ready to fight the Revolutionary War.

It was 1775 and the frugal king of Spain had finally decided to spend some of his own money to explore the west coast of America. Unable to get action out of the Mexican viceroy, he had sent over six naval officers to San Blas. It was their business to find out about the country northward.

Could the viceroy at least furnish chaplains?

Well, it was hard for him to do so, because there was a definite shortage of clergymen around San Blas.

Then he thought of the College of San Fernando—why couldn't it furnish the necessary quartette of padres? The school's guardian demurred. The proper function of the institution was to train missionaries, not sailors. The viceroy then put the voyages in the worthy light of converting heathen. So the guardian detailed four unwilling friars to act as chaplains on the four vessels of the fleet.

The friars were Miguel de la Campa, Benito Sierra, Ramon Usson, and Vicente Santa Maria. They had little zeal at the start, still less when the voyages were over, begging then to be excused from further spiritual activity on the ocean waves. And those first marine experiences might well have seemed to them enough, and more than enough. They did naught for the heathen but had their Christian hands full doing things for the Spaniards.

Friar Usson had little reason to complain, being back among the brethren by the middle of June. But Friar Santa Maria on the *San Carlos* had a terrible time. His ship's commander—one of the six the king had sent over—went as mad as a hatter, arming himself with a whole half-dozen loaded pistols in the crazy belief that everybody was against him, including the trembling chaplain. But, when transferred to another ship, the madman made it almost as bad for Friar Campa by trusting him and no one else and refusing to let him out of sight the whole night long. The only way poor Campa could get free to say mass at daybreak was to promise that Friar Sierra would take up the vigil in his place. (These two Franciscans, Campa and Sierra, before the voyage was over also had to pray for a Spanish sailor who ran off into the redwoods and presumably became a heathen and the father of heathens.)

The ship *Santiago* and the schooner *Sonora* were the ones charged with the actual work of exploring. The *Santiago*, with Campa as chaplain, was the ship of Captain Heceta, who has come down in history as a pretty important man in Spanish navigation. The thirty-six-foot-long schooner, with Sierra as chaplain, was captained by Bodega y Quadra and piloted by Lieutenant Maurelle.

The vessels went on to forty-two degrees north latitude—about the present California-Oregon line—where the charts said Aguilar had discovered the mouth of a river in 1603. Heceta expected so permanent a thing as a broad stream still to be there, though no other white man had set eyes on it during that intervening century and three-quarters.

The *Santiago*, towing the *Sonora*, came close into the

shore at forty-two degrees. It was June 7, 1775. No river.
The ships cruised south for two days. At forty-one degrees
and six minutes they found a good anchorage in calm waters
protected by a lofty headland.

This bold point was being discovered for the third time.
Sebastian Carmeno, a little-known Portuguese voyager, had
found it in 1595 but had mistakenly called it Cape Mendocino. Vizcaino in 1603 had also put it down as Cape Mendocino on his chart, whereon he additionally indicated a large
bay to the south which could scarcely be other than the
present Humboldt Bay. Pilot Maurelle, checking the latitude he saw on the Vizcaino chart, told Heceta that the sea-
swept mountain was the Cabo Mendocino of Vizcaino, or at
least it ought to be. So this was its third discovery. (A long
time later there was to be a fourth, more difficult and more
exciting than any of the others.)

On June 11th they took possession for the Spanish king
with a ceremony as duly prescribed by then as good manners
at table. And it had changed from Balboa's wading ritual. It
took place on the summit of the headland—Father Sierra
said on 'top of the hill,' Pilot Maurelle said on top of the
mountain. There they carried and set up the holy cross. As
they climbed, both padres chanted *Te Deum Laudamus.*
They unfurled the Spanish flag. The men fired a volley from
their muskets; the ships saluted with the cannon. Friar
Campa said mass and preached a sermon. Then he admonished the Indians to let the cross stay there, never to take it
down.

The natives were numerous, (the Yuroks, who had a big
village nearby). They were friendly. And they were not
timid. They put their fingers in the cooks' dishes of mussels.
They wondered if these bearded beings were people—and
what was it that made them wonder? Not the imposing
ceremony on the headland, not the ships, not the guns. It
was the fact that these strangers showed no interest in their

squaws—*prima facie* evidence to these simple savages that these Spaniards weren't mortal. (Padre Sierra, noting this in his diary, quickly defended the crew from any derogatory impressions by explaining it was due to Captain Heceta's non-fraternization order.)

The ships spent a week there. The savages were sad when these sailed away on June 19, 1775. They were never visited again, so far as anyone knows, by a Spanish ship. But a Spaniard stayed with them. Two sailors had deserted on June 14th. One, becoming lonesome or something, but claiming he was hungry, returned two days later. The other went out for good among the big trees, where all the police in Spain could not have found him. It is supposed that he saw a comely young Yurok squaw and that he let the Indians know there was at least one man in this crew of one hundred and six.

'The day being the feast of *Santisima Trinidad,*' the Spaniards named the place Trinidad—El Puerto de la Trinidad. The stream which they could see from the top of the headland—the Little River of today—they called Rio de las Tortolas.

Heceta's men did not fail to notice the enormous size of the trees. Said Padre Sierra: 'Near the river the party came across one very thick and very tall which out of curiosity they measured, finding it to be over forty-seven yards in height.' Said Pilot Maurelle: 'The hills were covered with very large, high and straight pines, amongst which I observed some one hundred and twenty feet high.' (What Senor Maurelle actually wrote was *sestenta varas,* more properly meaning sixty yards, or one hundred and eighty feet, but the translator, unfamiliar with the redwoods, evidently deemed the figures unreasonable and an exaggeration.)

Seventy-two years passed and there was an announcement mentioning Trinidad in a San Francisco paper. The next year, 1848, there were San Franciscan plans to go there, but before these materialized the discovery of gold caused Trinidad to fade out of the interests of men. Then, not quite two years later, gold caused it to leap back into their interests. Was there such a place? It was not uncommon to hear of locations on old charts and this might be as mythical as the rest. Certainly the earliest voyages to find it were without results. The following contemporary verses are satiric of the Trinidad excitement:

> *Ere long the country was o'errun,*
> *And gold could not be had,*
> *And many people then began*
> *To talk of 'Trinidad.'*
>
> *And some affirmed that they had seen*
> *A man, who heard one say*
> *He knew a person who had been*
> *In sight of that same bay.*
>
> *The story spread like any lie,*
> *A party sailed in haste,*
> *But soon returned—the reason why,*
> *They could not find the place.*

Trinity River gold diggers had to have their supplies brought by pack train all the way from Shasta City. Trinity River was thought to flow into Trinidad Bay. Find the latter and vessels could come far up the river toward the mines.

But why didn't somebody step forward who had unmistakably seen Trinidad Bay? Nobody did. A good many ships had passed up and down the coast from California to Oregon, yet there was no mariner to say he had ever set eyes on Trinidad Bay. A few stealthy fur traders and others had gone along the margin of the ocean on horseback or afoot —where was one of them to testify? The only evidence of its existence was a name some Spaniards had put down on a chart three-quarters of a century before.

All those California adventurers who invested so many ships and so much time and such a quantity of imagination seemed to be poor historical investigators. Either that or oldtime records were very scarce around San Francisco at the time.

Pilot Maurelle's journal had been translated from Spanish and published long before in English. Vancouver, the British explorer, had gone to Trinidad in 1793, eighteen years after Heceta. On top of the headland the English sailors found the wooden cross which Friar Campa and Friar Sierra had placed there. The Indians had duly observed the former padre's injunction to let it remain always, never to take it down. Had the deserting Spaniard been partly responsible for its preservation?—in his lonely hours, when a dusky wife and half-dusky children could not entirely console his heart, had he been accustomed to kneel there? In any case, he did not show up and ask for passage back to civilization; Vancouver made no mention of seeing him or any halfbreeds. The cross was by now 'in a certain state of decay,' but the inscription was still legible and one of Vancouver's men copied it: *Carolus III. Dei G. Hyspaniarum Rex.*

The Trinidad hunters of San Francisco had apparently never heard, either, of a certain contraband Yankee fur trader, an old smuggler by the name of Jonathan Winship who had spent twelve days at Trinidad in 1806 with a crew of Aleutians, hunting sea-otters for the Russians.

These two voyages, which should have made the finding of Trinidad sure, had passed into oblivion as far as the new crowd of explorers was concerned. But they probably had two recently published maps, Wyld's English map of 1845 and Mitchell's American map of 1846, both of which showed Trinidad as big as life on the northern California coast. The Trinidad adventurers, however, would have suspected that Wyld and Mitchell had put down the place on the strength of old Spanish authority and nothing else, and they knew that ships between Oregon and California—frequent since the Gold Rush—had time and again gone right by where Trinidad Bay was supposed to be without ever seeing it. The place had a will-o'-the-wisp quality; they looked for it without being absolutely certain that it even existed.

Still, the stakes were big. If Trinidad Bay could be found, what a bonanza in real estate! A city would spring up to rival San Francisco. And the men who got there first would be the ones with the town lots to sell.

Some men came down to San Francisco from the Trinity River mines in November, 1849, and chartered the *Cameo*, in which they made a voyage up the coast in December. They found no Trinidad Bay.

Two months later, in February of 1850, two other vessels went up there. They too were unsuccessful. Then in March the *Cameo* went back. The hunt was warming up. That same month not less than eleven other vessels went up to explore. Among these were the *Laura Virginia, California,* and *General Morgan.*

On March 16th one of the *Cameo* boats landed a party near Trinidad Head. Bad weather caused the ship to put out to sea. The shore party meanwhile discovered the elusive bay, snugly hidden behind two long sandspits and connected by a slender stem to the ocean. The *Laura Virginia* sailed along, seeing beyond the sandhills a strip of water that looked as if it might be a bay but unable to locate an entrance. The ship proceeded slowly, her captain increasingly uneasy at leaving that strip of water behind. When he too reached Trinidad Head he put a party ashore to find out if that had been the bay back there; he would pick them up in ten days if not signaled for earlier. As the *Laura Virginia* cruised outside, the *California* also appeared, and the original *Cameo* boat crew went out and piloted them both in. Later the *General Morgan* arrived. The *Cameo* itself did not return for some time.

The searchers learned that Trinidad Bay, which all of a sudden was so thoroughly found, had actually been discovered three months before by an overland party. On that March day in 1850 they saw a recent carving on a redwood tree:

Lat. 41° 3′ 32″
Barometer 29° 86
Ther. Fah. 48° at 12 N
Dec. 7, 1849   J. Gregg

J. Gregg, the real discoverer, was Josiah Gregg, medical doctor and author of a frontier classic, *Commerce of the Prairies*.

In the early part of November, 1849, he had set out with a party of seven men from the Trinity River mines, down the river to its supposed outlet into Trinidad Bay. The trip was slow and full of hardships. Friendly Indians said they would surely find unfriendly ones lower down the river, and advised them to strike out straight west across the ridges and through the canyons of the Coast range. They finally found themselves within twelve miles of the sea.

But the remaining distance was through redwood forests, dense and difficult to penetrate. Dr. Gregg, in spite of hunger and fatigue, 'frequently expressed a desire to measure the circumference of some of these giants of the forest, and occasionally called on some of us to assist him.' The only response he got was abuse. Nevertheless he stubbornly secured the measurement of one redwood with a diameter of twenty-two feet:

Through this forest we could not travel to exceed two miles a day. The reason . . . was the immense quantity of fallen timber that lay upon the ground in every conceivable shape and direction, and in very many instances one piled upon another. . . . To go around them was often as impossible as to go over them. We were

obliged, therefore, constantly to keep two men ahead
with axes, who . . . would chop into and slab off sufficient to construct a sort of platform by means of which
the animals were driven upon the log and forced to
jump off on the opposite side. . . .

At last they reached the sea. By then the men were not
interested in finding Trinidad Bay or anything else. They
wanted to follow the coast south to San Francisco. In rough
terms they condemned Dr. Gregg for wasting his time and
energies on scientific matters.

Dr. Gregg wanted to take the latitude again at the mouth
of Mad River; this angered the others, who almost went off
and left him. Hence the name.

Some distance beyond the stream they camped. Two men
went out to get drinking water. One dipped up some from a
slough. Dr. Gregg tasted it and didn't like it. The other
man came with a bucketful that looked better. Dr. Gregg
took a mouthful and then spit it out in a hurry.

"Where did you get that water?" he asked.

"About half a mile from here."

"You certainly did not get it out of the ocean."

"I dipped it out of a bay of smooth water."

And that source of the salty drinking water was Trinidad
Bay. Dr. Gregg engraved upon the trunk of a tree the inscription previously indicated: 'for the benefit, as he said, of
those who might hereafter visit the spot, if perchance such
an occurrence should ever happen.'

From the land side it was easy to see how the mariners
could pass by without observing a bay which was sixteen
miles long and into which in a few years there would annually sail over a thousand ships. It was more like a lagoon
than a bay. The south spit of low sand dunes and grassy
hillocks was somewhat less than a mile long and from eighty
to three hundred and fifty yards wide. The north spit was
ten and a half miles long and averaged about two miles

wide; and this, except for one stretch of sparse tree growth, was also composed of grassy hillocks and of dunes, but here the latter lifted as high as eighty-five feet. It was behind these two peninsulas that the bay could understandably be so well and so long concealed. The opening into the ocean was only a half-mile between the breakers.

Dr. Gregg died before reaching San Francisco, but the men from the early ships had a fine time selling city lots in the towns they started—Humboldt, Buckport, Eureka, and Union, which became the modern Arcata. A man from the *Laura Virginia* named the harbor Humboldt Bay. The Trinity River did not run into this; it ran into the Klamath and the Klamath ran into the Pacific without benefit of a bay. It did not afford a sea route to the Trinity mines, failing in the very thing which had given impulse to the discovery. But as those years changed into other years, what a little thing became the Trinity River and its exhausted gold, and what a big thing Humboldt Bay and its redwoods.

No one ever saw the relics of the holy cross on Trinidad Head; no one ever saw any white features marking Indian visages. After seventy-five years all the deserter Spaniard's begetting, if any, had been absorbed back into the Yurok bloodstream. It was as though he and Captain Heceta and Pilot Maurelle and the two padres had never been there. The daring of the navigators, the piety of the friars, the presumptive lust of the sailor—all had been equally erased.

5

RED HUMANS OF THE RED FORESTS

——————

THE ABORIGINAL dwellers among the big trees were about as provincial a people as primitive America had. A coast tribesman might go north, south, or east into the adjacent territory of a friendly neighbor because he was invited to a ceremony or because he wanted to buy a wife. Beyond he did not go; beyond was the end of the world.

Take, for instance, an old Yurok who was one of one hundred and thirty-seven inhabitants and occupied one of twenty redwood houses in the village of Pekwan, on the Klamath about thirty miles from the river mouth. When he finally laid himself down to die his geographical experiences had been unusually broad. He had journeyed up the Klamath to within eight miles of modern Happy Camp, where there was a big Karok village, a distance of about one hundred miles. He had made a trip down the river and southward along the ocean to Eureka, a distance of less than one hundred miles. He had ventured through the redwood forests north of the Klamath mouth a total distance of about fifty miles from his home at Pekwan.

The great timber went on and on just the same, but

among the huge columns a new language was spoken every fifteen or twenty leagues. A shaggy white man, the husband of a squaw, could spend years in a village learning to talk its dialect, then walk three or four hours through the redwoods to another village which couldn't understand a word he said. There was a place called by the whites 'Kentuck,' by the Hupas 'Howunkut,' by the Yurok 'Pia'getl,' by the Wiyot 'Tapotse,' and the three nations thus designating it so differently bordered one another.

Stand in a redwood forest by yourself and catch its shutting-in influence, the contraction it gives to space, the sense of its dimensioning and patterning the world. A few acres of trees seems to focus the universe. You arrive from a world outside that becomes indistinct in the overshadowing vividness. So it is perhaps not strange that Indian tribes would be cloistered in such narrow realms of the forest, not even having a creation myth but thinking the earth had always been as it was. Didn't the immortal trees confirm it?

While they occupied but a small tract of country, they knew that tract well. Each person carried in his head an accurate map of the tribal forest, being familiar with every landmark for ten miles around. The hunter would kill a deer, scorn to carry it home himself, enter his wigwam and say laconically to his squaw or to an old man of the lodge, 'Get um deer three bowshots up Red Water.'

There were about three times as many important Indian tribes occupying the redwoods country as California counties do now. Along the coast from north to south were the Tolowa, including Crescent City; the Yurok, from ten miles above the lower Klamath to Trinidad and Little River; the Chilula, on Redwood Creek going back to the Bald Hills but shut off from the ocean by the Yurok at the mouth of that stream; the Wiyot, with a strip thirty-five miles long and fifteen wide which included Humboldt Bay; the Mattole, owning Cape Mendocino; the Sinkyone, on the south fork

of Eel River with some country at the sea; the Yuki, along
Eel River; the Pomo, from Fort Bragg to Gualala, with
enough redwood holdings to make a millionaire of every
tribesman. Back from the ocean shore but still in redwood
timber were several other tribes.

The marked provincialism and separation of the redwoods
in other ways extend to the predominantly local grouping
of these native races, resulting in about the biggest Babel
of tongues in a small area since the Tower that started it
all. The great Athapascan family, the most widely distributed of North American linguistic families, was the only
one of national and continental scope to penetrate into the
redwoods. To it belonged the Tolowa, Chilula, Mattole,
and Sinkyone, but here the harsh and guttural Athapascan
had been modified into several dialects mutually unintelli-
gible. The Pomos belonged to the next largest family, their
own or Kulanapan, ranging outside the redwoods but only
into parts of four other California counties. The remaining
tribes were local in their linguistic classifications, limited to
small redwoods areas in their spread—the Yuki, the Wiyot,
the Yurok.

The great forest Indians were not noted for their deities,
though the Yukis and Wiyots had gods, the former believing
in a creator imaged like a man, Taikomolo, 'He-who-walks-
alone,' the latter in a certain Gudatrigakwitl, 'Above-old-
man.' The Yuroks had a culture hero without Supreme
Being status, 'Widower-across-the-sea.' But by and large they
acknowledged no sovereign in heaven and no chiefs on
earth; the man with the most hiaqua shells—their money—
was their biggest man.

The Yuroks, with the great ocean in front and the long
navigable Klamath inland, were the leading builders of
boats, selling them upriver to the Karoks and Hupas. For
tools with which to process the second largest trees in the

world they had stone hammers, stonehandled adzes with mussel-shell blades, and elk-horn wedges sharpened by being rubbed and whetted for hours upon rocks.

The Indians did not have to fell the trees. On the Klamath bar and for eighty miles along the coast were drift trees which had been brought down by a flooded current or undermined by the gnawing surf. To get a log of suitable length they did not attack it with their feeble tools. They bucked it off with fire.

They first split the big timber in halves. To hollow out the chosen part they spread pitch upon it and set it afire. When it had burned deep enough they precisely controlled its excavating work by clapping a piece of green bark over the blaze to smother it. Two Yuroks might work five or six months on a canoe, burning, adzing, scraping, and giving a final polish with stones. In the old days, such a laboriously manufactured craft might sell for ten or thirty dollars.

One of these canoes was occasionally large enough to carry a five-ton load, usually of fish, out over the violent bar, out to sea, perhaps in a heavy wind, and on twenty-two miles to Crescent City. They were carefully prevented from sun-cracking when out of the water and not in use by being hauled bottom-up on sandy beaches or dragged into shady coves or covered over thickly with leaves and boughs.

The average length was eighteen feet. There is a report of a canoe forty-two feet long built by the Tolowa tribe on Smith River. It would have been easy enough to find a redwood log from which to get a boat of such dimensions, but the dimensions themselves do not sound practicable for customary native use. Since the craft were employed a great deal more on the rivers than on the ocean, a boat like this that was more than twice as long as the regular ones would have been awkward for shooting swift rapids among upjutting rocks and for upstream transport of heavy loads. It was probably a hired-Indian arrangement for white men.

Redwood canoes were, curiously, used no farther south than Cape Mendocino, and inland on no rivers south of the crooked Eel. Though great logs lay in continued abundance on the beaches, the rest of the tribes of the redwood belt looked out boatless on a sea filled with food. Possibly they put together rude rafts of logs, but of actual boat-building out of single washed-up timbers there was none.

(The Yuroks anticipated the absence of tolls on modern highways by having free ferries. Even an enemy had to be taken across promptly and without charge. He would come to the riverbank opposite a village and yell. If on the other side there was no ferryman available except the fellow with whom he was on bad terms, the latter had no choice but to come and paddle him over. The situation was not to be made into an opportunity for them to tell each other what lowdown skunks they were. The traveler sat silent in the canoe with his back to the paddler. An Indian was fined if he refused such ferriage to an enemy.)

The average redwood house was about twenty by twenty-three feet, made out of vertical planking, with two ridges, an excavation in the center of the floor, a round sliding door, and an occupancy of seven or eight persons. The Yurok planks were split from redwood logs by means of the elk-horn wedges and somewhat smoothed with mussel-shell adzes. The walls were usually two planks thick. The roof boards were wide and from eight to ten feet long. The smokehole in the roof was the only window. The poorest Yurok would never have thought of using bark, as did some of the other tribes.

The sweathouse, from which squaws were excluded, was the place where the men spent most of their time in winter, not even sleeping at home. Yet, notwithstanding its communal purpose, it was smaller than the regular wigwam, about nine by twelve, very low, and with a floor excavation four feet deep. Gathering wood for the sacred fire, a matter of strict ritual, was at least a chore spared the squaws. The men went to the sweathouse 'to work, idle, meditate, sleep, or sulk.' For these winter bachelors, who condemned their spouses to what biologically amounted to a seasonal widowhood, this place was church, theatre, cafe, dormitory. While the winter wind made noises in the big trees, and all was frosty and chill outside, the bucks enjoyed a 'warm and cozy snuggery.' The Yuroks had a total of eighty-three sweathouses along the Klamath and upon the ocean front.

Some tribes did not go to the trouble of riving out puncheons but instead used slabs of redwork bark. The Sinkyone had two forms of such bark shanties—a round and a wedge-shaped lean-to. The Pomos laid bark into fat cone-shaped dwellings ten or fifteen feet across but only as high as a man's head. The Chilula used high-grade plank houses for regular residences but built temporary bark places for summer camping in the hills.

To house the tribes and give them sweathouses of bark or planks required a considerable amount of redwood lumber. The Chilula, for instance, had one-hundred-twenty-five houses and the Yurok two-hundred-sixty-three in their forty-seven towns. Yet these were almost entirely built of windfall and drift wood. The tragic prodigality did not start until the white man came with his steel tools.

The Indians used a small amount of their immense supply of lumber for other things. Redwood-root fibers went into baskets, and the Pomo squaws' double skirts were made of shredded inner redwood bark.

The Yuroks made a treasure box of redwood, a tapering cylinder two to four feet long, hollowed out from the top and with a lashed-on lid. They also fashioned two items of furniture, a redwood pillow for the sweathouse, and a round low stool three to nine inches high. Each lodge had several of the latter, mostly for use of the men.

An Indian went on using redwood to some extent after

he died. Frequently his grave was covered over with slabs. And very charmingly, according to Stephen Powers, he was lighted to the other world by bright fires. The gulf to the hereafter was bridged by a footlog. This was not a big redwood with the rough bark still on to make easy walking even in the blackest night. It was a very slender and very slippery pole. The Indians did not departmentalize the destination of dead people as is done in the white man's theology. All went to the same place, but a good or wicked life greatly affected the ease of getting there. The ghost who had dwelt righteously upon the earth could walk the slender, slippery pole with ease and speed; the fire that lighted the way for him needed to be of short duration. The one of evil deeds moved across the precarious footlog very slowly and with much difficulty; his moccasin soles had no resin on them; he couldn't keep his balance and was always on the point of slipping off. So the fires at his grave had to be specially bright and maintained for a long time.

Uneventfully these tribes dwelt among the redwoods. They didn't have very good times. Big things don't necessarily make life more exciting or more joyful, not big mountains or big rivers or big trees. The Yuroks and the Pomos and all the rest seemed to have a constant sense of being dwarfed. One traveler said he noticed very definitely an attitude of awe on the part of a tribe: while in the woods they seemed fearful, like children passing a graveyard in the dark, yet in canoes on the river these same Indians were resourceful, dashing, and bold. A psychologist could make an interesting study along this line, finding out whether those who dwell now among the redwoods are tinctured with a stronger melancholy than Americans who spend their lives in a less dominating environment—and also checking on whether a resistless insularity settles upon them as it did upon the Indian tribes.

Did the big trees have any influence in making the redwood Indians the most money-conscious natives of California? These tribes with their geographic astigmatism, their unawareness of a world a short distance off, measured everything in terms of a little shell that came from eight-hundred miles away. That white alien mollusk, no larger than your little finger, affected their lives a whole lot more than the trees which rose above them two and three hundred feet and stood around them in columns twenty feet through. By it they precisely calculated the value of a wife, a human life, a grief, an injury, a trespass.

What an absence of correlation of inhabitants with their environment! The biggest, cleanest, most inspirational forests of America were inhabited by the most venal aboriginal population.

A long way up the coast north of the northernmost redwood, beside a hundred flat beaches, around a hundred headlands, the breadth of two big commonwealths, farther than even a fast motorcar can go in a day, at the northwestern tip of the State of Washington is Cape Flattery—one of the remote and lonely places of the earth, a forlorn promontory stretching out west beyond all else of the nation's mainland except Cape Alava, seventeen miles south, which juts forth still another thousand feet toward Asia, toward the sunset. Here is where the ancient shell-money came from—money many times older than the dollar, older than doubloons or pieces of eight, older than Caesar's penny. Centuries before the white man arrived it was used in trade for a thousand miles around. It was mainly obtained from the wide general neighborhood of Cape Flattery, including Vancouver Island and Puget Sound.

It is only a small shell, considered extra-fine if it was as much as two and a half or three inches long. The examples in museums are yellow with age, but it is marvelously white when fresh out of deep water. It is shaped for all the world like an elephant's tusk. Its scientific name is *Dentalium indianorum*.

Among the northern tribes it was strung on a cord six feet long. This string, rather than the shell itself, was called *hiaqua*. Among the redwood tribes, where its scarcity and its value were greater, a string of 27½ inches was the rule.

In the early Atlantic colonies not all the shell-money came from one locality, though the best of it did—from Long Island. This Atlantic Coast wampum was much counterfeited by the whites, who made it out of 'stone, bone, glass, musselshells, horn, yea, even of wood and broken beads.' But the hiaqua shell-money of the Pacific Coast was not called wampum. And it was never counterfeited. It couldn't be.

The Indians themselves didn't make it. No white man was clever enough to imitate it, any more than the old alchemists could change cheaper metals into gold. Nature alone knew how to manufacture the hiaqua, and she did it sparingly and in seclusion. And the great ocean, and the tides of Juan de Fuca Straits, and the ebb and flow of bays and inlets, did not cast it upon the sandy shores. It remained remote and hidden, as gold does. It was scarce and hard to get, as gold is.

Alexander Ross, a clerk with the Astor party in 1811, said of the *Dentalium*: 'The higua is thin, light and durable, and may be found at all lengths, between three inches down to one-fourth of an inch, and increases or decreases in value according to the number required to make a fathom, by which measure they are invariably sold. Thirty to a fathom are held equal in value to three fathoms of forty, to four of fifty and so on.'

The haunt of the *Dentalium* was a sheltered harbor or arm of the sea, in deep water usually from four to eight fathoms deep, sometimes from fifty to sixty fathoms deep. It burrowed in the sand of the sea bottom, the small end downward. To gather it, an Indian fixed to the end of a

spear a comblike contrivance, which he thrust down into
the sandy bottom of the bay while his squaw rowed the
boat slowly along. If he caught a single shell upon a tooth
of the comb, he considered himself lucky. Very few indeed
would be the ordinary haul for a day. There was no use
looking for the hiaqua shells along the beaches at low tide,
for they were never to be found in this convenient manner.
They had to be fished for in deep water.

The redwood Indians, particularly the Yuroks, from about
ten miles north of the Klamath mouth to a few miles south
of Trinidad to Little River, counted their choicest strings at
eleven shells to 27½ inches. In the exact grading there were
strings of twelve, thirteen, fourteen, and fifteen to the 27½-
inch length. The latter was called 'young man's money.' If
it took more than fifteen to make a string, the shells ceased
to be true coin of the realm and were used as necklace beads,
'squaw money,' so reduced in value that it took ten strings
to equal a thirteen-shell string of money-sized hiaquas.

As nearly as the early whites could figure equivalents in
American money, the five grades of strings diminished
rapidly in value with the diminishing size of the shells, as
follows: eleven to the string, $50; twelve to the string, $20;
thirteen to the string, $10; fourteen to the string, $5; fifteen
to the string, $2.50; a bead string of shells too small for actual
money, $1.

Not many Yurok old men, and no young men, had as
many as two of the largest-size strings. If a man were that
wealthy he would be known all over the tribal dominions
and be talked about in the sweathouses by adjacent tribes.
A very prominent man might give one string for a wife, two
strings never. But a squaw purchased at such a price as one
of the eleven-to-a-string would have an enviable standing.
Social status went up or down according to the price paid
for the spouse. Children found it an affront to have a mother
who had been too much of a bargain as a bride. Sometimes

a bridegroom was like Jacob, and bought his wife on the installment plan, but here in the redwoods he had the use of her while he was paying the remaining amounts due. Marriage relations that might go wrong were all figured out in terms of hiaqua money—divorce, sterility, adultery, bastards. If the wife died young the husband had lots of wifehood due him from a sister or other kinswoman of the family; he had bought her for a lifetime.

The coveting of hiaqua shells was an important cause of living apart in the sweathouse. The Yuroks believed the precious shells would depart from a wigwam where mating took place. The man's avarice was greater than his lust. In gracious summer weather he could sleep in the arms of his squaw outside the house and not imperil his money. Hence the predominant birth of children in the spring. Yet, in contradiction, a Yurok who in anthropological euphemism could 'exercise his virility ten times in one night' was destined to be very rich. This was ruefully granted to be an unattainable ideal for modern men.

Also these sexually fasting Indians, though lacking an outright god, had among the lesser substitutes one *Wohpeku-menu,* who was very lecherous. He abandoned his son. *Kapuloyo,* in a high tree, presumably in the top of a lofty redwood, because he wanted to marry his daughter-in-law. Though Wohpekumenu stands high among roué deities, he was also rated as a benefactor. You see, the son escaped from the treetop, gathered up all the hiaqua money in the world, and escaped with it down the Klamath. Wohpekumenu overhauled him at the mouth of the river, and while he couldn't recover all the hiaqua, he got enough of it back for people to get along with in a scarce way.

A house of redwood planks was worth five hiaqua strings, probably of twelve shells or smaller; a slave, one or two strings; killing a man, fifteen strings; a bastard, five strings; seduction and pregnancy, five strings; adultery, five strings.

Think of all the power this tiny elephant's tusk of shell had during the five-hundred, or one-thousand, or five-thousand years it was used as money! How many men and women did it buy into bondage? What dangers were faced for it, what hardships suffered, what crimes committed? It was just a little mollusk of no value in itself. Yet consider all it was able to do over so vast a territory.

It was perhaps the most successful currency ever used by a primitive stone-age people. It was a good money according to economics (durable, divisible, scarce, portable, of a single substance) and it was proved good by centuries of use— perhaps the best before copper and silver and gold.

In four to eighty fathoms of water along Cape Flattery's shore still lives the little white mollusk. With its small end buried in the sandy bottom, the deep tides flow over and it is undisturbed, for the people who so highly valued it have turned to dust. Money once, old beyond reckoning, important beyond estimate—worth more than all the redwoods —it has become only a tiny shell again, quite valueless.

The isolationist Indians of the redwoods were also influenced by two messiahs from a long way off—Smohalla at the foot of Priest Rapids on the Columbia River, and Wovoka in Mason Valley, Nevada.

This tremendous pair of spiritual leaders declared the opposite of what was proclaimed from the white men's pulpits. They preached the emptying of heaven; described its becoming an obsolete realm; pronounced the end of it. They were responsible for the whirlwind spread in two periods of the Ghost Dance or Dreamer religion. The first period in the early seventies was the one which mostly affected the redwoods tribes.

The idea in both cases was that every Indian who had been put away in a grave since the far beginning, since the biggest redwoods were bushes, would come back to life upon a regenerated earth to be henceforth forever free from death, disease, and misery. It was Wovoka who said this would swell the population beyond the globe's capacity to hold it. But since nobody would be left in heaven and, without death, nobody would ever go there any more, heaven would properly be done away with and the earth, getting the vacant space, would be made large enough 'to contain us all.'

As for the palefaces, they would simply be extinguished. Smohalla believed the resurrection would make the Indians so numerous and so powerful that they could conquer the hordes of fair-skinned ones. Wovoka announced a kind of deluge for them. The multitude of reanimated ghosts, all young again, would go up in the mountains, leaving the whites down below to be drowned.

Wovoka, or 'Jack Wilson,' worked for a white man in Nevada. He grew up and married and was still nothing but a paleface's hired hand. He attracted no particular attention until he began to dream dreams and to see visions at about the age of thirty. The time was to come when tribal delegations would reverently visit him from more than a thousand miles away. A government ethnologist went to see him on a snowy New Year's Day in 1892. The messiah was out in the white-covered sagebrush hunting jackrabbits. He was taller than most Paiutes, nearly six feet. He wore white man's clothes and shook hands with his visitor.

Sagebrush prophets, he and Smohalla, and what a little plant the sagebrush is compared with the redwood! But out of the great red forests there never came a leader of men's beliefs like unto them. The slabs that covered the graves in the redwoods cemeteries were taken off to make it easier for the dead to uprise—and the expectation of this glad Judgment Day did not burst out of the Indians' own exalted souls there among the enormous woods, but needs must come fourth-or fifth-hand from two exalted souls upon the treeless plains.

The designation of the doctrine came from its aspect of trance communion, from the belief that prophets visited the dead in dreams: hence the names Dreamer religion and Ghost Dance religion.

Wovoka's father was a dreamer in the earlier period. The Dreamer religion did not have to go far from the Paiutes to reach the Modocs at Tule Lake and in the Lava Beds— and Captain Jack's band of extraordinary warriors were the first outsiders evangelized, perhaps partly accounting for their remarkable valor and astonishing success in the Modoc War. Thence by successive contagion it spread to the Shastas, to the Korak on Klamath River, then into redwood country to the upriver Yuroks and across the Siskiyous again into redwood country among the Tolowas in the Smith River and Crescent City region, and in continued redwood invasion down the coast to the lower-river and ocean Yuroks.

The force of the religion collided with that other force which possessed the Yuroks—the passionate coveting of hiaqua shell-money. The epidemic first stirred the upriver Yurok and then left them more than a little cold. The first Korak dreamer was a woman. She was visited from a distance by tribesmen eager to hear the new and wonderful gospel. Among them was a considerable delegation of Yuroks as eager at the outset as the rest. But when the woman dreamer proclaimed that wealth and hiaqua shells would have no place upon the regenerated earth and in the new scheme of things, the mercenery Yuroks lost interest and went home.

An uncle and his nephew found hard evangelistic going among the lower-river and ocean Yuroks. The uncle was a Tolowa Indian, the nephew a Yurok living a few miles up the Klamath. First the older man, then the younger, became a dreamer. They said a ghost dance must certainly be held for the Weitspus at the junction of the Klamath and Trinity, or the dead of that vicinity would not come back to life. But in fading zeal the Yuroks never got round to holding the ghost dance there. So the Weitspus dead stayed dead and nobody seemed to care much.

The movement reached the redwood Pomas from the south. The Ghost Dance religion, strictly as such, failed to live or to be revived during its second spread in the nineties, but it mixed with and put its stamp upon the religion in that redwood area for a long time.

Thus a people who dwelt in narrowly circumscribed commonwealths among the big trees were affected by two foreign influences, the far-off origins of which—Cape Flattery, Priest Rapids on the Columbia, and a Nevada sagebrush valley—were not grasped by their limited geographical imaginations.

In turn, the redwood forests and their people did not send any influences out over the Indian world. The big trees did not breed any material or social culture at all in keeping with their own majesty.

6

THREE OLD VISITORS

———————

PADRE SIERRA AT TRINIDAD, 1775

June 9, 1775—The Schooner *Sonora* which was proceeding ahead of us in the Frigate *Santiago* in search of a place to anchor, found a port with a good shelter, and following in her wake we anchored at four o'clock of the afternoon.

June 10—A number of the inhabitants came out to see us. We went into some of their houses, which showed their poverty stricken condition. [The Yurok village of Tsurau occupied a sheltered place behind Trinidad Head. Said Padre Campa, the other friar with Heceta: 'The houses were few in number, not exceeding seven, and were built of planks with very low doors, oval in shape and more like the entrances to dog kennels than anything else.']

June 11—We went on shore with all the officers and the greater part of the men of the Frigate and Schooner, and on the beach worshipped the Holy Cross which had been constructed for the purpose of being placed on top of the hill. [Redwood must be regarded as the natural material for the

51

cross, yet why was it so much decayed when Captain Vancouver found it eighteen years later?] We made our way to the summit, not without difficulty, as the path was rough and steep and in places even dangerous. [The Spaniard of those times must have been fairly energetic. By anybody's standards it is a tough climb to the top of Trinidad Head. A road now starts on the east side, ascends along the south side, and ends up at the lighthouse on the west side. From above the road to the summit the land is apparently still as wild as Padre Sierra found it—a thicket of bushes crisscrossed with small down-timber.] The day being the feast of the Santisma Trinidad caused us to give that name to the port. From the top of the hill we saw a river to which was given the name Rio de las Tortolas [Little River].

June 14—Padre Campa asked the Indians if any other ships had come there. They answered that none had.

June 17—A topmast for the foremast was cut and brought back to repair it, as the one brought from San Blas had been sprung and repaired. [The first recorded use of redwood for spars.]

June 18—The Commandant Captain Bruno Heceta accompanied by the pilot of the Schooner went to explore the Rio de las Tortolas. The Indian canoes are not large, being four yards long at the most, but are well built, with two prows, generally of a single log, half decked at stem and stern except the poop, which has a piece added on top to prevent the entrance of the waves, and are very safe. They could be made larger, as there are plenty of large pine trees available. Near the river the party came across one very thick and very tall which out of curiosity they measured, finding it to be over forty-seven yards in height. The trees come down to the beach. The hills are covered with great pines. [The modern traveler can see some of the great stumps of the very redwoods which the old Spanish friar beheld nearly two centuries ago.]

A REDWOODS RAILROAD, 1880

Hear sadly of things which you could have seen but now can see no more, for what follows is a very old railroad timetable as given by a Nebraskan, George A. Crofutt, in 1880.

In the preface to his guidebook, presumably written back in Omaha, he said that 'we have stood beneath trees four hundred feet in height and forty-eight feet in diameter; have strolled amid the redwoods where they grow so thick that, were they felled, the ground would be covered to a depth of sixty feet.' This is a nice piece of exaggeration. There never was a redwood tree quite that high: three hundred sixty-four feet is about tops.

He then proceeded with chatty comments about the redwoods for prospective passengers over the North Pacific Coast Railroad from Sausalito on San Francisco Bay to Duncan's Mills on Russian River. After mentioning Sausalito, Tamalpais, and Fairfax, he coupled with Nicasio his first reference to the big trees. Then, as he took the train down the canyon beyond Lagunitas, he told some more. Taylorville was accredited 'with some tall redwoods along the creek and on the side of the mountain to the left.' He didn't have anything further to say about *Sequoia sempervirens* until the train pulled into Valleyford station, but then he commented: 'Years ago the section we are now entering was the southern border of the great redwood forests. Here the lumberman began his labors, and as years passed, step by step, he penetrated this great lumber region, leaving in his track stumps, fire, smoke, and finally broad, rich fields from which he subsists while persistently following up his receding prey—the redwoods.'

The next stop was the occasion for a reference to a redwoods Paul Bunyan who does not seem to have been perpetuated in later legends. The place was Howard, and of it he said: 'The principal business at this station is burning coke. Passing on, we enter Dutch Bill Canyon, called so in early days after Mr. Howard, who there wrestled with the big redwoods that it then contained. Redwoods now appear on each side, as also sawmills.'

Tyrone Mills was the next station on the narrow-gauge line. From there the train rolled on a downgrade 'through towering redwoods three hundred feet high' to Russian River; on through 'a perfect forest of towering redwoods'; on to Mosco Mills station, opposite the mouth of Austin Creek, 'abounding in redwoods'; on to Duncan's Mills 'in the midst of great forests of redwoods' eighty miles from San Francisco—the end of the North Pacific Coast Railroad, along the line of which a million feet of redwood lumber was manufactured every week in 1880.

VOYAGE FROM RUSSIAN RIVER TO CRESCENT CITY, 1888

George Davidson's *Coast Pilot* for 1889 was known to navigators along the redwood coast as 'Davidson's Bible.' He knew as did no other person the shoreline bordering the big trees. He spoke scornfully of the Gold Rush ships which often 'arrived with only school atlases' to guide them. As early as 1852, in an old paddlewheel steamer, he tried to land at Cape Mendocino, that focus of myth, adventure, and disaster, that strange dividing line in the action of the great ocean.

In selected and abbreviated form, here is what someone on a small schooner might have seen in 1888 all along the front of the redwoods, with the ocean at times washing the roots of the trees:

Russian River—The shore is bordered by rocks twenty to a hundred and thirty feet high. The mouth of the river between the high cliffbanks is about half a mile wide. The valleys of tributary arroyos and streams near the coast were filled with a very dense growth of heavy redwood, which has been greatly depleted and transported hence by rail to San Francisco.

At Fort Ross Anchorage the high coast hills crowd close upon the seaboard, covered with forests of redwood, pine, and fir, which gradually come down closer to the shore as we approach. Coasting vessels load firewood, tanbark, redwood posts, and farm produce for San Francisco.

Fort Ross to Point Arena—The distance is thirty-six and a half miles. The timber comes close to the shores, and the hills to the coastline are covered with forests. A large traffic in lumber is carried on at numerous very small coves. At Saunders Landing there is no cove whatever; the cliffs are bold and about a hundred feet above the sea. The chute is quite long, carried from the ninety-foot cliff over a chasm to a small rocky islet forty-nine feet high, and then projected over the edge of the islet to five fathoms of water, where the schooners lie to load. The lumber is hauled from Schooner Gulch to this chute, together with wood, ties, and posts. At the south point of Arena Cove the lumber chute is a very large and long structure, coming from a distance down and along the face of the steep slope. It stretches out over ten feet of water, and a vessel lies with her stern under the chute. An annual average of fifty schooners load lumber, posts, tanbark, produce.

At Gualala under the north bluff, broad open to the sea, cables are passed from the sixty-foot cliff to the schooner's masts, the ship being fastened to heavy moorings. Engines on shore lower or hoist the loads along the cable.

Point Arena to Cape Mendocino—For the first half of this distance the forests reach almost to the shoreline. There continue to be numerous coves for the anchorage of lumber schooners. At Mendocino Bay a schooner stands outside the harbor and waits for the signal. If the flag is at the masthead, the ship comes in; if it is half-mast, it means the anchorage is too rough or there is room for no more vessels. The Noyo River, forty yards wide at the mouth, has a bar outside the entrance. Sometimes, when there is a good head of water, the bar washes away, so that a bark is said to have loaded in the river and been taken out at high tide.

At Rockport, a small indentation of the shore, the land is here at about an eight- or nine-hundred-foot elevation. Then the redwood forest begins and is very dense. From the nearest rock a chute is projected out forty-five yards. A vessel lies broadside to the chute. The lumber is piled on the rocks, but even at the height of fifty feet the sea after a southeaster will wash it away unless it be lashed down.

Northwest from Kuluna Cliff the sands have blown in on the shore for a breadth of thirty to a hundred and thirty yards, for a length of nearly three miles, and for a height of as much as thirty-five feet. This is quite a feature for recognizing the locality. A Sandwich Island brig went ashore directly under the cliff. The cargo of lumber was partly saved by people living in the vicinity, but before they could haul it away a landslide buried the greater part of it under several hundred tons of earth and rock.

Cape Mendocino to Crescent City—In summer weather, when the forest fires to the north are in full blast, the smoke is very thick along this section of coast. Cape Mendocino may be so completely hidden as to be dangerous for vessels to approach it. Eel River is an uncertain entrance, though in 1877 the steamer *Continental* made sixty passages over its bar. Eureka on Humboldt Bay is the great lumber center of the region. Trinidad, thirty-eight miles north from Cape Mendocino, has redwood trees of enormous size in the vicinity. The stump of one was twenty feet across, and a dozen trees standing in the particular area averaged over ten feet in diameter. Here in 1793 Captain George Vancouver obtained from the Indians some crude knives that were apparently pieces from old sabres which they said they had secured from the north. One was marked with an *L*.

In fourteen and a half miles appear the Gold Bluffs, where in early days the black beach sands were feverishly worked for gold. For several miles the ocean is bordered by bold, rocky cliffs. Within three miles of Crescent City Bay there is a change to a low sandy shore.

In his study of the redwoods coastline, Davidson noted the remarkable inshore eddy current running north of forty-two degrees latitude, almost like a swift river in the ocean. This drift was responsible for the first extensive distribution of the redwoods, far beyond the region of their growth. It is well known that the redwood groves cease a little north of the California line, just a few miles over into Oregon. Yet redwood logs and trunks of redwood trees were washed upon the beaches along the whole of the northern shores. They were found on the low strands between Tillamook and the Columbia. The coast from Grays Harbor to Cape Flattery was well marked by redwood logs. In these sections so far distant from where the great tree grew, it was familiar to the Indians. Logs were observed among the drift timber in 1886 on Vancouver Island, and in that year on the beaches of Wales Island, Alaska, in latitude fifty-four degrees and forty minutes—meaning the redwood timber had drifted in this northward ocean current a total distance of not less than eight hundred miles.

The great Pacific had made this big tree known to tribes who had never seen it lifting its three-hundred-foot height up toward the clouds, and who must have wondered much whence such huge driftwood came.

7

FORT ROSS

———

THE FIRST white men to make substantial use of the redwoods in construction were the Russians—'the cold, impassive Muscovites'—at Fort Ross. They were not behind other whites in their ability to drive a good bargain with the Indians. In 1812 they bought the site for 'three blankets, three pairs of breeches, two axes, three hoes, and some beads.' The Spaniards disputed their claim to this settlement eighteen miles above Bodega Bay and eight miles above the mouth of Russian River, and the Russians did not at first include the land in the sale in 1841 to John A. Sutter. But the latter persuaded the Fort Ross superintendent to antedate the contract with a statement that the Russians were putting the Fort Ross land in with the other things he was buying for $30,000. It was upon the shadowy and questionable possession 'thus acquired by certificate of a subordinate officer' that the possibility of a valid Russian claim to land along the coast 'became a stalking spectacle among American settlers in later years.'

The Russians had the largest collection of redwood structures in California, as many as would be found in an ordinary village, fifty-nine in all. The Kodiaks, or Aleuts, had little huts of the ruddy lumber. The fort was nearly square, two hundred and fifty by three hundred feet, and its whole circumference of a fifth of a mile consumed a large quantity of timber. The palisade logs were fifteen feet high, with three feet in the ground. Three log houses had a total of twenty-two rooms. Two blockhouses were given thirty portholes. There were three warehouses, a barracks, and a Greek chapel.

The latter, built of split boards, was still in good condition in 1895. One of the bells hung for half a century in the Petaluma fire station. The chapel was restored in 1928 and the bell given back to it. One of the blockhouses was rebuilt. The state division of parks took official control of old Fort Ross in 1929.

In the considerable amount of shipbuilding carried on by the Russians at Fort Ross, redwood did not prove to be a good material for vessels. It was not given an entirely fair chance, since the workmen were inexperienced and the timber was used before it was seasoned enough. Of the four largest ships launched before 1824, two were constructed at least partly out of redwood. The *Volga,* which sometimes carried the Aleuts and their *bidarkas* in the poaching sea-otter hunting, was of one hundred and sixty tons and cost 36,189 rubles. It was launched in 1822 and had become unseaworthy by 1827. The other boat which contained a substantial amount of redwood was the *Kiakhta,* of two hundred tons, launched in 1824 and still in service six years later. But five or six years was about as long as a redwood ship held up. Something like a dozen smaller vessels were made at Fort Ross for the use of the Russians themselves, and several small brigs were made and sold to the Spaniards.

The first transportation of redwood as fuel was carried on by the Russians. This was to reach big proportions by 1890, when schooners carried many cords to San Francisco. The Russians took wood in bidarkas to their detachment on the bleak Farallon Islands off San Francisco; this seemed to have been troublesome business, for they hit upon a substitute of burning oiled bones for cooking.

Sutter had purchased a schooner from the Russians, and in this he hauled away several windows, doors, and other lumber from Fort Ross to use in finishing his buildings at New Helvetia.

William Bennitz had charge of the Ross property from 1843 to 1867, first as the agent of Sutter, later as lessee, and finally as owner. In 1861 the walls of the palisades were still in a good state of preservation, together with the buildings inside the enclosure, including the chapel and blockhouses.

In 1891 a visitor reported the passage of a county road through property once enclosed by a heavy stockade twice the height of a man. The barracks had become a saloon, one of the houses a hotel. The blockhouses had lost their roofs and canted over because of the wormeaten condition of the timbers. The Greek chapel continued to stand erect, but was 'no longer used for holy purposes.' The orchard fence was still fairly sound.

Then the visitor went into the redwoods—a second-growth forest grown up from stumps cut by the Russians in 1811. Only a half-dozen of the big first-growth trees still stood in the Fort Ross grove. The stumps made him realize that the forest of big trees among which he walked was a new forest. He had a pocket rule with him, enabling him to measure a tree that was four and a half feet through. J. W. Call, who then owned the property, assured him that some of these second-growth trees were five feet through—reaching that size in sixty-five and not over seventy years. Said the visitor: 'We are thus exact and explicit in reference to this forest of new growth because we know there is a widespread fear that in consequence of the rapidity with which our redwood forests are being converted into lumber, that species of timber will ultimately become extinct. Right there, overshadowing old Fort Ross, is the refutation of such fallacy.'

A horseback tourist along the coast in 1912 found Fort Ross at that time to be a community of about three dozen people. The stockade was still standing after exactly one hundred years. The chapel was in fair condition, but the earthquake of 1906 had shaken it down; the roof, with its cupola and belfry, had fallen to the ground, though it was still intact. The commandant's house was still used as a hotel. An oldtimer at the Fort had tried to get volunteers to come and repair the chapel, but only two or three had responded to the summons.

8

SEA OTTERS AND GOLD

———

TWELVE DAYS AT TRINIDAD

CAPTAIN JONATHAN WINSHIP, the smuggler, in his retired old age raised flowers on the East Coast, and died among his roses. This horticultural demise was preceded by much adventure, which included twelve exciting days of hunting sea otters for the Russians at Trinidad.

The sea otter was the marine furbearer so much coveted by the mandarins and high functionaries of China that a single skin once sold for the equivalent of seventy-seven dollars. A short-legged, webfooted animal about five feet long, mostly body and hence wrapped in a considerable area of thick, fine, glossy fur, the sea otter used to inhabit the ocean out in front of the redwoods in commercial numbers: Today it is not to be found there, or hardly anywhere.

Captain Winship, with his brother Nathan as mate, entered into a contract with the Russian governor, Alexander Baranof, in Alaska. The latter had no right to commission a hunt for otters in a Spanish dominion such as

Trinidad was then. It was the case of a contrabandist making arrangements with a still bigger one.

Winship's vessel, the *O'Cain,* carried a hundred Kodiak hunters and fifty bidarkas for them to hunt in. On board was plenty to eat, with twelve Indian women to cook it. Provisions included a thousand pounds of whale meat and a number of casks of whale oil, a beverage which the Aleuts considered delectable. The hunter boss was a four-syllabled Russian, Slobodchikof, with whom Captain Winship quarreled before the trip was over, but not at Trinidad, where there were more pressing things to occupy them. The hitherto peaceable redwood Indians, who had so tractably carried up the cross for the padre, resented the expedition in a dog-in-the-manger way, for they didn't much hunt for otters themselves.

The *O'Cain* arrived on June 10, 1806. The first anchorage was off Big Lagoon, which Captain Winship and his crew discovered and partly explored, and named Washington Sound.

The numerous and hostile natives complicated matters. Hunting had to go on under the ship's guns. Field pieces had to be brought ashore to protect the camp. One Indian was killed. A number of skins were secured, but the quantity was not sufficent to offset the difficulties. So the *O'Cain,* on June 22nd, sailed away to the Farallons, after only twelve days in the vicinity of Trinidad.

Other sea-otter ships with American captains visited Trinidad, but also briefly—the *Leila Bird* in 1804 and the *Mercury* in 1808—and a Russian mariner, Captain Golovnin, in 1818. Trinidad seemed to be at the northern edge of the southern habitat of the animals. The Russians said they were found between Cape Mendocino and Trinidad, 'though not in great numbers.' In front of the redwoods it was not the best hunting.

THE GOLD BLUFFS

On the Redwood Empire Association's tourist map the Gold Bluffs are item of interest No. 220. They lie north of Redwood Creek's village of Orick, about two and a half miles off the Redwood Highway. An acknowledgedly poor auto road leads diagonally to the spot, branching off about two miles north of Orick and crossing Little Lost Man Creek.

If you have something of the Chinaman's disposition to resift the dirt wherein fortunes were once found, you can satisfy it fully here upon a beach which for a short time was declared by promoters, and believed by listeners, to be the most extraordinary goldfield that had ever been known, so rich that the share of each member of the Pacific Mining Company owning the main patch was estimated to be worth $43,000,000.

The land back of the shore, in obstinate specialization, grew no other wealth than the lofty trees. In front was the limitless sea of salt. But in a narrow strip between the two was a compensatory concentration.

News of the Gold Bluffs in January of 1851 caused in San Francisco one of the wildest excitements which have swept that city. The placer stream was nothing less than the great ocean itself. The beach sand, all mealy with gold, was the paydirt. In a sense the gold had already been washed by the sea waves—the ocean was a mighty miner's cradle 'that had been rocking and washing up gold from the bottom of the sea for unknown ages, and had chanced to throw it in tons and shiploads beneath the hitherto undiscovered Gold Bluffs.'

You can see the black sand to this day. Maybe the tides and the billows have washed some of the rich topping away. Maybe, on the other hand, they have laid down other rich deposits. Even while the beach was being mined the prodigious broom of the surf would sweep the topping off and sweep it back in quite unpredictable and capricious moods. By mixing up the enchantment of the past with hopes for the present it remains a good spot for amateur gold-hunting. From time to time, since the great days, mining beach-combers have come expectantly to this dark strand to have at least their loneliness delightfully beguiled.

In April of 1850 a band of five prospectors came up along the redwoods coast in the brig *Cameo* to the mouth of the Klamath River. Landed there, they set out afoot to see what they could find, and they found a remarkable beach at the foot of high bluffs.

Why didn't they at once come away with the astonishing riches they happened upon? Well, they considered it. But how much gold could a man carry any distance on his back? Seventy-five pounds, at most a hundred. Why be contented with such insignificant amounts when numberless tons of it lay all about, more than a thousand men could remove in a thousand years? They would remain and watch over it until they could get a ship and fill it with their wealth.

They waited, five men in possession of the richest gold deposit upon the earth. They kept the secret for half a year from the outside world.

And that world, notably the part of it in San Francisco, was beside itself when it heard. By January of 1851 men in the city were listening with credulous ears to reports of the immensity of gold in front of the redwoods forest and the ease of its getting. 'No digging even was required, since one only had to stoop a little and raise as much as he wished of the stuff, half gold, half sand, from the surface of the beach.'

Meantime promoters had got hold of the discovering five. Heading the promoters were General John Wilson and John Collins. They formed the Pacific Mining Company.

Wilson and Collins had plenty of samples of the wondrous black sand. They showed it—in sealed bottles. The golden particles were unmistakably shining there, as innumerable as stars in the Milky Way.

'Gold Bluffs' was in every man's mouth, in huge posters on the sides of buildings, in the newspaper shipping advertisements, in the announcements of eight vessels shortly to sail thither. A reporter of the *Alta California* interviewed Collins, who spoke of great distances of the beach being literally strewn with pure gold, which was mixed with a certain kind of black sand in amounts ranging from ten cents to ten dollars a pound—and one of the original five discoverers had accumulated two and a half tons of this precious ebony granulation. Mr. Collins had measured a patch and done some conservative calculating; it was a patch belonging to the Pacific Mining Company; if it held out to be just one-tenth as rich as the parts observed and tested it would yield, not in terms of the whole company but to each individual and separate member of the company, $43,-000,000. 'No wonder people raved, and either invested a few thousand dollars in shares of this company, or sold or forsook their all, and made sail for the Gold Bluffs.'

One skeptical newspaper granted that the sand was there in immeasurable tonnage, and would remain there unless the bottom dropped out of the earth and it fell through to China, but whether the gold was in it in such quantities was another matter. Its voice and the voices of a few others were lost and drowned in the credulous clamor.

Those who went in the eight vessels and in various trips of the *Chesapeake,* now bought by the company, almost at once looked with dismay upon the manufactory of multimillionaires. Most of them were not long in returning, goldless, disgruntled, 'ashamed of their hopes and credulity.' The gold was far from being ready-washed by the ocean, with little remaining to do but put it into pokes and pouches. They learned from the early miners, and soon found out for themselves, that the black sand had first to be separated from the gray, and then the gold itself from the black. And the ocean took a hand, diabolically removing the black sand patches. Heavy rollers wrapped them up and took them off, dispossessing the miners right under their melancholy gaze. They were told by the company to be of good cheer because still heavier rollers would soon bring the patches back again, but they 'got tired of waiting for that event and hastily fled the place.'

Thus the bubble burst.

But what of the bottles of black sand and the particles so innumerably shining therein? Wasn't this concrete evidence for those who went and those who stayed at home but bought shares in the company? The sadly returning adventurers and the dismal shareholders alike cursed 'the cruel wags that had exhibited in San Francisco sealed phials of dingy sand largely mixed with brass filings.'

There was gold, all right, but the specks were too fine to be profitably separated from the heavy black sand. The ocean had done a job of over-washing. The deposits, while lying in the greatest richness under the Gold Bluffs, existed in stretches most of the way from Crescent City to Eureka, in front of seventy-five miles of redwoods. Very conveniently you can walk over, and prospect if you like, a considerable acreage of the characteristic black sand at Trinidad.

The procedure was to wait for the tide to recede and then shovel up the rich patches left by it. This could be sluiced at a creek nearby. Thus a few men could make reasonably good wages from the quantity of small particles secured, but there was not enough for such numbers as rushed there to get it.

J. G. Bruff has left a firsthand account of a trip he made to the Gold Bluffs in January of 1851, before negative reports had punctured the excitement.

He went on the *Chesapeake* owned by the Pacific Mining Company whose realty holdings by the edge of the sea were exuberantly priced at all those millions. At sunrise on January 21st the ship entered Trinidad Bay, where Bruff found Trinidad 'quite a thriving little place.' Indeed, in that early period it was the leading town among the northern redwoods, with about thirty buildings, part of the impulse for its growth coming from the Gold Bluffs. In fact, there were two town developments underway by a pair of rival ship captains.

The next morning a Gold Bluffs official and another important man mounted very small mules. The ten others, including Bruff, walked. At Redwood Lake—no longer called by that name—they were ferried across at the cost of two dollars a head. As they went on they had to take the beach at flood tide, the periodically farthest reach of the breakers sloshing at their feet.

For a stretch of a few miles underneath the Gold Bluffs, the Pacific Mining Company had three stations, the lower, the middle, and upper. The lower station had just been abandoned. The *Chesapeake* lay off the middle station, the main one, consisting, in the way of headquarters, of two log cabins and two tents. Between the ship and the shore a buoy was anchored, with a line extending to the beach. Casks of goods were floated to the buoy, attached to the line, and then dragged in by men on the shore. The miners were numerous enough to require seven hundred pounds of flour. Several casks of bacon escaped in the surf, eventually to be food for the fish.

Bruff failed to describe the actual gold operations. These didn't look good enough to cause him to stay.

On his way out, at Trinidad, a miner gave him an earful about a fallen redwood that had been really high. It was not merely a giant footlog but a regular bridge across Mad River on the trail from Humboldt Bay to the Trinity mines in the interior. Teams and wagons crossed it, and it had no railings. The tree was fortunately flattish on the upward side (one of flatiron growth, correcting a lean), and being fifteen feet in diameter at the butt it was of course adequate for vehicles. The size was reasonable enough, but the miner gave him an extraordinary report of its height before it fell across the stream and broke in its upper reaches. Said Bruff, 'This magnificent tree was supposed to be six hundred feet in height.'

The miners that crossed the bridge got their gold far outside the redwood forest, and got an abundance of it. The great trees had the one big, abortive stampede to the Gold Bluffs, and escaped other digging. Trinidad, partly receiving its early vigor from the one winter of excitement, is a quaint, somnolent place now, with the noted headland back of it. Those working in the three or four trading establishments along the highway know little about the sea otters, and the black sands once all mealy with gold, so tenuous and easily broken is the connection with history.

Here and tributary to it were the manifestations, scant and short, of two exploiting activities which had such immense proportions elsewhere. In this land were no furs and no gold as men count them in their search for profits. The only riches the redwoods had were themselves, substantially nothing to put in a buckskin pouch, nothing to put on a mandarin's back.

9

MENDOCINO AND HUMBOLDT LOGGERS

A STAGECOACH visitor to the Mendocino logging camps in 1873 relates a terrifying sea story. The lumber schooners at that time took all kinds of risks coming into the small Mendocino coves or loading along unindented cliffs, as George Davidson mentions. One bluff indeed had an indentation, but it was one of forbidding nature, a huge cavern that pierced and mined the rock in a great opening, into which the breakers roared in a storm or at high tide and in which the wind whistled and shrieked, bottling up a fury of violence and sound.

A schooner stood off this place with its cargo of redwood lumber. A sudden gale blew up and the anchor broke. The crew hoisted sail, but the vessel was unmanageable in that heavy wind and heavy sea, and headed willy-nilly toward the great cave in the cliff. She sped into it with all sails set. Her masts 'snapped off like pipestems,' and the prow thumped into the opening with the heaving, white-crested swell of the sea. Two of the crew standing forward were killed by the ceiling of the cave. Five others rushed to the stern, the cave not being deep enough to accommodate the whole ship. There they clung until rescuers on the cliff above lowered ropes and saved them.

This visitor found that the redwoods loggers were mostly bachelors, living in shanties that used little of the lumber which they got out. But he judged these ten-by-twelve dwellings to be ample for male comfort—huts, kennels, snuggeries, he variously called them.

As he looked about and observed and interviewed old-timers, he heard about a man in the neighboring county of Humboldt who cut down just one giant on his place and got enough lumber from it to build his house, his barn, and to fence two acres besides. He learned of a schooner which was loaded with a full cargo of shingles from a single redwood. He was shown the stump of a tree from which enough ties had been cut to make a mile of railroad. He was told about logs too big to be handled all in one piece, which had to be blown apart with dynamite—not an uncommon practice.

This tenderfoot was caused to stare and gasp by the way the fallers could lay a tree precisely where they wanted it. For his delectation they planted a stake a hundred feet or more away and drove it into the ground with the falling column. He couldn't find it afterward, nor could they— 'Druv plumb through to Chiny,' they explained.

The dying noise of the redwoods was something that echoed long in his memory: 'When such a tree begins to totter, it gives at first a sharp crack; the cutter labors with his axe usually about fifteen minutes after this premonitory crack, when at last the huge mass begins to go over. Then you may hear one of the grandest sounds of the forest. The fall of a great redwood is startlingly like a prolonged thunder-crash, and is really a terrible sound.'

An eight-foot tree was a good day's work for a chopper. The loggers ground their axes once a week, usually employing the Sabbath for this purpose. And there was hardly another time for them to do it, for in the 'seventies they worked twelve hours a day.

He noted a somewhat distressing peculiarity of redwood which hasn't been otherwise much promulgated and which is contrary to modern claims that one of its good points is little shrinkage. Anyway, in the poorer seasoning practices then he found, or thought he found, that while it wouldn't contract perceptibly across the grain it did so lengthwise, like a railroad rail in hot weather. So he pointed out that, in weatherboarding with it, the careful carpenter might be accused of unworkmanlike cracks at the joints and corners.

The Russians were not the first to saw redwoods into lumber. The first real lumberman was John Dawson of Bodega, a ship's deserter in 1830 who later wed a Spanish girl. He was whipsawing the big logs by 1835. At Humboldt Bay in 1850 an old sidewheel steamer, with paddlewheels turned to pulleys, powered a contraption called a sawmill. A year later some Mendocino Chinese, in the contagion of Yankee ingenuity, turned out planks by rigging up a Muley perpendicular saw operated by the incoming and outgoing tides. By 1854 Eureka was manufacturing more than twenty million feet of lumber a year. In 1876 a total of 1100 vessels crossed the Humboldt bar.

Ships under various flags were in time hauling redwood lumber to the far places of the various continents. Some of those sailing from Eureka in 1910 were the Norwegian *Sark,* to Adelaide with 1,345,048 feet of rough-clear redwood; British *Iran,* to Calcutta with 1,204,996 feet of railroad ties; American Barkentine *Aurora,* to Mexican ports with 1,221,728 feet of railroad ties; British bark *Antiope,* to Sydney with 1,081,865 feet, some of it dry door stock and some of it shingles; *Nehalem,* to South Africa with a half-million feet of railroad timber—a previous shipment having been used for the South African mines; British *Bankdale,* to Peru with 802,864 feet of redwood ties; *Sequoia,* to Hawaii with one-third million feet.

Wasteful were the early logging practices. The timber, being both very large and very soft, was much damaged in falling. Beds often had to be prepared, adding to the expense, for a ten-foot tree taking two days to fall might require a week to fix up the bed for it.

The bark had to be peeled off, for the thickness and texture of this would put a saw out of commission in short order. After falling and before yarding-out, the ground was burned over to destroy the immense amount of debris. Said one observer:

> Nothing is more appalling than the sight which greets the eye upon emerging suddenly from the tall, stately green redwoods upon the scene of desolation which follows the logger. The whole country is a blackened, charred mass. The very soil has been burned and shows the result of intense heat. Every living green twig, every vestige of life has been wiped out. Redwood reproduces itself from the suckers which spring up around the stump, and the effect of fire evidently makes little difference, proving the sublime struggle nature makes for reproduction.

The waste in manufacturing redwood lumber ranged from a third to a half. The wood varies in grain and color; the side of the tree exposed to the wind is harder than the protected side. The average yield to the acre in Mendocino County was 35,000 feet; in Humboldt and Del Norte Counties 60,000 to 100,000. High ground partly accounted for the better yield in the north. Groves appearing the same might have entirely different values for producing lumber. Swamp-ground trees, from an excess of moisture, are more likely to have rottenness and defect and be hollow-butted.

Redwood uses listed in 1915 included balusters, newels, porch rails and posts, columns, moldings, clapboards and shingles, doors, flooring, siding, shiplap, barrel staves, tank and silo stock, laths and lattice, grape stakes, fence pickets, railroad ties.

There was a redwood barrel factory at Arcata. Fort Bragg in 1913 shipped a carload of redwood tanks to the San Diego Brewing Company. Fifty carloads of box shooks went out of Eureka in 1914 for the canning establishments, some to the Mississippi Valley. The Union Lumber Company at Fort Bragg shipped large quantities of redwood sawdust to the interior lands of Bacchus for packing grapes. About thirty thousand cords of tanbark, redwood undergrowth, was shipped from Eel River and Bull Creek.

Back of Crescent City a special and peculiar variety of redwood was reported in 1907. Outwardly the trees looked like any others, but the wood itself was white and remarkably clear of knots and imperfections.

Sometimes an accidental twist or curl was given to a young tree, continuing in the growth to form 'curly redwood,' with spiral whorls in the grain, very ornamental and much sought-after for fancy work.

Swamp redwoods may show an interesting excrescence known as 'redwood fungus,' appearing as a huge knot or wart but being wholly a growth of the bark and not having any distinct grain. When cut into slabs it has a mottled, deep-red color, all filled with little bird's-eyes. It was in demand at good prices for panelwork and billiard tables. These knots in the tall, growing trees often were covered with lodged leaves to form a soil, so that they became lofty gardens of ferns and trailing vines, 'very pretty' up there in the air, adding delicacy to bigness.

10

LOGS PASSING IN THE NIGHT

———

CAPTAIN HUGH ROBERTSON of
the Robertson Raft Company was in the Pope & Talbot
lumber office in San Francisco. With him was John M. Ayres,
his assistant in the business of transporting logs by means
of great towed rafts, of shipping five schooner-loads at a time
without a schooner. But in the dark midnight disaster had
hit him hard, not in the violence of storm-heaved billows
through which the straining hawser went till it parted; instead, mysteriously, as if while his back was turned, a thief
had noiselessly and viewlessly taken his trailing cargo away
from him and been able to hide so big a thing, still to hide
it when daylight came upon the level plain of the sea.

Though a hundred men could have taken passage there,
no one had been on the turtle deck of that tremendous hud-
dle of logs—no saboteur to make the raft, and himself with
it, a derelict in front of the rocky coast of southern Oregon.
The helmsman of the steering steamer *Czarina* had observed
the flashes and the eclipses of Cape Blanco light. Before
daybreak he would see those of St. George's Reef and Trinidad along the redwoods coast. He did see them, and sooner
than he expected, with the *Czarina* speeding along minus
her heavy trailer.

An eight-hundred-foot raft tied together with a hundred and seventy-five tons of chains, and containing logs (no redwoods) worth a fortune—5,000,000 or so board-feet—had been lost upon a quiet sea.

Captain Robertson, John Ayres with him, was discussing it with the Pope & Talbot officials, to whom it was also a matter of concern, for their mills would have sawed the logs.

It was a castaway monster, nearly a sixth of a mile long. No whale, dead and abjectly floating, was ever so big. It had a fifty-foot beam, a twenty-six-foot draft, and lifted its expansive hogback a good many feet out of the water.

Yet for nearly five weeks after it was lost its huge bulk had been to the sea no more than a needle to a haystack. It had not been seen piled in wreckage upon a beach. The *Czarina* had looked for it for two days. Two tugs had scoured the ocean for two weeks.

What could have happened to such a mighty piece of flotsam?

Even while Captain Robertson, John Ayres, and the Pope & Talbot men talked, in walked a sailor.

In fiction what follows would be condemned as coincidence. But it is fact, as true as responsibly veracious men remember, as true as in their remembrance they can tell.

The sailor walked in and asked, "Is this headquarters of the company that lost a log raft at sea?"

"Who are you?" asked Robertson.

"Formerly a fireman on the steam schooner *San Pedro*, sir."

"What does the *San Pedro* have to do with the raft?"

"She was towing it, sir."

The sailor explained that the schooner was compelled to leave the prize because she ran out of coal.

"All them logs made a heavy load, sir."

"We know."

The ship had hurried north to San Francisco to refill her

bunkers. She was in the harbor now but would lose no time in returning to bring the raft in as salvage.

"Where is it?" .

"We left it not far off San Pedro Harbor, sir."

"What's your interest in telling us all this?" asked Robertson cagily.

It developed that the sailor had consumed too much in an Embarcadero saloon. When he returned to his post on the *San Pedro* in his unsound condition, he was promptly fired. He was simply evening up the score by telling.

Robertson gave him a hundred dollars. "Stay in San Francisco," he said.

The apostate sailor's tip seemed on the square, certainly worth following up. Captain Robertson spoke to Ayres, "Follow the *San Pedro* when she puts out after refilling with coal."

Ayres immediately chartered a tugboat and gave her captain a primary order, "Keep the *San Pedro* in sight." He gave the captain a secondary order, "Keep well back of her."

The tugboat stayed as far as possible behind the schooner but never lost her to view. The crew followed her running lights at night. They watched her through a telescope by day. When they neared the location the sailor had indicated, the tugboat captain spurted up at all speed to overhaul the schooner with his faster craft. This made the schooner captain suspicious, and he headed the *San Pedro* west. But the tugboat was not thus to be put off the right course; she kept straight on due-south.

In an hour there was the lost raft, as intact and tight as ever in its chains. The tugboat made fast to it and, towing it, started back to San Francisco. Meantime the thwarted schooner had come alongside and demanded and been promptly denied salvage rights. Six weeks after the raft had been lost it was tied up safe and snug in San Francisco Bay.

In due time the Pope & Talbot mills sawed it into lumber.

It had got loose along the shores of southern Oregon. The schooner, with its frustrating shortage of coal, had come upon it no great distance north of San Pedro. The same south-flowing ocean current which the Manila galleons knew, had drifted it five hundred miles in five weeks' time.

How did the raft break loose from the *Czarina* in the first place? Nobody exactly knows to this day. Captain Robertson was day watch, ever keeping a vigilant eye on the great mass of logs. Mark Schwager, assistant foreman, was night watch. On this particular occasion, at midnight, he had gone below for coffee. For all the chains that bound the raft together, it was pulled along by a big manila towline. When Schwager came up from the galley, the rope did not go out of the spindle taut; it dangled there.

The *Czarina*'s captain refused to stand by till daylight. He declared he was short of provisions and put into Eureka, the redwoods capital. Later he went out and searched two days, and then, eagerly enough, headed for San Francisco.

The raft had come down from Seattle, successfully rounding Cape Flattery. The year was 1900.

What caused the big manila hawser to break? A cut would have been too-obvious sabotage. The seamen's union, afraid the log rafts would put the lumber schooners out of business, had with bills and resolutions protested to Congress that the mammoth ocean behemoths were a menace to navigation. Whether there was any connection between all this and the midnight event must, as one reporter has said, 'be left to the imagination.' After all, the wrist-sized manila towrope could have broken in an entirely natural way, considering the tremendous strain upon it even in a calm ocean. But the sea, often a good saboteur itself, did not in this instance hurl the great sticks against the crags but, taking the raft into a ruddering channel, right neatly substituted for the *Czarina*.

During the period of these self-tightening rafts, patented by Captain Robertson, a total of a hundred and ten were taken seven hundred miles from the Columbia River to San Diego, carrying almost as much lumber altogether as is cut in the redwoods in a year. On the run there were but three serious misfortunes, all of them along the coast of the redwoods—a curious fatefulness for competitive timber floating past, this Douglas fir from the north. Two disabled rafts were towed into Santa Cruz. The last of the hundred and ten broke in two in the sea. But even then there was no dissolution; the great chains still held and the raft was towed in two parts into Fort Bragg. There it was sawed into lumber and duly shipped to San Diego.

The Hammond Lumber Company, from 1902 to 1922, safely landed fifty-three rafts in San Francisco. The steamer *Arctic* reached the port from the Columbia River with a big one in tow in fourteen days. During a score of years the loss was only six per cent.

All the while the schooners continued to carry the redwood trade. There was an abortive effort by Captain Robertson to raft this huge timber to San Francisco, and one raft was actually built, in 1891 at Fort Bragg, but it couldn't be launched from the shipways on which it was put together. So the redwoods schooners did not have to meet the new competition, and it continued to devolve upon such Mendocino navigators as Captain 'Midnight' Olsen, so called because he could put his ship into one of the 'dog-holes' of the coast in the blackest midnight.

One Robertson raft, the only one built at Coos Bay not far north of where the redwoods stopped, met with misadventure upon misadventure. The tug *Ranger* started out with it, but both tug and raft put ashore to keep from going over the bar in low tide. High tide came in the night. In trying to make fast in the blackness, the tug broke her rudder. Four days later they started out again. The raft willy-nilly went ashore and stayed there twenty-four hours. No sooner was it floated than it grounded hard and fast on the South Spit, the breakers of a rough sea piling over it in the night. The tug, with a six-hundred-foot hawser, kept hold of it, however, till ten o'clock the next morning. Then the raft floated off, but, in reversal of the towing, dangerously took with it the tug, which had to cut loose. When found the next morning, it lay piled up on the north side of the jetty but still held together in the embrace of the chains.

In three days, with the aid of a lifesaving crew and with some reorganization of the mass, it was pulled away from the jetty. But by now a hurricane was upon the sea. The tug was run ashore to have enough anchorage to keep the raft from drifting out into the billows. Next morning the tow was started on its way once again, but grounded on the middle quicksands.

Two tugs now worked at it for five days. Sardonically, after they had failed, it floated off by itself. Another tug, the *National City*, with more power than the *Ranger*, took it in tow.

The raft got across the bar on a December day. But success was short-lived. Along the California coast they ran into a winter gale, near Cape Mendocino, where winds can blow swift. The raft went to pieces in the sea. Some of the great chains released their hold and sank to the bottom. Some were dragged to the shore by the cast-up logs, to become red and scaly with rust. Off the redwoods coast still another big raft had met its doom.

11

FIVE PEOPLE

HONEST HARRY MEIGGS

H<small>ARRY</small> M<small>EIGGS'S</small> vision expanded to match the gandeur of the redwoods but it expanded to the discomfiture of a good many citizens. That grand environments create grand men is a conception more poetic than factual; otherwise an ambitious hombre would merely have to annex himself to a big mountain, a big river, or a big forest and grow big by happy and easy contagion. In four instances of a conspicuous correlation between the magnificence of *Sequoia sempervirens* and its inhabitants, three were sent into exile—a great soldier, a great writer, and a great builder. The fourth, a great inventor—John Dolbeer, who devised the donkey engine—stayed on.

Meiggs, whose sobriquet of 'Honest' wasn't exactly like Lincoln's, had his first experience with the redwoods in the San Antonio forest where Berkeley and Oakland now are. In 1851, at the age of forty, he bought an unfinished sawmill there. But the boundaries of this tract of timber were too narrow for him. The next year he built a sawmill on Big

Creek near Mendocino City, where the redwoods were without limit. He rapidly became one of the leading manufacturers and dealers in the industry. With headquarters in San Francisco, he kept putting up sawmills and planing mills till he had a dozen; at the city's North Beach he built a wharf one-third of a mile long; he owned several sloops and schooners; he hired five hundred loggers for the logging camps in Mendocino County which furnished timber for his operations.

He also became a large speculator in San Francisco real estate, and therein lay his ruin, if a necessary flight from one nation to become rich and renowned in two other nations can be so characterized.

A depression hit; the bottom dropped out of Honest Harry's real estate. He forged great quantities of city warrants, which his position of alderman enabled him to do, and borrowed money on these at an interest rate of ten per cent a month.

He was generous, genial-mannered, and popular. These qualities delayed but did not finally prevent the rise of ugly rumors. So he decamped, but did it in a manner becoming a man of redwoods dimensions.

In 1854, two years after he had built his first Mendocino sawmill, he fitted out 'in a lavish manner' his own ship, the bark *American*, put his family aboard, told his acquaintances he was going to take a cruise about the Bay, and in the night sailed out of Golden Gate, leaving San Francisco victimized to the amount of about a million dollars.

In a few months the *American* arrived in Chile. At first the Chileans were suspicious of the foreigner and his schemes. During the period of their suspicion the $8200 with which he landed was reduced so completely to nothing that he had to pawn his watch. But Chilean trust immediately succeeded his visit to the pawnshop, and within five months he was prosperous.

He built railroads for Chile until Peru practically commanded him to come north and build theirs. So he left Chile, where he was the great 'Don Enrique,' where he had spent a dozen years gathering in vast wealth, where he lived in a $600,000 house in Santiago. In Peru, employing as many as 20,000 men at a time, he built the Central Railway, the highest in the world, across the Andes. His contracts within a decade amounted to $125,000,000.

He bought up his bad San Francisco notes cheaply, to change 'Honest' from a term of satiric contradiction to one that was real. In further nostalgia, he induced the California legislature to pass an act dismissing all indictments against him. This the governor vetoed, but the legislature passed it again over the former's head. However, it didn't seem quite enough to the exile to clear his way for a free and honorable return, so until his death at sixty-six, in 1877, he lived on in South America, the industrial hero and railroad king of two republics of that continent.

In all three cases, the men who had to leave the redwoods held strong remembrances of the trees as they neared the end. The great soldier dying of cancer told how he had expected to come back to the country where they grew. The great writer (of whom more in another chapter), living in England, turned to them across two-score years as subjects for his later stories. And Harry Meiggs, the great builder become rich and renowned in the countries whither he had fled, wanted laws fixed up for his return.

CHETCO JENNY

Chetco Jenny, a noted white man's wife, lived at the northernmost edge of the redwoods. South of her village the great trees stretched densely and then scatteringly for a total distance of five hundred miles. North of her village a traveler could go on interminably without seeing a redwood. This Chetco River terminus to the Oregon groves was at its mouth about six miles north of the California line and twenty-five miles north of Crescent City. How different were the opposite boundaries of the forest in human terms—Father Junipero Serra laid away in a redwood coffin in the utmost south, and in the utmost north an Athapascan squaw eating some of the heart of the white husband she helped to kill.

The husband was Ben Wright, married to other squaws before Jenny and with the blood only four years old on his hands from massacring forty-eight Modocs. When he was appointed Indian agent in southern Oregon, he had Chetco Jenny with him as wife and interpreter. With him also was a half-breed named Enos, formerly with Fremont, dissembling faithfulness . . . and biding his time.

Enos stirred up Chetco Jenny and 'aroused flaming jealousies in her Jezebel breast.' From the government she received a salary of five hundred dollars a year for being interpreter. Wright could talk Shasta very well and some other inland dialects, but not the tongue of Chetco Jenny's people.

This white Indian agent, who looked much like an Indian in dress and in the wearing of long, glossy hair, did not the least suspect the terrible jealousy of Chetco Jenny or the treachery of Enos. He was lured to the village of Gold Beach. There the pair killed him. The year was 1856.

His heart was cut out, roasted, and portions of it made a repast for the two. Wright could live with three squaw wives and despise Indians. Chetco Jenny could live with a white husband and do this. How little transference may be possible in the closest of unions.

Enos was later hanged at Port Orford. Chetco Jenny promptly dropped out of the records of history.

U. S. GRANT

The half-year that U. S. Grant spent in the redwoods had no effect on them or on their settlements, but it was a turning point in the great destiny of Grant. In back of what seemed unfortunate circumstances at the time, but which proved to be fortunate ones in disguise, was the leading citizen of pioneer Eureka, one James Ryan. In histories and promotion literature his name leads all the rest as the successful founder of redwoods lumber manufacture. Captain Grant, even at thirty-one (his age in the redwoods period), was not highly energized. This man Ryan was. He not only ran the first paying sawmill, but kept a store, and his predilections for activity caused him in addition to be a pilot, bartender, Indian trader, alcalde, surveyor, and, it is declared, a preacher. The vital man of affairs furnished the means for the indolent army officer's undoing.

Conspicuously among the commodities of Ryan's Store was a barrel of whiskey, always there, always on tap.

Fort Humboldt, only nine months in advance of Grant's coming, had been established as a post for protecting the settlers against the redwoods Indians. (In the northern precincts of Eureka on Route 101 there is a sign directing motorists to the site.) The fort was located in what was then Buckport, an extinct village of early days. It had no impressive palisades and fortifications, only some earthwork. Eureka itself was in its infancy, only three years old in 1853, but in a robust infancy, with about a hundred ships a year coming into the harbor. The redwoods stood close around this settlement of unpainted houses. And the captain's actions were not in keeping with their dignity, only his silence was, only his brooding.

Responsible chroniclers tell of two results of the affinity between the barrel in Ryan's Store and the slouching, moody West Pointer, speaking in monosyllables. One was that in an absurdity of imagination he got hold of three buggies and three horses, segregated vehicles and animals, connected up two buggies as trailers of the first, hitched the three horses tandem, and thus went through the streets of Eureka. The other was that while paying off his men he himself had too obviously anticipated the proper spending of his own pay at Ryan's.

Grant was not in charge at Fort Humboldt. Over him was Major Robert Buchanan, a stern believer in keeping leather polished and buttons in their buttonholes, and in upholding all things appertaining to military ritual. Martinet Buchanan had put up with a great deal from his slipshod captain, but this was too much. Grant was advised to resign, and he did. In any case, he was homesick for his wife and small children back in Missouri. He was tired of barracks life. And he was definitely fed up with the major.

It is more than a manner of speech to say he was obliged to leave. Historians have reflected upon what might have happened if he had remained in the army. He might have commanded a regiment in the Civil War.

He had nothing against Eureka, the redwoods, or the over-vitamined Ryan. He hoped to come back to the Pacific Coast sometime. But for the next decade, as he told a friend, agriculture was his objective: 'Whoever hears of me in ten years will hear of a well-to-do Missouri farmer.' In ten years it was 1864, by which time his glory had reached quite around the world.

He himself, in his *Personal Memoirs,* wrote one paragraph about his redwoods sojourn:

The death of Colonel Bliss . . . which occurred July 5th, 1853, promoted me to the captaincy of a company then stationed at Humboldt Bay, California. The notice reached me in September of the same year, and I very soon started to join my new command. There was no way of reaching Humboldt at that time except to take passage on a San Francisco sailing vessel going after lumber. Red wood, a species of cedar, which on the Pacific coast takes the place filled by white pine in the East, then abounded on the banks of Humboldt Bay. There were extensive sawmills engaged in preparing this lumber for the San Francisco market, and sailing vessels, used in getting it to market, furnished the only means of communication between Humboldt and the rest of the world.

It was April of 1854, after approximately six months at Fort Humboldt, when he resigned, but his pay and allowances amounting to $92.50 a month continued till July. 'I left the Pacific Coast very much attached to it,' he said, 'and with the full expectation of making it my future home.'

Humboldt County settlers' literature has not remembered to quote this statement of the redwoods country's most eminent convert.

THE LAND FRAUD KING

The Homestead Act was the loophole, bigger than a barrelhead, through which 'timber shoplifting' became a bigscale operation far less condemned by the public contemporaneously than now retrospectively, all the more so because the former couldn't easily see its one-for-all policy. In 1903 a Eureka journalist referred sarcastically to the 'roolins' of the Interior Department, to 'Calamity Sparks who sat in the department chair with his club and hatchet,' and to the interpretations which made 'the law black one day, and white the next, with the facility of a prestidigitator performing sleight of hand tricks.'

The 'swamp angels,' the cattle kings, the timber barons, all used the homestead subterfuge. One Nebraska stockman had to bring in Civil War widows far and wide by train. In the redwoods it was much more convenient. Dummy homestead entries could be made by sailors loafing in the Eureka bars.

The most spectacular entrepreneur of the redwoods land frauds, who in time languished for seventeen months in jail, wrote his confessions while he languished. This man, S. A. D. Puter—Steven A. Douglas Puter—was raised, and raised the hard and honest way, among the redwoods themselves.

At the age of two in 1859, Puter was taken by his parents to Humboldt County in the heart of the redwoods. Here, on a homestead on Mad River—the stream which Route 101 crosses just north of Arcata—he had his home until he was thirty-one years old.

He who was to guide so many others in magnificent looting of the public domain had his first experience with that domain as a hard-working axman for a deputy United States surveyor in running the lines of several townships in the big Humboldt timber. His wages as axman were modest enough, sweat-of-the-brow tiddlywinks, as he very quickly learned, in comparison with available rewards for a bright young man. Applicants for claims later paid him $25 each for locating them and $25 extra for building a cabin as required by the government—cabins from redwoods on the place, twelve by sixteen feet, about the cheapest housing project on record. Entrymen often had not a single night's sleep in these structures, which represented the minimum in architecture next to those of the red Indians. But less than a year later the absentia owners, alleging a continuous residence, made final proof. Puter had a fourth association, his third profitable one, with the public's redwoods—as a real estate broker. He sold the claims for the entrymen to a Eureka capitalist at prices from $800 to $1200 a claim. Then the Eureka capitalist sold them in a contiguous lump at $25 an acre to a big capitalist company, which in turn sold them at a still higher price to an operating company that began to cut the trees and manufacture planks and beams and railroad ties.

These transactions did not yet entirely turn young Puter from the ways of honest work. For twelve years he had made a hand among the actual redwoods loggers, part of the time as a teamster driving twelve-horse outfits hauling logs over a skidroad to the landings.

Next the deputy United States surveyor gave metes and

bounds to a dense body of redwood timber in the northern
part of Humboldt County. As soon as this was thrown open
to entry, the same big capitalist company, through its agents
in Eureka, began to hire men to file on the whole tract, for
the Homestead Act had been improved most conveniently
by a Timber and Stone Act in 1878.

Said Puter:

> I have known agents of the company to take at one time
> as many as twenty-five men from Coffee Jack's sailor
> boarding house in Eureka to the county court house,
> where they would take out their first papers, declare
> their intention to become citizens of the United States,
> after which they would proceed direct to the land office
> and make their filings, all the location papers having
> previously been made out. Then they would appear
> before a notary public, and execute an acknowledg-
> ment of a blank deed, receive the stipulated price of
> $50, and return to their ships, or to the boarding house
> from whence they came. The description of the tract
> filed on was afterwards inserted and the transfer of title
> completed to the corporation.

An agent of the compay went to Great Britain and sold
the whole tract to the so-called Scotch Syndicate.

Everything was going fine for the company. To make it
go finer still, they sent their own lawyer to the national
capital to circumvent the land laws without so many inter-
mediaries.

Better if they had let well enough alone. The General
Land Office got suspicious and sent out an investigator.
Puter said the company took care of him. Two others ami-
ably found no evidence of fraud. The fourth, an appointee
of Grover Cleveland, was different. Under Special Agent
B. F. Bergin, the smooth land dealings ceased to be smooth
any more. His report caused about two hundred entries to
be first suspended and then canceled. Involved was title to
60,000 acres of redwood timberland in Humboldt County,

valued at $20,000,000. Says a historian: 'The case was contested with all the ability and power that vast wealth could command, and more than four hundred witnesses were examined during the trial, which was won for his Government by Mr. Bergin.'

The jails claimed a number, but not yet Puter.

(*The Valley of the Giants,* by Peter B. Kyne, perhaps the best-known novel to come out of the redwoods country, drew on such actual marauding for its fictional villainy.)

The canceled entries were afterward filed on by bona fide settlers. Even so, Puter was able, much later, to sell 30,000 acres of the tract to a Minnesota millionaire, the 'most selfish, covetous and avaricious landgrabber' with whom the experienced Puter ever had dealings. His indignant description seems to have come less out of outraged ethics than out of withheld commissions. Puter was to get fifty cents an acre for buying the tract at an average price of $9 an acre. He said he was 'bamboozled' out of this, actually getting but a thousand dollars, and that only after a dozen trips to Humboldt County, livery stable hire, hotel expenses, and a year or so of time devoted to the wealthy Minnesotan's interests.

The law did not catch up with Puter for his redwoods operations; it did for his Douglas fir ones in the northern forests. He stayed in the Portland jail for seventeen months, until he was pardoned by President Theodore Roosevelt. His disclosures, written while in jail, were published in 1908.

BUILDER OF THE CARSON HOUSE

Lumber from the greatest lumber tree in the world is for the most part used hiddenly. From its magnificence in the living forest it goes to obscurity in manmade structures— in the ties that trains pass over, invisibly in the mines, in foundations that are not seen, time after time in supporting but concealed places. It is not possible to point out great or beautiful buildings and say they were made of redwood. This for nearly a century has been largely the fate of a wood which, without garniture, delights the gaze and never affronts it.

The most notable dwelling in the redwoods region is itself not indigenous in its surface materials. What has kept it so solid and enduring is redwood. What the eyes linger upon is mostly not.

The Carson House in Eureka is one of the best examples of late-nineteenth-century dwelling architecture in the country, and is said to be the most photographed residence in America. It makes a favorite postcard for tourists in the drugstores and curio shops all along the Redwood Highway. Said Chet Schwarzkopf, 'Up to Eureka came Hollywood to film the epic saga [*The Valley of the Giants*], not once but three times. The Carson home was the center of the story.'

Finished in 1886, it has the decorations, bay windows, towers, and cupolas of the period. Its main cupola was not merely decorative. From there the owner, William Carson, could look out across Humboldt Bay and out beyond the breakers of the ocean to see the ships coming from distant ports to his mills.

Possibly it was the architects, possibly a cosmopolitan sense of reciprocity, that caused redwood to be relegated to the unseen parts of this house that was the fulfillment of a long dream. Carson called in the leading architects of the time and gave them, very much to their own surprise, a free hand. They had carte blanche to furnish the best according to the taste of the 'eighties. From South America came mahogany, from the Orient teakwood, from eastern America hardwoods. In this he could have simply been an export merchant buying from the continents and regions to which he sold, in an interchange admitting the limitations of his own goods for finish-work.

But the lumber that he sent out in schooners to the far

places, was it not more than merchandise, more than something he shipped for ties and did not care to use as wainscoting for his own house? For thirty-five years, many of them with ax and saw and bull-team goad in his own hands, Carson had been making redwood lumber. Knowing it as few men do, its every texture and every hue, had he failed to see that a redwood plank is as beautiful as a mahogany one? Or in his laissez-faire attitude toward the architects had he ruefully but silently let them use what was acceptedly stylish?

Whatever the reason, the Carson House failed to be an example of complete redwood construction, failed quite to be the 'Mansion of the Giants' as sometimes called. Underneath the alien surfacing much redwood went into it, timbers from Carson's own mills, into the foundation and other parts to make it permanently solid and unsagging, to keep it as erect through the generations as one of the trees.

William Carson was a pioneer who came to Humboldt Bay soon after its rediscovery, at the very beginning of lumbering. With John Dolbeer he was a partner in the Dolbeer & Carson Lumber Company, which remains one of the most important firm names in the redwoods industry. They were so successful that, a few years previous to his house-building, they bought 20,000 acres of redwoods forest. Though his operations became vast and prosperous, he remained a working industrialist, close to labor and the dignity of labor, and so complete was the popular goodwill toward him that his great house was received with much the same gladness as if it had been a fine public building.

It has been kept up with uninterrupted care. Its striking nineteenth-century lineaments, with scarcely a trace of nineteenth-century age, cause it to appear a startling reassertion and rebirth of a past era.

12

SEQUOIA SEMPERVIRENS

A REDWOOD TREE is the loftiest thing alive. Nature builds higher—mountains, sheer canyon walls, bleak headlands rising perpendicularly from the sea. Man also—the Great Pyramid, skyscrapers, the Eiffel Tower. But these are dead. The ascending redwood bole is full of the juices of vitality; the cloud-mingling brush of its foliage is bright with animation. Many reach up two hundred feet; a number exceed three hundred feet; and one, in the transcendent elevation of life, is three hundred sixty-four feet. 'They tickle the feet of the angels,' said a man as he gazed with thrown-back head, not irreverently.

Walk through a forest of big trees, especially between Klamath River and Crescent City, and by their tallness they have the effect of making rough ground ahead seem smooth. There may be dips, and gullies, and ravines, but the sight does not take in the various planes wherein they are rooted, or the corresponding rises and dips of the tops. The normal up-and-down reach of vision is filled with big columns that pass out of range above and below. As you look in this way while on the move, you may, almost unconsciously, descend a slope or stumble over an abrupt jumpoff, so strong is the illusion of level ground.

These heights have all the greater impressiveness because they have been attained by such resolute undeviating aspiration. The bushes and saplings stand erect, as if at the command of a drill sergeant. Throughout their long existence they never stand any other way. They lean enough to require wedging when the lumberman fells them, but not enough for the eyes to detect. They make a beeline for the clouds, drawn straight up and up during a hundred or a thousand years, as if magnetized from above by a force stronger than all the side-pushing of storms and seasons. If in too-great gregariousness they collide, there is still no compromise; both go up together at right-angles to the earth, as precisely as a carpenter's studs from the sill. If one is defeated and dwarfed by the more vigorously expanding girth, the greater shade of the other, it stands there defeated but it stands unbending. Moreover, it stands opportunistically, perhaps for four hundred years while growing only a fiftieth of an inch a year; then, if something happens to the smothering neighbor, it at once begins to grow sixty times as fast.

This universality of the redwoods upright posture increases their hold upon the imagination. Here a whole forest, with seldom an exception, does what no nation of men has been able to do, where a few rise and remain erect but most are stooped.

Against what might naturally be expected, in view of such great heights, the roots of a redwood are unusually shallow. The towering trees merely sit balanced upon the ground, instead of being anchored in it—nothing but colossal ten-pins when the storms and winds come rolling, all the more on account of their leveraging height. Yet even on the Mendocino coast, where gales blow farther in a minute than a modern automobile travels, they have stood, and have stood up straight, through the centuries. Josiah Gregg told' about getting into a mass and crisscross of fallen logs that was like a jam in a stream, but in the main one is surprised at finding the forest floor not more littered—and what litter one does find is in some measure due to old age and the inevitable lying down to die. For all that the redwoods seem to be set up so precariously, nature has given them an extremely solid footing.

The roots, while shallow, are widely outspreading. These subterranean guy ropes may have the coverage of an acre or so. Where a fallen tree makes a footlog across a wide stream, the upturned base, with roots and clay mingling to form a sort of reinforced concrete, rises up in a vertical and rounded wall like the end of a big Quonset hut. In addition, almost every redwood is flaringly buttressed at the base. This serves as a kind of balancing apparatus. When a tipping starts above, the buttress starts getting bigger and shoulders the tree back. The whole lower bole grows preponderately in the direction of the lean; hardly at all opposite. Cut such a one down and see how a cross-section of its timber has a flatiron shape.

The more *Sequoia sempervirens* is observed, the more astonishing appear whole sets of immunities, one ready when another fails—immunities to vicissitudes and, most strikingly, to extermination itself. When there is too much solicitous sentimentality by outsiders for their preservation, a practical local person, who may have had to fight re-encroachments upon his little field or meadow, is likely to remark, "You can't kill a redwood."

And there is much evidence on his side. A big specimen may produce as many as a million seeds in a year. These are so tiny, so little from so much to spring, that it takes 123,000 to make a pound; and so unobtrusive are both cones and seeds that some redwood residents believed for a time the trees had no seeds at all. The cones, egg-shaped and purplish-brown, are only about an inch long; whereas those of the sugar pine will run fourteen inches long. Four or five of the seeds nestle under each cone-scale. They take hold quickly of the life they are going to keep so long. Planted in April, they may be ready for permanent places in the forest in November. They are likely to start off too fast; in the Scotia nursery root-pruning is sometimes needed 'to hold them within bounds.'

In one instance the fact that redwoods have cones was made dramatically manifest to a forester of the Pacific Lumber Company. He had energetic harvesters, the squirrels. From one colossus they dropped down three hundred pounds of cones; each week he picked them up; the next week they had another supply for him. This particular tree produced that year a total of 5,000,000 seeds. No wonder the squirrels sought its harvest.

Negatively, the seeds have a low percentage of germination, not more than twenty per cent, ordinarily much less. That squirrel-harvested tree's five million seeds would not at best have started in excess of a quarter-million seedlings —enough, however, to reforest five hundred acres, nearly the area of a pioneer's donation claim. Affirmatively again, a clinging cone has been found to be fertile after sixteen years, and three-year-old saplings have borne good seed.

But this prodigious seed fecundity is only a secondary source of propagation. The tree mainly reproduces itself through sprouts. It is the only conifer which does this. The sprouts have all the response and vigor of horticultural slips. They will appear fast upon the heels of devastation, they will grow enormously in a single season, they will emerge like grass, and even in advance of it and of weeds, from a burned-over area. Around one stump in the path of a fire, three hundred sprouts sprang up. And they do not have merely a transitory existence. Two or three feet high, often more, at the end of the first year, they may in the years allotted to a man grow one hundred-sixty feet high and over three feet through. Once, at the Scotia nursery, not only were the roots clipped but the tops also. Just for curiosity the cuttings were stuck in the earth. Forty per cent of them rooted and grew, were later set out in a cutover area, and went right on toward becoming big trees.

Even this is not the last of the tree's versatile anchorages upon the future. It commonly has burls, full of little eyes, every eye an adventitious bud, as quick with the instinct of life as a potato eye. You can buy a little piece at a novelty shop, put it in a dish of water, and soon have a fern-like bouquet. Burled piling of a railroad trestle has been clothed for a year with shoots.

While entomologists are schooled and trained to protect other forests, the redwood has a natural insect resistance. A kind of powder post-beetle and two fungi inhabit but do not imperil the tree, except one of the fungi indirectly. Man is redwood's only legged enemy.

Fire, that terrible scourge of other trees, causes tremendous damage, but does not as a rule permanently destroy. Some have thought that the sheathing of thick bark serves as an asbestos protection, and it does to a large extent. But much redwood is in mixed stands, and the accompanying growth—on the upper slopes, fir and tanbark; on the lower, spruce, hemlock, cedar, yew, alder, cascara, knobcone pine, laurel, cypress—are inflammable and produce a consuming heat. The rotten hearts of ulcered giants especially are attacked.

In addition to the tree houses along Route 101, there are many trees in the forests with hollow butts. One, a dozen feet through, has been scooped out with fire so that it stands on a twenty-inch rim all around, except for the four-foot doorway; it still goes on living. What a tenacious hold upon the eternal! The old English botanist who, in 1804, gave the redwood its species name of *sempervirens* found the best word in all the Roman vocabulary to describe it.

On the lower Klamath stood a hollow stump, thirty-eight feet in diameter, in which it is declared a packer in the 'seventies corralled his whole outfit of thirty-three pack mules. Lumbermen call these hollow redwoods 'goosepens.' In their capacious size, they have served husbandmen as implement sheds, chicken houses, and horse barns. And they have been used for less worthy purposes; in the days of Prohibition several of them housed moonshine stills. In a few instances suicides, instead of using gas or jumping off a height, sought out in some final fascination these remote charred chambers in which by their own hands to give up the ghost. The disappearance of each would remain a long mystery until some forest wanderer happened upon the body.

Yet the redwoods are not immune to death, which comes earlier than much irresponsible publicity would have the visitor believe. (Even the Redwood Empire Association allows a considerable amount of exaggerated age-estimating in its literature. The lumber companies, the foresters, and most of the local residents are more practical in reporting redwoods longevity.) In print the trees frequently antedate the birth of Christ, which is barely possible; according to Arthur Brisbane, 'they were old when Socrates drank his hemlock,' which is contrary to any sober determination of their venerableness.

Size and age do not always go together. At the Columbian Exposition in 1893 there were two sections of redwoods logs plainly showing the ring counts—one fourteen feet through was from a tree eight-hundred-seventy-five years old, the other sixteen feet through was from a tree two hundred years younger.

Foresters made the following age count of the trees on a thirty-acre tract:

YEARS OF AGE	NUMBER OF TREES
201 to 300	108
301 to 400	89
401 to 500	81
501 to 600	102
601 to 700	67
701 to 800	38
801 to 900	34
901 to 1000	31
More than 1000	17

About twice the age of Methuselah seems to be the maximum. Some reports have been made of trees two thousand years old, but these are few and secondhand and without confirming details. An actual birth certificate is not possible until after the tree is down. The means of telling are the annual growth rings, furnishing evidence as reliable as the teeth of a horse. The Mendocino County specimen (described in the following chapter in this volume) was, with its 1728 years, about the oldest by dependable ring-count chronology.

The redwood therefore, among American trees, stands not first but about third in longevity. The *Sequoia gigantea* may have a life-span two and a half times as great, and even an occasional gnarled juniper may be hoarier in age. Yet seventeen centuries, combined with its amazing capacity for regeneration, make it extraordinarily *sempervirens,* certainly the most so of all in the sense of a forest and not of individual trees.

And it is not exactly dead after it dies, so great is its resistance to decay, particularly underground. When he knew that the end was close, Father Junipero Serra ordered the mission carpenter to make him a coffin out of redwood. He of the great spirit must have had some solicitude for his mortal body, to wish it encased so lastingly. While ordinarily, in such reverent use, the wood's permanence is inferred, it chanced that the vicissitudes of this celebrated grave caused that durability to be directly known. Father Junipero died at San Carlos in 1784. The roof of the church fell in 1852. The parish curate was unable to find the grave three years later under the debris. But in 1882, ninety-eight years after burial, it was found, and the preserved condition of the redwood coffin made it identifiable as that of the noted padre, disproving the rumors of removal to Spain soon after burial.

Fog is the *sine qua non* of the redwoods. Without it they do not grow; with it they are radiant, still youthful-looking at the age of a thousand years. In the account of the Dawn Redwoods it was noted that this moist climate was still a requirement in remote Central China. Some early inhabitants thought that redwoods caused fog, instead of the other way around.

Sometimes the fog is low, sometimes high—trunks may be in the sunlight while the summits are in mist, or the tops may be wrapped in vapor while the ground is clear. It saturates the boughs to such an extent that in a dense forest one may believe a delicate rain to be falling. Writers have found these sea fogs very interesting and have frequently mentioned them. Botanist Archibald Menzies, near Cape Mendocino in April of 1892, noted in his journal, 'The extreme points we saw were not very detailed on account of the thick hazy weather.' Bayard Taylor acknowledged their departure soon after breakfast, '. . . the morning-blanket of gray fog, which the hills of the coast range never kick off till nine or ten o'clock.' Said Robert Louis Stevenson, 'Where their shadow touches, color dies out of the world.' Benjamin F. Taylor agreed with the other Taylor that they were off and gone by the middle of the morning: 'It is only fog from the Pacific that rolled in last night. It will all be neatly reefed by ten o'clock in the morning. You see it swinging about below in wreathy gay gauze, like a woman's veil in the wind. It comes from the salted sea, a sort of pickled relish.'

Departing so accommodatingly after coverleting the trees in the night, the fogs mostly leave bright daytime weather and a forest in full view to the summer traveler.

13

THE TREES ON EXHIBIT

"THE BIGGEST plank ever sawed," exclaimed one of twenty-eight million visitors to the Columbian Exposition at Chicago in 1893.

It was a board sixteen feet, five inches wide, big enough to form the flooring for a sixteen-foot room, 'and no Parisian rug was ever figured to look so beautiful as its polished surface, the grain curling in beautiful and intricate shapes.' Added an Englishman, 'A grand specimen of what can be cut from trees which may be numbered by hundreds of thousands if not by hundreds of millions.' Three redwoods were shipped to the fair, with some extra exhibits, including this plank and redwood shingles from old Fort Humboldt where Grant had been stationed, shingles that were 'sound after forty years' exposure.'

Durability featured a redwood exhibit twenty-one years later at the Forest Products show in Chicago and New York. The chief item was an old Humboldt barn built sixty years before. Inside this, visitors could also see old pieces of tanks, old fenceposts, and other old and weathered samples. The barn, never painted in its threescore years of existence, didn't have a board that wasn't in good condition. The miniature forest outside was surrounded by a fence no rail of which was less than forty years old.

To the St. Louis Fair in 1904 the owner of the Stump House at Eureka shipped a thousand canes made from redwood bark. At the World's Fair in San Francisco in 1939, Humboldt County had a model sawmill, on a scale of one inch to a foot, this scale being carried out even for the shingles on the roof. There was a well-stocked log pond, the logs being sections of redwood limbs. A bull chain continually dragged these up to a mechanical sawyer, who stood at the controls to operate the carriage. The mill was reconstructed for the California State Fair in 1947.

At the Civic Auditorium in San Francisco in the summer of 1948 was exhibited a redwood two-room house called 'The Rancher,' having 913 feet of floor space, with resawn redwood rustic siding and redwood shingles—a 'lifetime' home, factory-built and taken by truck to building sites in twenty-eight sections and various bundles of lumber, in a total amount of fifteen hundred to three thousand board-feet of redwood.

Along the Redwood Highway a folk sculptor has dramatically left his handiwork at a few places, notably at the 'Trees of Mystery,' where he carved a heroic statue of an Indian on a horse, both animal and rider with their heads down. He chopped and whittled the whole out of a single tree, the stump of which is now a pedestal for the statue. All the tools he had were a jacknife, ax, and saw. This itinerant sculptor also carved some big California bears for passing motorists to see.

One of the most interesting of permanent exhibits is outside the offices of the Union Lumber Company at Fort Bragg. It is a section of the largest redwood log known to have been grown in Mendocino County, felled on Big Creek in 1943. Its estimated age was 1728 years, by sober determination and not by the extravagant guesses frequently met with. Height of the tree was 334 feet. Diameter of the stump was 21 feet 2 inches. The log made 140,800 feet of lumber. To fell it required a saw twenty-two feet long. The time to saw it down, the actual working time, was sixty hours, or seven and a half days. It is indeed an impressive relic of venerablness in a living thing. It had already been standing more than two and a half centuries when the Roman Empire ended, and more than three and a half centuries when Mohammed was born. It was 1105 years old before Marco Polo returned to Venice, 1405 years old when the Pilgrims came to Plymouth Rock, 1561 years old when the Declaration of Independence was signed.

The Little River Redwood Company of Humboldt County has a standing tree in their woods of which they have made a lumber scale, with allowances for falling and for twenty-two inches of bark. It is 208 feet high and 20 feet through. When cut it would be made into fourteen logs to produce 361,336 board feet of marketable lumber, or enough to completely build twenty-two average-sized houses.

Humboldt and Del Norte Counties have catalogued their particularly big or particularly tall specimens, five in the former region, two in the latter. In North Dyerville Flat, Humboldt County, is the tallest tree in the world, that 364-footer. At the time of its dedication in 1931, the Save-the-Redwoods League was careful not to be rash in claiming it as the highest, for the world is a big place and in one part of it there was just possibly a competitor. It was a common saying that an Australian eucalypt, starting out the same time as a baby, would grow fifty feet while the baby was growing three. Reports were abroad that some of these lofty gums of Australia and Tasmania approached a height of 500 feet. Indeed, Webster at that time soberly stated, '*Eucalyptus angydalina,* the peppermint tree, is the tallest known tree, often attaining a height of over 400 feet.' So the Down Under region was investigated. It was learned that until

1880 there had existed a 375-foot eucalypt, but it had since died or been cut down and the tallest one left was at Melbourne and was only 326 feet high. Timber cruisers talk hopefully of finding a still loftier three, but so far they haven't by several feet. The North Dyerville redwood stands in the supreme altitude of a living thing. Its girth, however, does not (as is often the case) match its height, for it is only forty-seven feet around and fifteen feet through. It would make a little more than half as much lumber as the Little River tree, only about 125,000 feet.

Two literary trees are included among the lofty ones, the Samuel G. Blythe and the Irvin S. Cobb trees, respectively 340 and 335 feet high. The former is only a little over and the latter slightly less than 11 feet through. Still taller is a redwood in Bull Creek Flat which is 345 feet high and fairly big withal—72 feet around and 16 feet through and scaling enough lumber for twenty houses. The Big Redwood Tree, on Prairie Creek, is 90 feet around but only 200 feet high.

The two Del Norte trees are both big and high, and rank well with the greatest redwoods. The Mill Creek giant is 16½ feet through and 340 feet high, with a lumber content of twenty dwellings. The other, north of the wide Klamath River in Big Tree Park, is 16 feet 2 inches through and 280 feet high.

At one of the big trees the American traveler's predilection for leaving his initials behind has been officially and fully humored. Both an old log lying inside the tree's enclosure, and the fence itself, have been completely covered with tourist calligraphy, so a fourteen-inch board, eight feet long, has been placed on top of the latter to carry the overflow of jackknife engraving. This tree in time, if it has not done so already, will surpass the famous rock on the Oregon Trail which testifies that the signatory disposition was well implanted even in the covered-wagon wayfarers.

Resort owners have made good use of the peculiarities of the big trees to entice and feed the wonder of the tourist.

There are two featured 'drive-thru' trees. (This motoring experience is free.) Two of capaciously hollow butts are points of interest. Tree House, excavated by an ancient fire, has a ceiling fifty feet high, 'the world's tallest one-room house'; the tree ascends above it 250 feet and is still growing in apparently vigorous health. Chimney Tree was also hollowed out by fire, in its case from the base to the broken-off top; four regular-sized trees, rooted high up, are growing out of the bole.

How, in the case of the redwoods, life is ever fed by death is strikingly evidenced in two places. On the south fork of Eel River, which Route 101 follows for a long distance, twenty-two redwoods are to be found growing vertically from a fallen one. North of Crescent City is a similar phenomenon of a corpse suckling new life. It is called the Never-Dying Redwood; fourteen trees have sprung up vertically out of a prostrate redwood log.

It is an interesting experience to watch the great modern mills manufacturing the huge logs into lumber. The public is invited at Eureka, Fort Bragg, and Scotia. The Pacific Lumber Company mill at Scotia is the biggest of all, and, being right on Route 101, the most convenient to visit. The establishment year after year extends hospitality to motoring multitudes, and is efficiently prepared for it. You go to the employment office for a permission slip. With this, which as a rule nobody subsequently asks to see, you are given a redwood pencil and a little rectangle of thin redwood on which are printed directions for your visit.

There are overhead walkways running the whole length of the mill, which is as large as a city auditorium. In this way you can look down from above on all the operations. It is a sort of two-ring exhibit. The two sides ceaselessly carry on in parallel activity and noise. Two carriages, each with a man at the controls, shove the whining saws through the log and then dart back swiftly to begin again.

You first wach a log being slowly dragged up out of a pond as big as a lake. You see it being ripped into thick wide boards and sent on rollers to the next station. You can follow it through until it is made into lumber, with men at various controls to send each plank where it belongs. You see some of it emerge at last as small-dimension stuff, causing you to wonder what difference it makes, except in quantity, how big a tree the lumber comes out of, because it is all so much the same after the milling.

You can follow the process still farther in a neighboring building, where the lumber is made into various products.

Across the pond is a big peeling shed. Hand-peeling still has to be done, for even the long modern saws cannot manage the bark, but in modern practice it takes place at the mill instead of in the woods. Machinery turns the logs, which used to be the work of peavies in men's hands, but the bark is still pried loose and off with crowbars, two young men working together on a big log. The integument makes an elephant's hide seem thin; it is up to sixteen inches thick.

A chute goes from this peeling shed to the bark shed, bigger than a dairy barn. The bark that once was waste is now shredded and processed into a number of commercial products. These shredders and driers of the Pacific Lumber Company cost half a million dollars, but even before the war bark by-products amounted to about a third of a million a year. A big buyer is Westinghouse, which uses a processed bark for insulating electric water-heaters. On the athletic fields of universities it is used for running tracks, placed as a resilient filler under layers of cinders and clay. Its insulation purposes are extended to cold-storage warehouses, dairies, fur vaults, butcher boxes, farm iceboxes, sound-deadening. The Company also manufactures Palco Pete's Mulch, which keeps open the pores of soil and lasts for years. Numerous other articles are made out of the thick tree rinds—pincushions and wipes; table, lamp, and bathroom mats; cork jackets and fishing floats; mattress filling and carpet substitutes. In the processing, the bark is finely shredded and cleaned of dust and solid matter. Then its red volume, soft and fluffy, is pressed and packed into hundred-pound bales for market.

When you have finished looking, you don't go and thank the management for the courtesy. They wouldn't appreciate it; it would simply make double work for them. You get in your car and drive on south or north along Route 101, full of admiration for modern lumbering efficiency, philosophizing on how ingenious and clever man is in making small neat things out of big rough ones.

Along the way you may observe a moving exhibit of trucks heavily loaded with three or perhaps only a single log, or of trains at a crossing or where the thoroughfare parallels the logging railroad. There is an old picture of a tiny locomotive pulling seventeen flatcars, each loaded with a single huge log. Scenes like that are not likely to be yours in these times, but as you come into the Eel River country you may well see a train of nineteen flatcars carrying an average of three logs each.

Quite the most active redwoods resort you will find along the Redwood Highway is the one suspensefully billboarded as the 'Trees of Mystery.' It is located about five miles north of Klamath River and sixteen miles south of Crescent City. As you approach it along the highway, a loud and metallic and very chummy voice comes to you from a loud-speaker. Nothing is said about the price of admission in the roadside advertising or in these megaphone buildups. Vocally you are beguiled through the entrance, which is a hollow redwood log through whose tunnel you can easily walk erect. It is not native to the place, but was hauled from seventy miles away and, since it weighed fifty tons, the hauling was a good deal of a problem for the construction company that did it.

The management has applied the Robert Ripley principle to the business of displaying trees. Some of the oddities over which much is made scarcely warrant the interest of a sober and discriminating citizen. An octopus tree, with roots that have seized upon the fallen trunk of a redwood, is declared to be the largest octopus tree there is—10 feet through, 150 feet high—and the redwood log it grows upon is accredited with an age of five thousand years when it tumbled down, five times what it probably was. There is also the world's largest cathedral tree, sanctified with a prodigious amount of synthetic sentiment. An organ plays Joyce Kilmer's *Trees.* Here is posted the redwoods poem by Joseph B. Strauss, builder of the Golden Gate Bridge. There are benches for meditation and mayhap for prayer. Couples get married here often, it is said.

Soon after this you emerge from the Trees of Mystery. And lo, as you exit you find yourself inescapably right by the cashier. She is very explicit. You pay fifty cents a head and proceed through a novelty store. As you walk away with your companion to get in your car, the chummy megaphone voice calls out a cheerio: "The two gentlemen just leaving—happy vacation, fellows."

The oldest man-made exhibit, dating back more than a century and a half, is not in America but in London, in the herbarium of the British Museum. This is the scientific specimen collected by Menzies, Captain Vancouver's botanist. Collected in 1792, it was classified by Lambert in England in 1803 and called *Taxodium sempervirens,* in the belief it was related to the Southern cypress. Endlicher, a German botanist, was the one who changed its name to *Sequoia* forty-four years later, in honor of Sequoyah, the half-breed who invented the Cherokee alphabet. He anglicized his name to 'George Guess,' but his Indian one thus bestowed has been handsomely perpetuated.

14

ENORMOUS STUMPS

—————

MAN, CONDITIONED by thousands of years of tillage, ever looks upon the earth with a plowman's eyes. He goes out among the big trees and digs the toes of his boots into the soil and picks it up and feels it and crumbles it and smells it. Loam that can produce such gargantuan timber ought to be rich enough to grow heavy crops of wheat and alfalfa and corn. And so his imagination sees the trees removed, the great stumps all blasted out, and cultivated crops growing bountifully and profitably upon the forest floor.

So lovely is this inward vision that it dominates the actual sight of the great reddish pillars reaching so far up toward the clouds.

Man, the inveterate husbandman with his incurable mania for clearing land, has habitually moved into the forests and made farms out of them. The chambers of commerce in the Great Plains region can properly declare that prairieland is the American's ideal. Everywhere across the nation he has tried to make all other land like it.

What man grows and takes to market or threshes or husks or puts in silos, is very precious; what God grows wild is in the nature of a weed, even if it is a redwood tree.

Captain George Vancouver was a soil examiner in the red-woods country as early as 1793. As he walked about in the neighborhood of Trinidad he was a mariner turned agricultural agent. He made the following report: 'About the outskirts of the wood the soil, though somewhat sandy, appeared to be tolerably good mould lying on a stratum of clay.'

The first whites to try out the soil for agriculture were the Russians at Fort Ross, from 1812 to 1841. They did nothing to root out the stumps, but planted in little patches in a catch-as-catch-can way. Their scattered small fields totaled one hundred seventy-five cultivated acres sixteen years after they had built the fort. The potatoes of Alexander Kuskof, the superintendent, yielded a hundred-fold, other gardens sometimes two hundred-fold. Some reports were of two plantings a year, but of only five or six tubers to a hill. The wheat crop was only five- or six-fold, and the fogs that were so good for the redwoods made the grain rust. The Russians and Aleuts were said to have been the worst farmers in the world, but they at least astonished the indolent Indians and the *mañana* Spaniards with their prodigious energy.

One of the most spectacular jobs of clearing was carried on several decades ago by Charles Willis Ward, who had been a New York businessman. At tremendous expense he created Carlotta Ranch upon two hundred thirty-two acres where once had stood a grove of especially large redwoods, having diameters up to a score of feet. In this instance the owner came into possession of the foundations of the forest after it had been made to vanish by others. He bought the land and the stumps. The latter were numerous and they were large. But he had 'plenty of energy, ability and money . . . the magic words which evolve rich agricultural lands from redwood forests and silage from stumps.'

Said the Dairy, Land, and Development Edition of the *Humboldt Times,* Eureka, in 1916:

> When this ranch was bought it was largely covered with giant stumps, some over twenty feet in diameter and equally high. It looked like a Herculean task to remove these mammoths but dynamite solved the problem. It required one hundred and fifty pounds of the explosive to remove the largest and an average of fifty pounds was used. After being blown up the debris was hauled into a gulch and used for filler, the land was raked, plowed and leveled and then planted to alfalfa and corn. The finest stand of alfalfa in the county is the result and on this land comprising one hundred and thirty-five acres, which cost $350 per acre to clear, alfalfa will run six tons to the acre per annum with five or six cuttings. The illustrations show the scene of the transformation from the original logged-off land to the level, productive sandy loam soil thirty feet deep and rich beyond compare.

Three of the nine pictures showed the original logged-off condition of the land—such as to make the local dynamite agent lick his chops. One showed a man and a team of horses beside a stump which loomed up, in comparison, like a building.

If the stumps had been let alone, if the dynamite man had not made his handsome sale, if Mr. Ward had not been so indomitable, then the shoots about the stumps would eventually have made another forest, as was demonstrated at Fort Ross. But it would take threescore and ten years to grow trees four feet through, and in that time each acre would produce four hundred and twenty tons of alfalfa. Which would pay the most taxes, the hay or the trees?

Not everyone could afford to wipe off in a quick operation the vestiges of a great forest, as did Charles Willis Ward. Back in the period before World War I it was the custom of ranchers to buy from the big timber companies tracts of logged-off lands in the fog belt good alike for growing redwoods and red clover. The settler would sow his clover and other forage crops right in among the stumps, letting his livestock roam and graze at will. In time, as he had the energy and could afford the dynamite, he would get around to blasting out the stumps. The land thus secured was declared by one rancher of the redwood country to be the 'richest that lays outdoors'—not hard to believe, seeing the tremendous crop of timber that could grow on an acre.

Clearing logged-off redwood land is such a matter of individual prowess and resourcefulness, such a dismaying project outside common practice, that the agricultural advisers simply have not recognized it with printed literature. Each man with the preposterous courage to attempt it finds himself in an operation with special and formidable problems.

In current practice the clearing agents, in addition to the farmer's own sweat and muscle, are dynamite, bulldozers, tractors, and fire. Dynamite, an old ally in the redwoods, is still used the most. The bulldozer, which here meets something to challenge its omnipotence, is employed to some extent. After the stumps have been cracked and split with dynamite, a tractor with a winch does good work in pulling out the pieces that are still big and resistant. Burning out the stumps is a different problem from that in the Douglas fir region, because of the redwood's incombustible characteristics. In clearing, by whatever method or combination of methods, the roots cannot be left in the earth to rot, because of the redwood's further characteristic of long durability underground. They would endure to obstruct and stop the plow of the farmer's grandson. So they must be removed at the outset below the plow level.

Present-day costs are so high that cleared land must be greatly needed or coveted. A big lumber concern, combining most of the methods, recently cleared an area at a cost of $650 an acre.

Says W. D. Pine, State of California farm adviser at Eureka: 'It does not pay to clear this land for agricultural purposes except by one trying to hew himself out a home on a few acres, or by one who owns bottom land on which redwoods have grown. Most of this bottom land is overflow land from the rivers, very fertile, and, once the stumps are removed, is quite valuable. At one time much of our good dairy land was covered with redwood and spruce stumps. The hill lands or prairie or uplands are not cleared to any great extent.'

15

DIFFERENT LUMBERMEN NOW

—————

WHENEVER a redwood died a retinue of lesser trees died with it. It was like a pagan king taking his entire menage along into the other world. This was the case for over a century. A tree several yards through and from two to three hundred feet high, thickly beset by other trees, could be brought down only with tremendous havoc in the broad path of its fall. Furthermore, it was likely to break up and be made worthless unless there was prepared for it a soft bed, which upon uneven ground might require enough wood to suffice a householder for a year. The bark, as thick as modern paving and yardaged like the carpets in a mansion, covered up and smothered out new growth. When the donkey engine and wire cables and highlines took out the thrashing, smashing logs, they left wide swaths of havoc. The densest-wooded land in the world was laid bare, no green thing remained, complete desolation followed the logger. He didn't *per se* enjoy the destruction; it made extra work for him; it was entirely owing to the nature of the huge and lofty tree which only yielded its life at the expense of all other life. He finally burned the wreckage to get clear space in which to chop and saw.

Even in the selective logging of today a giant still frequently involves other trees in its ruin, and goes to earth in a crash rather than in an isolated fall. But its descending pathway, nearly the length of a city block, is picked with greater care; it may with extra labor be felled against a lean to minimize the damage of its downward passage. And enough small conifers to make Christmas trees for a city continue to give up the ghost to furnish soft funeral couches for the tree's fall.

The power saws of today have made the felling of the giants and their segmenting into logs much easier and faster than in the old crosscut days. The evolution from pioneer to modern methods was described by H. I. Bower, veteran logger of the Pacific Lumber Company, in an experience paper for the Pacific Logging Congress in 1936:

> In the early days, redwood timber was felled entirely by ax, as the only saws then available were too short for the purpose. At first pole axes were used, with double-bitted ones coming into favor later.
>
> Fallers, or choppers, as they are known locally, work in pairs. An outsider is often impressed by the number of tools a set of choppers carry around with them in a redwood operation—two axes, two eight-foot saws, one twelve-foot saw, two dozen plates, one dozen shims, ten wedges, two sledges, one pair of gun sticks, one plumb bob, twelve springboards, six pieces of staging.
>
> Areas are felled as units. The chopping boss—bull buck—plans the strips. A set of choppers may work anywhere from a month to three months on a strip. The timber as far as possible is felled uphill, heavy leaners being an exception. The chopper's primary concern is to fall the tree with the least amount of damage.
>
> After determining the direction of the fall, smaller trees, called 'bedding,' are felled into the layout to build up the low spots. The undercut is now put in. The back cut is the next step. . . .
>
> Hand buckers working on contract were used entirely up to 1923. They were paid on the basis of the square foot area each cut made. Rates were from seven to ten cents a square foot.

The first power drag saw used in bucking by the Pacific Lumber Company was brought in by two brothers in 1923. The number soon increased to ten. The saws are owned by the men themselves. When peeling operations were transferred from the woods to the mill and the practice of burning before logging was abandoned, the bucking whether by hand or power was made more difficult due to the presence of more debris and slash. In some cases the logs were entirely buried. The logs were now covered with bark anywhere from two to sixteen inches in thickness, which did not help the bucking any. At present about forty-three drag saws are being used by the company.

So satisfactory and fast was the handpower of expert buckers and fallers that it did not rapidly become obsolete and hasn't entirely yet. Ray Shull of the Hammond Lumber Company entered a contest against forty other fast buckers. Two thousand people watched him win. He was twenty-three years old, six feet, five inches tall, and weighed two hundred pounds. He sawed off a 3-foot redwood log in just a little over 3½ minutes. But Charley Buck beat him another year by sawing through a 32-inch log in 2 minutes, 49⅘ seconds—with exactly 304 strokes of the crosscut. Peter Morelli, at a 'Days of General Grant' celebration in Eureka, won the log-bucking contest by severing a 30-inch log in ⅗ of a second over 3 minutes.

After the long postwar strike of redwoods workers, the fallers and buckers had become scattered and scarce. Said the logging superintendent of one of the big sawmills: 'In recent years few young men have been trained for this work and the age level is getting too high for security. Logging superintendents have clung to hand falling and bucking methods but power saws may have to be introduced.'

Usually the cost of felling trees goes down the bigger they are, but it is the reverse with the redwoods. The cost rises sharply beyond a hundred inches of diameter.

Falling operations can now very rarely be watched by the

public. For one thing, logging has receded back from the main-traveled roads; for another, visitors would be too much in the way. To be present at the crash of one is an experience that never quite fades from the eyes and ears, but it is hardly so awesome and terrific as the (previously quoted) description by the Mendocino visitor in the 'Seventies. Either the colossals don't fall so hard and thunderously as they did then or the modern audition is more realistic. One tree which the author saw felled was not lacking in proper dimensions—nine feet through and three hundred feet high. A power drag-saw went through it in about half an hour. Before the final severance a good deal more time than that was spent in driving wedges and shims into the cut, for the tree that looked as erect as a flagpole was four feet out of plumb at its three-hundred-foot top and was being felled the other way. Raising the bottom one inch at the cut took out the four-foot lean at the top, but that necessary inch, and another inch to make it bow a little in the right direction, required a great deal of sledge-hammering. The bull buck, probably in his forties, easily did as much of it as his two half-as-old assistants put together. As the tremendous tonnage resisted lifting, he remarked, "I've been doing this for twenty years and haven't been fired yet, but maybe I will now." But he finally brought it down, placing it (not so precisely as they used to do in Mendocino) with the top about three yards to the right of where he aimed it. This error caused some delimbing of another tree. When a visitor ran up the prostrate column and approached the tree of the collision, he was called peremptorily back. "Widow-makers," the bull buck explained, indicating precariously hanging limbs liable to fall at any moment.

The Caterpillar Tractor Company, for its proving grounds at Peoria, Illinois, bought a monstrous log from the Pacific Lumber Company. It was 100 inches in diameter, 24 feet long, contained 11,708 board-feet of lumber, weighed 57,100 pounds and was 1500 years old by ring-count. In its journey of 2500 miles across the country it made a full load for a railroad flatcar. At Peoria it was to be hauled by tractors under varying ground and grade conditions as similar as possible to the actual conditions which logging tractors met in the redwoods.

The tractor has been a big factor in 'selective' logging— taking the big timber and leaving that below a certain size, something which was possible in the case of only a few trees under the system of steam-logging with donkey engines and wire cables. The tractor driver must be skilled and he must be interested in order to avoid the reserve trees. It is his responsibility to do so. "If the tree were cut down," he is told, "you would have to avoid the stump anyway."

It takes time and patience to train a good driver, but it is a sight to watch him when he becomes really good. Under him is a seventeen-ton tractor. Behind is a four-ton skidding arch; behind, twenty tons of logs. Ahead are stumps, the reserve trees, and a steep grade. But in his hands and in their correlation with his quick eyes, the great machine is as maneuverable as it is powerful. It and its cumbersome load miss the stumps. This the watcher expects, because stumps with their formidable air of solidity have always turned aside the approacher. The triumph of the progress is the escape of the standing trees.

When he has dragged out his last load there is still a forest, not so majestic as it was, but green and living and full of promise. Perhaps in fifty years this driver's grandson will be driving a tractor there. He will need to be better still, for he will have to miss two sets of stumps, in addition to a thick growth of young trees yet unborn.

A big redwood is imperious and advantageous, a main-chancer and self-aggrandizer, a Turk among trees. Its stature, like many a great man's, doesn't result from tender concern for others. It hogs the soil, the root moisture, the sunlight, every nurturing thing about except the sea fogs. In a community way, its ineffable grace disguises a nature compounded of the noxiousness of a million weeds.

The large specimens make a splendid show of being hospitable to other growth, not only to smaller redwoods but to a mixture of other trees—fir, spruce, hemlock, tanbark oak, laurel, alder. But these are only glorifying accessories, welcome in lowliness but suppressed in competitive bigness.

The casual visitor doesn't know this, but the lumberman does, and trades on it in his selective logging. A little tree, disproportionately old for its size, which may have taken thirty years to put on an inch of diameter, soon shows a remarkable acceleration of growth after the lordly overtopper is removed. It may then expand its girth at the rate of an inch in five years, or even in two. And this period of being dwarfed is also a period of conditioning for choice lumber. When its new freedom makes it ready to cut, it will be clean-boled for fifty or seventy-five feet and half of its planks be without knots.

The dwarfing should not give the idea of trunks that can be circled by the sweatband of a man's hat. The giants keep the other growth very small in comparison with themselves, but the lumberman's reserve trees are not mere poles or saplings; they are often up to three feet through. 'Some trees being left now,' says Immanuel Fritz, 'would be regarded as "super-duper" choice timber in regions of smaller timber.'

In the growing of redwoods as a crop in perpetual yield, lumbermen count on a cutting rotation of about fifty years. On the best sites an average 20-year-old redwood is 8 inches through and 51 feet high. On good sites, at the age of 25, it is 9 inches through and 53 feet high. At this rate the best sites would in fifty years produce 116,000 board-feet an acre, good sites 95,000, medium sites 76,000. Most of the second-growth sites are good and medium.

Redwoods lumbermen started an important amount of timber growing as early as 1920, being thus in no sense additionally tardy in what was a tardy national impulse toward conservation. They saw that they were simply putting themselves in the cutover-land business, and this in all conscience was not profitable. It took thirty-five acres to keep a cow, two acres to keep a sheep. The rental was from nine to fifteen cents an acre. They banished the cows and the sheep, and for several years in the 'twenties annually planted something like 25,000 acres of cutover land, using several million trees from a number of large redwood nurseries.

Not all the denuded areas are being reforested, and there is only about a fifty-per-cent practice of selective logging, but the redwoods industry has gone a long way toward a sustained yield, a continuous production.

The original redwood belt contained 1,454,000 acres, about twice the size of Rhode Island. Three-quarters of a century of logging, from the pioneer 'fifties to 1925, had reduced to stumps a little more than one-third.

It is estimated that 41 billion feet are still standing. About 3 billion of this are withdrawn from commercial use and 5 billion are classified as recreational. Of the remaining 33 billion all but one billion are privately owned. At the present rate of cutting this will last sixty or seventy years.

In the half-century period 1899-1948, lumbering consumed 22 billion feet, totaled from the actual figures for forty-five of the years and estimates for the other five, including 1948. At ten-year periods the redwoods were eaten into as shown on page 122.

The total production reports are likely to give the impression that more redwood is being logged than is actually the case. Only three times has the annual cut gone beyond

YEAR	NUMBER OF FEET
1899	360,167,000
1909	521,630,000
1919	410,442,000
1929	485,606,000
1939	345,003,000
1948	600,000,000

600,000,000 feet, and only thirteen times beyond half a billion. There has also grown up in the redwood region a distinct Douglas fir industry, and in 1946 the cut of fir and other species was greater than that of redwood.

All the redwood area is far from being tied up in tightly clutching hands. Important tracts are constantly being bought and sold. In 1937, 35,000 acres in bankruptcy went for $800,000; and three years later the Pacific Lumber Company secured 22,000 acres in a solid body twelve miles long and seven wide, enough to supply this largest of all redwoods mills for twenty years. Most of this forest had been homesteaded in the 'eighties in 160-acre tracts and soon no less than a New York governor and his associates had bought up 6000 acres, which they kept till 1902. Delinquent taxes amounted to $26,000 on 4500 acres sold in 1944. There were purchases in 1945 of one tract of 25,000 acres and another of 13,420 acres, the latter for $700,000. This same year the American Redwood Company of Gualala in Mendocino County announced for sale a forest that contained 238,000,000 feet of standing redwood and 38,000,000 feet of down redwood besides 200,000,000 feet of Douglas fir, pine, and alder.

Over four-fifths of prewar redwood lumber was cut by nine big sawmills, the rest by about fifty small mills, which by 1949 had increased to approximately four hundred, nearly half of them sawing redwood in varying quantities.

Though there are eight or ten plywood plants in the region, their peeler logs have included little redwood. The tree which supplies the widest of all solid planks has presented problems of knots and glueing and drying to prevent its use for plywood in commercial quantities. Nor has it had to suffer the still greater ignominy of having its utmost bigness reduced to the utmost littleness to make pulpwood. The twenty-five shingle mills of the region, manufacturing the oldest commercial redwood product, have now formed into an association.

Still without economic value, still left in the woods, is the slash, a vast litter and a great fire hazard—limbs, tops, decayed parts of aged trees, chunks, brush. But in many logging operations the debris no longer includes the bark, the manufactured uses of which have been pointed out. Its mulch properties were discovered by John Alexander of Eureka, who, trying to solve the riddle of the tree's longevity and decay resistance, thought he found it in the bark. After successfully making plastic shingle boards out of the dust, he went on experimenting. He put some of it in a patch of dirt where nothing had grown well. Thereupon green shoots, immune to insects, shot up with surprising vigor. His formula was an inch of redwood-bark dust mixed with four inches of topsoil. The mulch did not turn to dirt, but kept its separate identity without decaying.

Early in the war the redwood sawmills had seven thousand employees. During and after the war, with many new mills, the number increased to ten or twelve thousand. On January 14, 1946, the Lumber and Sawmill Workers of the American Federation of Labor, consisting of about four thousand men, went on strike. One operator referred to it as being 'against our woods and mills.' For the trees, at least, it was a respite, the longest they had had from axes and saws since the coming of the Americans. For six months they put on thousands of feet of lumber; none was taken from them. The mills stood idle. That brief half-year measured the complete sanctity given to the redwoods, though the strike itself went on and on for a total of twenty-seven months, the union pickets not being withdrawn until April 13, 1948. Long before that the mills resumed production, and have since operated without a union agreement.

One plank in every seventy sawed each year in the United States is a redwood plank. This, if sapwood, is a creamy white; if heartwood, a ruddy color which deepens in direct sunlight. It may be one of nine grades, descending from 'Vertical Grain Clear Heartwood' to 'No. 3 Common.'

Of those seventy planks it will last the longest, declares the redwood lumberman, who will mention a log his mill sawed once. This log was found with a tree twelve hundred years old growing astride it. It had been dead wood that long, but it could be used for lumber. "It's still lasting somewhere in a building," says he.

He will also claim that, of the seventy planks, it has the most uses in modern life. It makes many bleacher seats, as in the stadiums of the Universities of Pittsburgh, Michigan, Minnesota, Iowa, Virginia, Louisiana, and McGill. The Stanford stadium used 450,000 feet, but four or five of the biggest trees could have furnished it all. Baseball fans sit on redwood in the American League parks at Chicago and Boston.

Another use is for tanks too numerous and varied to list. In the liquor industry redwood has a place with oak and chestnut. Nearly all California wine is made and aged in redwood tanks, some of them holding 50,000 gallons.

The common grades of redwood lumber are mostly marketed green in California. Siding is the biggest item in the eastern market, being principally employed for tank stock. Exports have long been worldwide, the most consistent buyers being Australia, New Zealand, Central America, and South America.

The manager of the Redwood Export Company points out

that, for several decades, Peru—where Honest Harry Meiggs was once railroad king—has been a customer for redwood railroad ties because of their proved durability in high, dry altitudes. In Central America the United Fruit Company is an important customer for its banana divisions; between 1939 and 1949 a Panama subsidiary used six million feet.

Since the early 'thirties the Redwood Export Company has sent representatives widely abroad to turn up business. One went to France, where the import duty was just $2 a thousand. Over a million feet was sold. But in about a year the duty was raised to $23 a thousand. "That," says the export manager, "ended the dream of the conquest of France."

Said Benjamin F. Taylor of the Santa Rosa Baptist Church in 1878: 'That house was made of a single redwood; and the interior, from the floor to the ribbed ceiling, was once wrapped in the same bark jacket.'

The church was nearly new when Taylor saw it, having been built on Ross and B Streets in Santa Rosa four years earlier. It is very much still standing. The fact that a single redwood furnished all the lumber was kept a secret from the congregation and the public until the church's dedication. The idea of a church-from-one-tree was that of Rufus Murphy, a redwood sawmill man from Guerneville, who supplied the lumber (the tree yielded 78,000 board-feet), and swore to the unique construction in a statement witnessed by a Santa Rosa attorney.

Big trees.

16

A MILLION TOURISTS

IN ANY scenic western region the tourist is a person around whom chambers of commerce build their activities, for whom much accommodating state legislation is passed, on account of whom highway departments are able to keep the lush gasoline taxes, though other state functions may drag along impecuniously.

The prospective settler with a hundred dollars in his pocket soon sees what a cold world it is. The tourist with a hundred is struck by the warmth and hospitality everywhere.

This person, who might excusably become a little heady at all the evidence of his desirability, has had a big influence on saving the redwoods. He is in holiday mood and spends what he has. Enough of this money now comes into the three principal redwoods counties of Mendocino, Humboldt, and Del Norte to make it one of the major sources of income, a lumber revenue *sans* the agency of ax or saw.

Honeymooners visit the big trees in thousands of pairs, and with them the essentially unexciting nature of the recreation is unimportant. Older people come in thousands of other pairs, and sedentary gazing is for them also sufficient.

But the rank and file of on-the-go Americans, before a week of undiluted redwoods aesthetics is up, are likely to suggest, "Let's go into Eureka to a movie."

In the mountains the tourist can at the very least get recreation with his legs as well as his eyes. At the sea three additional senses are delighted, by the surf in his ears, the saltiness in his nostrils, the sea foods tasted; and he can walk and wade, and swim and boat and fish and clam-dig and pick up agates, and any boresome hours in between can be charged up to a tan that will be the envy of the office. "But, dern it," complained a visitor, "what can you do in the redwoods after you've seen 'em and bought all the trinkets you want?"

Indeed, one redwoods resort advertises croquet, another horseshoes, a third table tennis, hardly enough for strenuous trippers even against the background of the majestic trees. An auto court puts as a fillip to its advertising, 'Enjoy the quiet redwoods.'

This noticeable absence of auxiliary delights made the tourist administrators and advertisers aware that travelers came but went and went too soon. They were en-routers, instead of more profitable sojourners. But the fault was in the promotion rather than in the intrinsic lack of supplementary assets. After all, the whole redwood belt is close along the sea; back of it is a high, wild mountain range; two famous western rivers flow through it. Redwoods country has all these and the redwoods too, and has begun increasingly to let the country know it.

The appeal to hunters is beguilingly played up. Big-game men used to come to hunt grizzlies; Joaquin Miller has told about one hunter being mauled on the ground and another treed, the grizzly alternately giving the two his attention. Gone now, he was the inhabitant who most nearly matched the great woods where he dwelt. In the 'lonesome land' to the east, in the Coast range mountains, lesser bears still feed in the clearings and cougars still lie in wait above the deer trails. It is also declared by the Mendocino people that bears and mountain lions 'are especially good in the hills off the coast'—between Route 101 and State Route 1, the Shoreline Highway.

Mendocino County claims to lead all other California counties in the annual take of deer. Quail-shooting there and duck-shooting in the marshes around Humboldt Bay and in the big lagoons, attract hunters. 'From ducks to bucks, from hares to bears' is the poetic way the Eureka Chamber of Commerce puts it. Chinese pheasants, that now widely distributed alien, have been imported into the redwoods country, although the hunter cannot expect to flush them and bring them down right among the big trees.

Fishing, and a great deal of it, is in the streams, in the ocean, and in the three lagoons along the highways. Fishermen from afar visit the Klamath River for steelhead and salmon—trollers, and casters with spinner or fly. At the height of the season people line up along the edge, each sportsmanly allowed sufficient elbowroom, while others sit on the bank behind, waiting their turns. The Eel River, which the Redwood Highway follows for so long a distance, is with its tributaries noted for steelhead, salmon, and trout. Some of the pools have names as well known as those of prominent buildings in a city. A promotion picture shows a redwood log in the background on Van Duzen River, a rubber-booted man in a pool with a trout on his hook, and a woman on the boulders at the edge with her rod bent and her line taut. Mendocino County itself has thirty-odd fishing streams; there are, altogether, hundreds of miles of trout watercourses.

Deepsea fishing accounts for many pleasant man-hours at historic Trinidad, near the Humboldt Bay jetties, and along the picturesque Mendocino shore. Clam Beach at the mouth of the Little River, where three thousand people have dug in a single early morning, is a famous place for razorbacks. The Mendocino abalone beds are extensively advertised, a number of resorts listing this as a special attraction. Humboldt Bay and the mouth of Eel River are crab-fishing localities. Surf-fishing requires no elaborate gear; many use mesh nets or window screening on hoops.

Motorboating, rowboats, and canoes; saddle horses and bridle paths back into the big woods; golf courses; the lagoons, the rivers, and the ocean for swimming; wildflowers for the amateur field botanist; airplanes for flying over the lofty trees: a whole list of non-redwoods things exists in extensive repertoire to afford the visitor variation from the majesty of the trees and to give a vacation to his other senses as well as to his eyes.

The redwoods country is reached by three highways marked in red on the oil-company maps: Route 101, the Coast Highway, from the north or south; Route 199, dubbed part of the Redwood Highway, from Grants Pass on Route 99 to Crescent City; and Route 299, from Redding on Route 99 to Arcata on Humboldt Bay. There are some others in black, notably State Route 1, the Shoreline Highway, from north of San Francisco to a few miles north of Fort Bragg.

There is a long segment along the coast, from Westport to Eureka, which is accredited on some maps as possessing a sort of automobile route, but the outsider attempting it from the north will find himself in a cul-de-sac where small redwood logging and lumbering establishments are all that break the primitiveness of the country. Driving across the mountains crookedly and narrowly from Route 101 he will wonder if every next turn won't be goodbye, after several experiences on sharp, hidden curves meeting hell-bent trucks loaded with redwood logs. The trip is begun in a tame redwoods grove; it ends in an uncivilized grove where the nostrils breathe in at a whiff the saltiness of the sea and the resinousness of the forest; and as the traveler takes in the doubly fresh oxygen he thinks how many times and how close he has just come to joining the big-tree serenity and immortality.

The black-lined Klamath River route—California 96— starts nine miles north of Yreka from Route 99. Smack on top of the Coast range at Weitchpec it turns north and west on the map, a black line made with a still finer pen. It is all right to stop and look at this mountain entrance to a mountain road, to look at it covetously and misgivingly; and it is decidedly all right to yield to the latter mood and go on. The route proceeds roughly and tortuously, but gloriously, through Wiregrass Prairie, along French Camp Ridge, across Robbers Gulch, through the Bald Hills (a peculiar prairie country just beyond the threshold of the great forest), and ends up at the coast at Orick on Redwood Creek.

Usually the visitor will go south a considerable mileage, through the Hoopa Indian Reservation and along the Trinity and into the Trinity Hills to Willow Creek, and there join Route 299 from Redding to Arcata. The national government built this road, but kept the curves, which are so continuous that for long stretches one can be blocked helplessly behind an antisocial lumber truck. One follows this route about 175 miles before the redwoods show up; they are driven through in half an hour, then one passes the big redwood mill at Blue Lake and comes to a whole covey of mills at Arcata, joining Route 101.

An explorer's variation of this Klamath River approach to the redwoods is to leave the Grants Pass-Crescent City highway at O'Brien's Store and cross the high Siskiyous at the only place a car can get over them, other than along the Pacific Highway or Route 99. Traffic is limited to jeeps and the various mountaineering varieties of automobile, although on the Oregon side it is being improved. 'One place where Kilroy wasn't,' says a rude sign at the top. Side trails are marked—Dunne Mt. Trail, George Ranch, Althouse Cutoff Trail, Hell Hole Trail.

A night drive of fifty-one miles to Orleans is an unusual experience. Here in truth is a winding thoroughfare, and the windings are short and continuous, and it is properly speaking a one-way road. It is hazardous in the daytime. Two stage drivers and several oil-truck drivers resigned because their nerves couldn't stand it. But it is safe enough in the night. The approaching headlights can be seen a long distance. Motorists are courteous in drawing off to the side to let you pass; you catch the contagion of their good manners and turn off a proper share of the time, so there is no narrow-squeak passing. In the way of fauna you are likely to see in the glare of your headlights, during the course of the drive, two toads, one burro, two cows, two deer, one rabbit, and one chipmunk.

Quite as pleasant as the journey itself is the day's end at Orleans, the remote mountain village which, from 1856 to 1874, was the county seat of now-extinct Klamath County. Hunters fly in for vacation weeks in this 'lonesome land.' Harvey Van Pelt, who runs the Orleans Hotel, is a man of cultivated manners and cultivated speech. Here you do not sit down to a meal aloofly, but with whoever else is eating at the same time; of all the dining rooms along the gateways to the redwoods you remember this one the longest and the most nostalgically. Mr. Van Pelt was for some years a state cougar hunter, and estimates that he has killed about sixty of the big cats.

There is another crooked and rugged lateral across the mountains from Red Bluff to Laytonville on Route 101, and a straighter one, California 28, from Sacramento to Albion on the Mendocino coast. The roads across the mountains from Route 101 to the Shoreline Highway are all crooked but very scenic routes. One railroad—the California Western—goes across from Willets to Fort Bragg; a passenger in a motor 'Skunk' can have a thrilling ride through the redwoods. The railroad's original 115 bridges in 34 miles have been reduced to 44 now. Enough redwood lumber has been hauled over these to build a city.

The foggy redwoods coast, so unbroken in its gloom to the old Spaniards passing in the dark, has that darkness unceasingly punctuated now by six lighthouses. Their varying combinations of flashes and eclipses are interesting to the motorist, who may pass from one range to another of their beams during a swift nighttime journey. From south to north, the beacons are Point Arena, built in 1870, a white, black-galleried, cylindrical tower, with a light 150 feet above the water and visible for 19 miles; Point Cabrillo, 1909, white, octagonal frame tower, 84 feet up, seen 15 miles; Cape Mendocino, 1868, white, sixteen-sided, pyramidal tower, its 422 feet making it the loftiest of all and its 28 miles making it the farthest visible; Table Bluff, 1856 and 1892, a square tower attached to a dwelling, 176 feet above the waves and penetrating 20 miles of darkness; Trinidad Head, 1871, white, pyramidal tower 196 feet above the water, seen 20 miles (this is convenient to visit; as an automobile takes you up, you can see how high and steep and rough was the climb of Heceta's padre with the holy cross of redwood in 1775); and St. George Reef, near Crescent City, 1891, square, pyramidal tower at an elevation of 146 feet and reaching out 18 miles in neon-like versatility, with eclipses five times as long as the flashes of alternating intensity.

The redwoods capital (population 21,380) is Eureka, 'the westernmost city in the United States,' with a forty-acre redwoods grove inside its limits. The logging and lumbering industry does not have a record of building gracious towns; one in the Douglas-fir region proclaimed itself the most civilized because it wore the most dinner coats per thousand inhabitants. Eureka, though not wholly concealing the economics that made it, is far from being like that. Of the logs-and-planks urbanizing up and down the commercial forests of western America, it is the most pleasing, the least characteristically marked by its leading product, with predominant aspects of a cultivated place and with a personality of its own, not too quick to grab for ritualistic modernization, not too eager to erase the evidences of its hundred years. Its being a lumbering center is agreeably modified by its being also an important seaport. By the time the town was a quarter-century old, a thousand ships were coming to it a year. Provincialism never had a chance to get rooted.

Arcata, also on Humboldt Bay eight miles distant, with a population of little over three thousand, is for its size at once more modern in its business section and more old-fashioned in its residences. The latter stand in attractive dignity in the town, at its edges, and out in the country surrounding. This is Bret Harte's old town, and the location of Humboldt State College. The hilltop affords a fine view of Humboldt Bay, which so many navigators failed to see from the decks of passing ships.

Perhaps next to Eureka in interest is Fort Bragg, right by the sea on the Mendocino coast, very trim and neat, yet keeping an atmosphere of individuality. Here the Labor Day celebration, 'Annual Return of Paul Bunyan,' brings competing lumberjacks from far and wide. Mendocino's Ukiah and Willets on Route 101 are prosperously up-to-date. The latter is the highway's southern 'Gateway to the Redwoods.' Crescent City, near the northern limit of the trees, has an agricultural personality appearing dominantly from out its sea-edging and redwoods-flanking. Practically ghosts as municipalities now, Trinidad and Mendocino City are wrapped about in the charm of their history. Long would be the roll call of all the redwoods towns; Humboldt County alone has forty-nine besides Eureka and Arcata, ranging in size from eighteen hundred to twenty-six souls.

17

THEY CAME AND WROTE

———————

FRAY FRANCISCO PALOU

Rᴇᴅᴡᴏᴏᴅs ʟɪᴛᴇʀᴀᴛᴜʀᴇ is at least old. Padre Palou wrote the following in December 1774:

Near the crossing there is a grove of very tall redwood trees, and a hundred steps farther down another very large one of the same redwood, which is visible more than a league before reaching the arroya, and appears from a distance like a tower. [The crossing is now Palo Alto, and the tree still stands, a landmark in the area. *El Palo Alto* has been designated the insignia for both Stanford University and the city of Palo Alto.]

We descended afterwards a very high range of hills all covered with redwood trees, very tall, thick and straight. In a valley which was very full of these trees, I saw one extremely large one which had its heart burned out, forming a cave, and one of the soldiers, mounted on his horse, rode into it, saying: 'Now I have a house in case it rains,' and it is true that neither he nor his horse would have been wet however hard it might have rained.

134

BAYARD TAYLOR

"Who cut down the magnificent trees that stood here?" asked Bayard Taylor.

"The Pikes."

A Pike, Taylor wrote on to explain, was the omnipresent fellow from the Missouri region—'long, lanky, and sallow . . . expectorates vehemently . . . has an implacable dislike to trees.'

Taylor, on his second journey to California, in 1859, made two trips of brief redwoods observation, one south and one north of San Francisco Bay. On the southern trip:

> We bowled along merrily and presently Redwood City, the county-seat, came in sight. Ten miles ahead towered the solitary redwood, two hundred feet in height—the old landmark of the valley. . . .
>
> For some ten miles our road led over the level floor of the valley. The land here appeared to be tolerably well divided into farms, the fields fenced with redwood, regardless of expense. I was glad to see that the fences were all substantial post-and-rail—none of those hideous worm-fences. Redwood timber has a great durability in the moist soil. Col. Fremont saw a redwood post at the Mission of Dolores, which had been in the ground seventy-five years, and had only rotted to the depth of half an inch. Nearly all the frame houses are built of this timber, and I never saw without pain its rich, *beautiful* natural color—intermediate between that of mahogany and black walnut—hidden under a coat of paint. If it could be preserved by oil, or a transparent varnish, nothing could be more elegant.

On the northern trip as far as Healdsburg:

> I perceived that we were already in Russian River Valley. Tall, dark redwoods towered like giants along the slopes and summits. . . .
>
> Fancy a country composed of mounds from one to five hundred feet in height . . . studded with trees— singly, in clumps, or in groves—which surpass, in artistic

perfection of form, all other trees that grow. Headlands crowned with colossal redwood were thrust forward from the ranges on either hand, embaying between them the loveliest glens.

'This,' said I, 'is certainly the last created portion of our planet. Here the Divine Architect has lingered over his work with reluctant fondness.'

WALT WHITMAN AND OTHERS

The redwoods have not extensively inspired poets. They can claim but one great poem, that by Walt Whitman printed elsewhere in this volume. It was first published in *Harper's Magazine* in February, 1874, and was included in *Centennial Songs* in 1876. This was a time when the early Mendocino logging operations were attracting the attention of magazines. Originally Whitman had the trees 'over a hundred feet high.' Apparently he became aware, or was made aware, that he wasn't putting them high enough. The whole poem is one hundred-five lines long, the thirty-five in this book comprising, however, all that are actually about the redwoods, the rest being meditations, prophecies, and philosophizing.

Joaquin Miller has in his long poem *Californian* a few redwoods lines, including. 'This side yon blazing evening star, seen through that redwood's shifting bough.'

The *Overland Monthly* in its career ran only a few verses on redwoods, the best being by C. E. Barns, who was a kind of John the Baptist for the conservationists: 'Vandal breeds, swing wide, strike deep and bring your landmarks low—and on your graves hands yet unknown for every chip shall cast a stone.' Sam L. Simpson, a man of considerable poetic standing up in Oregon, tried his hand but obviously didn't know much about the trees, for he placed miners with rockers and long toms among them. Joseph B. Strauss wrote a twenty-line poem that is popular in the region itself, two lines being: 'The greatest of Earth's living forms, tall conquerors that laugh at storms.'

These lesser singers, whose poems gushed from the heart, weren't as careful as the great Walt to get things right. Though no redwood has been found over two thousand years old, the builder of the Golden Gate Bridge had them existing 'through fifty centuries of kings,' and the *Overland* contributor required an old tree to declare, 'Ere Tyre and Ninevah was I.'

ROBERT LOUIS STEVENSON

In the summer of 1880, during his honeymoon stay in the Calistoga region. Robert Louis Stevenson set down three short chronicles of the redwoods. The longest, making a chapter in *Silverado Squatters,* was the report on the Petrified Redwood Forest which mainly featured an embroidered human-interest sketch of Charley Evans, the finder and excavator of the great fossils.

Another Stevenson story concerned a Mendocino City dentist who suddenly got tired of looking after loggers' teeth and 'flamed forth as a captain of banditti.' This amateur gang, for their initial project as road agents, pulled off a sensational robbery. Marshals and posses chased them for days, if not for weeks, 'among the intricate hill country.' The ex-dentist and several of his followers finally 'bit the dust.'

(Though usually provident with his material, later putting the Monterey country into *Treasure Island,* it does not seem to have occurred to Stevenson that a manhunt among the big trees would in his hands have made exciting fiction. The redwoods people themselves, in relish for this sort of romance, transported Black Bart to a redwoods setting. Tourist folders listed 'Black Bart Rock' as a point of interest on the Redwood Highway, until a road relocation crew in 1948 bulldozed it off and away.)

The third chronicle consisted of two descriptions of Sonoma County denuded of its once lofty trees:

'He showed me where some young redwoods were already spiring heavenwards from the ruins of the old; for in this district all had already perished: redwoods and redskins, the two noblest indigenous living things, alike condemned.

'Alas! if they had left the redwoods, the pines, in turn, would have been dwarfed. But the redwoods, fallen from their high estate, are serving as family bedsteads, or yet more humbly as field fences, along all Napa Valley.'

BRET HARTE

Three years after Grant left the redwoods, they received another distinguished sojourner, a young man as neatly garmented as the army captain had been carelessly so—Bret Harte.

To this day Bret Harte probably stands out as the best-dressed man in American literature. This sartorial elegance was not an affectation that followed spectacular success in letters. When in 1857, at the age of twenty-one, he took up residence among the big stumps at Arcata on Humboldt Bay, he was looked upon as a dude. There, where he lived three years with his sister and brother-in-law, he managed to pick up enough money for clothes, though he usually had little for anything else.

As a tutor he made $25 a month. He also taught school in the regular way and worked for a while in a drugstore, or, as it was then denominated, an 'apothecary shop,' and served as printer and writer for the town's newspaper, the *Northern Californian*. Early in his stay he dedicated himself to literature, and while he seems to have been satisfyingly conscious of it as an occupation, it was not so apparent to his industrious neighbors. He went along for three years at catch-as-catch-can employment, turning up nothing for himself in the way of a definite career.

In February of 1860, during the editor's absence, Harte placed the paper on the side of the Indians and against the citizenry regarding the Gunther Island massacre of about sixty peaceful natives. A month later he left, and though the editor said some pleasant things about him in a printed farewell, his departure was necessary. A neat young man of twenty-four, a slouchy captain of thirty-one, both to become the most celebrated of all redwoods dwellers, both expelled.

Bret Harte's literary output during the three years he spent on Humboldt Bay did not amount to much in quantity, and held little promise in its quality. He contributed to the San Francisco *Golden Era* 'A Trip Up the Coast,' about his journey from San Francisco and his impressions of the Humboldt Bay region in 1857. He wrote a poem on Mad River, the stream just north of Arcata.

Later (in proportion to an output of fifty-five volumes) he did not greatly feature redwoods settings in his stories and not at all in his verse. But after he was old, an expatriate living in England, he turned back to the big trees somewhat for material. *Under the Redwoods* was written when he was sixty-five, a year before he died.

There is one full-length novel, *In the Carquinez Woods* (1883), which contains some excellent redwoods descriptions, including the sentence, 'He called aloud to her; the vacant Woods let his helpless voice die in their unresponsive depths.' He turns the trees to account in his plot by having the hollow butts serve as hideouts and by featuring a forest fire.

Among the shorter pieces were 'A Drift from the Redwoods,' which he sold to a French magazine that published it under the title *'L'Epave de Bois-Rouge'*; 'A Treasure of the Redwoods,' with the opening sentence, 'Mr. Jack Fleming stopped suddenly before a lifeless and decaying redwood-tree with an expression of disgust and impatience'; 'The Heritage of Dedlow Marsh,' supposedly with a Eureka setting and having in it a Fort Redwood and a Logport, and describing the mighty drift upon the beach: 'Over a space of half a dozen acres the flotsam and jetsam of years of tidal offerings were collected, and even guarded with a certain care . . . the blackened hulks of huge uprooted trees, scarcely distinguishable from the fragments of genuine wrecks beside them'; and 'Three Vagabonds of Trinidad,' the three being a dog, a young Indian, and a Chinese boy in perishing conflict with the whites—one of his last writings, his brief memorandum of its composition stating, 'For *Punch* supplement. 4000 words. Begun Feb 1, 1900, London. Finished Feb 14, 1900, Camberley.'

All his material was derivative except the redwoods. Though he did not correct the romantic impressions in England that he had driven a stage and even been robbed by road agents, and had dug for gold, his white hands had never been calloused by the haft of a pick or the driving lines for six horses. Arcata, while he lived there, was still something of an outfitting center for the Trinity mines. So in that way at least he had vivid contact with the life he was afterward to put in volume upon volume, and he knew as one of the best of observers the geography of the regions where he placed his stories.

His redwood tales, buried in his collected works, are little-read any more. One, 'The Man on the Beach,' published in 1878, is given here, reduced from its original twelve thousand words to the dimensions of a short-short, to make conveniently at hand and perhaps freshly welcome at least one story by the most celebrated writer to put the redwoods in fiction:

The traders at Trinidad Head, themselves individual and eccentric, were profoundly indifferent to all other forms of eccentricity or heterodoxy that did not come in contact with their own. To the general public 'The Man on the Beach' was considered a sufficiently distinguishing title.

The bleak northwest tradewinds had brought him

mornings of staring sunlight and nights of fog and silence.

A woman's face was always before him—the face for whose sake and for cause of whom he sat here alone.

Before the fogs came he had found surcease and rest in the steady glow of a lighthouse upon the little promontory a league below his habitation . . . it spoke to him of a patience that was enduring and a steadfastness that was immutable.

Later on he found a certain dumb companionship in an uprooted tree, which, floating down the river, had stranded hopelessly upon the beach, but in the evening had again drifted away. A day or two afterward he recognized the tree again from a 'blaze' of the settler's axe still upon its trunk. He was not surprised a week later to find the same tree in the sands before his dwelling, or that the next morning it should be again launched on its purposeless wanderings. And so, impelled by wind or tide, but always haunting his seclusion, he would meet it voyaging up the river at its flood, or see it tossing among the breakers on the bar, but always with the confidence of its returning sooner or later to an anchorage beside him.

Such was the mental and physical condition of the Man on the Beach on the 1st of January, 1869. [On that New Year's day—in fourteen pages—his Aunt Mary from the East, with a Parisian dress clinging 'over her well-bred bones artistically,' and Cousin Maria, 'crisp and pretty,' came up in a livery-stable rig from Eureka to see him and get him to come back to civilization. Cousin Maria was ruefully not the girl who had exiled him here. Of the latter Aunt Mary said, 'While we shut our eyes to your very obvious relations with that woman . . .' The upshot of it was that he did *not* go away with them 'to enter once more the world they represented.']

The second winter of his hermitage drew near to its close, and with it came a storm that passed into local history, and is still remembered. It uprooted giant trees along the river, and with them the tiny rootlets of the life he was idly fostering.

[In the night, his cabin upon the highest point of the sandpit, was isolated from the mainland.] The low swale on one side was a seething mass of breakers, while the estuary behind him was now the ocean itself.

[Next day in the bright sunshine] he saw the old

uprooted tree, now apparently forever moored and imbedded in the sand beside the cabin. As he walked
toward it he heard a strange cry, unlike anything the
barren sands had borne before. Between two crossing
roots was a bamboo orange crate, almost intact. [In this]
was a living child. [One baby, the 'Luck' of Roaring
Camp, had caused Bret Harte to wake up famous, and
here was another.] As he lifted it from its damp en-
wrappings he saw that it was an infant eight or nine
months old. His nearest neighbor was Trinidad Joe, a
logger three miles up the river. He remembered to have
heard vaguely that he was a man of family.

The door at which he knocked opened upon the
figure of a buxom woman of twenty-five . . . 'I'm Bessy
Robinson, Trinidad Joe Robinson's daughter.'

Trinidad Joe pondered: 'Them brigs lays there course
well inshore. If an able seaman had fallen from the
yard-arm he'd sunk in sight o' the ship, and thet baby
ez can't swim a stroke sails ashore, sound asleep, with
the waves for a baby-jumper.'

[He left the baby and did not revisit Trinidad Joe's
cabin during the next two or three days. Then came
Bessy on horseback, with the child: 'Dad's over in
Eureka buying logs, and I'm alone . . . This yer baby of
ours is sick.' So he mounted the horse and set out to
Eureka for a doctor.]

Two facts were in his mind. One was that he was
about to open communication with the wisdom and
contemporary criticism of the settlement, by going for
a doctor to administer to a sick and anonymous infant
in his possession; the other was that his solitary house
was in the hands of a self-invited, large-limbed, but
rather comely young woman.

[After the doctor had recommended the greatest care
for the infant, Bessy announced she would stay on till it
was better. Meanwhile he put up at Trinidad Joe's
place. With the baby all right again, with it and Bessy
back home, and with himself restored to his cabin, he
still saw much of Bessy and repaid her kindness to the
child by tutoring her. One day Trinidad Joe brought in
a copy of the San Francisco *Herald*]:

'It is now ascertained that the wreck was the American Brig *Pomare,* bound hence to Tahiti. The body of
the woman has since been identified as that of the
beautiful daughter of Terpsichore—whose name was
prominently connected with a mysterious social scandal

last year. The body of her child, a lovely infant of six months, has not been recovered, and it is supposed was washed overboard.'

[It turned out thus]:

"And you will still be mother to the child?"

"*Her* child?"

"No, dear, not hers but *mine*."

They were married in the autumn.

MOVIES AND PLAYS

The most popular novel to be written with a redwoods setting is *The Valley of the Giants* by Peter B. Kyne, published in 1918. It is still read as a book, and continues to be pretty good box-office at suburban theatres. It was filmed three times among the redwoods

Frenchman's Creek was filmed at Little River on the Mendocino coast. The movie-made sailing ship was anchored in one of the coves used by redwoods lumber schooners. The scenery, simulating that of quite a different kind of coast, left out the redwoods.

California Giants is a technicolor industrial picture which has been widely circulated by the California Redwood Association.

The Redwood Empire Association likewise has a film, slanted at tourists, which has been shown as far away as China—*Redwood Empire Travel Thrills*.

So much for the movies.

The Bohemian Club of San Francisco, founded in 1872 by a group of theatrical and newspaper men, has long owned a large redwood grove on Russian River which serves as one of the most renowned outdoor theatres in America. It is a tradition of the club to give a play each midsummer with the big trees as a setting.

The Bohemian Grove stands in a ravine, the steep side of which forms the backdrop of the forest stage. The acoustics of that big-tree-filled arroyo are excellent; voices carry farther and more distinctly than in a conventional theatre.

The redwoods lend themselves to unusual dramatic effects. The 1904 club play was *The Hamadryads,* which worked out the illusion of figures emerging from the trunks of the great trees. When *St. Patrick at Tara* was given in 1909, there appeared in midair a cross of shimmering light twenty-five feet high. *The Atonement of Pan,* the Grove play of 1912, secured an impressive finale by using colored fires to illuminate the woods above the stage.

Striking representations have also been secured with the aid of the huge timber, as in *The Green Knight* in 1911, when the knight sat on his horse in the center of a triangular grouping of the great boles so that one (having three joined trunks) was behind him and the other two framed him right and left.

The play for the midsummer of 1948 was *Maternus,* based on events in Rome in 189 A.D. The Bohemian Club has in its membership so many men of distinguished achievement that the 'spear carriers' of *Maternus* included three generals, one admiral, and a number of navy captains.

18

BACK INTO THE PUBLIC DOMAIN

———

ROOSEVELT REDWOOD FOREST

Dᴏ ʏᴏᴜ ᴡᴀɴᴛ the federal
government to create the Roosevelt Redwood National
Forest at a cost of twenty-five million dollars a year?

Representative Helen G. Douglas of California—wife of
the motion-picture actor—introduced a bill to that effect
in Congress in 1946, and with earnest persistence reintro-
duced it in 1947.

This new national forest would take in 'the natural habitat
of the California coast redwood *(Sequoia sempervirens)*,
within the counties of Del Norte, Humboldt, Mendocino,
and a little of Sonoma, a strip of country from six to thirty
miles wide and extending southward from the Oregon-
California line for more than two hundred miles.

The area would contain 2,385,000 acres with 521½ billion
board-feet of timber, 36 billion of it redwoods.

There would be four memorial units focusing around the
present state park holdings, administered by the National
Park Service for scientific, educational, recreational, and

inspirational purposes. The rest would be scientifically managed by the United States Forest Service to provide a perpetual yield of timber. Sawmills and the like, now operated by private industry, would continue to be private, and would be allowed to cut the average of the last twenty-five years, gradually increasing to possibly twice that much. And if the cut doubled it could stay at the two-fold figure perpetually, because of scientific methods to sustain the growth.

A study of the situation shows that, of all the redwood lands that have been cut over so far, fifty-six per cent are growing little timber or none at all, meaning that more than half the logged-off forests have been wiped from the hills and out of the valleys and arroyos. Yet, for all this wasteful death, it is declared there could still be a resurrection day. These lands 'have a tremendous growth potential,' and would be restocked so that, as at Fort Ross, there might be trees four of five feet through in seventy years.

Seventy years is how long the present old growth will last at the expected cutting rate of 600 million board-feet a year, representing 10,000 acres of mature forest, nearly 1000 acres a month. The great trees that have been standing for hundreds of years would all be lumber by then. Following which, second growth would continue to sustain an annual cutting of a little over half the present figure.

If, however, the United States Forest Service were intensively managing this timber as a crop, the allowable cut would be 510 million board-feet a year for the first thirty years, followed not by an abrupt decline, as is the present forecast, but by an increase.

At the prewar level, the redwoods accounted for the direct employment of over 6000 people and indirectly supported over 30,000. In 1940 one-fifth of the total population of the four counties in the redwood area gained a livelihood from recreational offerings and services to the visiting public.

It is claimed that the proposed government control would

reduce fire loss, particularly by tighter regulation both in the matter of logging slash and in the burning-off to make grazing lands. 'A majority of range owners consider burning of the lands essential to the production of livestock feed.' It is frankly acknowledged there would probably be a thirty-seven-per-cent decline in grazing use of the redwood area in forty years.

Increased employment is predicted under the national forest plan. Under present practices, one redwood acre will grow enough in a year to give one man a half-day's employment. Under such intensive management as is proposed, this acre could grow enough timber in a twelvemonth to hire him for four days.

Those who might expect to lose are listed in three main categories—those concerned with excess profits in lumber, those engaged in timberland speculation, those using summer grazing in the redwood forests. It is granted that other individuals might be discomfited by the intention of the bill to eliminate unattractive signs and commercial advertising in the highway strip, and undesirable lodging and eating places 'jammed up against the highways'; to provide better standards of service and architecture, and give campground and trailer landlords the competition of free campgrounds.

Representative Douglas explains that, in thirty or forty years, only three or four per cent of the total redwood area has been brought into the public domain. 'Perhaps fifty per cent of the original stand has already been cut over once,' she says, 'and while second growth is coming along in some places, it will never match the first growth in scenic beauty. Even now second growth is being cut in a manner that may well destroy all hope of recovery.'

ORGANIZED CONCERN

In the experience of many western communities adjacent to reserved scenic areas, the controls which preserve have also ritualized out a good deal of the pleasure which attracts. The proposal for a redwoods national park was accompanied by one proposer's remark, 'And a national park needs lots of space.' Most of them do, being built around one wonder or group of wonders, but the redwoods are unique in not having to follow the pattern. Along their stretch could be made a hundred parks or five hundred. To concentrate them is unnecessary and scarcely desirable. For convenience and enjoyment, the present scheme of groves is preferable. These should be made bigger and more numerous, but no more formal in management.

There are five organizations concerned with redwood information, publicity, legislation, and action—the California Redwood Association, the State of California, the United States Government, the Redwood Empire Association, and Save-the-Redwoods League. All three of the non-government groups have offices in San Francisco.

The California Redwood Association is composed of the nine biggest owners and operators, who before the war produced from eighty to ninety per cent of all redwood lumber but below that now, with the influx of small mills. The functions of the association are primarily trade-promotional, with extensive activities in technical service, grading, research, statistics, traffic, forestry, and general information.

The association is interested in growing, manufacturing, and selling redwood lumber. It is farsightedly interested in redwoods as a crop. The men in it are the ones who actually know the most about the trees. A number of them have given back or unprofitably sold back to the public domain some of the finest old-growth tracts. An increase of groves is possible, for big acreages have recently been sold and sold at small stumpage prices to other companies, and these could just as easily have been bought for public use. To alienate a whole region from industry for the supererogation of a national park might understandably be a more expensive matter.

The 1948 Redwoods Logging Congress discussed better logging roads to facilitate winter logging, re-logging practices and possibilities, reduction of logging losses, salvaging clear cants from rotten center logs, centralized bark-peeling, fire protection, second growth, operation of the State Forest Practice Act.

The commonwealth of California, without ignoring proper safeguards, keeps something of a hard head in listening to its Elysium-makers. A bill in 1947 for five million dollars to purchase state forests did not get out of committee, but there was an appropriation of a hundred thousand to raise and sell seedlings in lots of a thousand or more and seeds in the quantity of ten pounds or more. In responsible information, in the laboratory, in research, in training men of socialized outlook for careers in the redwoods, in suitable legislation such as the State Forest Practice Act, California has met its responsibility to the trees. About 50,000 acres are now in the state redwood parks.

In advance of what may eventually happen in the matter of the proposed Roosevelt National Forest, the national government has 14,492 acres, about 800 million feet, in the Northern Redwood Purchase Unit, not a part of any national forest. Six Rivers National Forest, with the supervisor's headquarters at Eureka, contains from 50 to 75 million feet upon 3,000 acres along the thinning-out inland edge of the redwood belt. United States foresters are doing much valuable redwoods work in research and services.

The Redwood Empire Association is tourist-promoting in its purposes. Its empire is much bigger than the actual redwoods area, including eight California counties plus

Josephine County, Oregon. When the Golden Gate Bridge was formally opened, the association's president arranged for something much more substantial than a ribbon to be cut as a symbol of the linking of San Francisco and the rest of the world with the redwoods. He had placed at the north portal of the bridge three redwood logs. The champion of all buckers was there to represent Douglas fir, a champion was there to represent Idaho pine, and Ray Shull of Mendocino County was there to represent the redwoods. One had a Simmonds crosscut saw, one a Disston, one an Atkins. In a contest these three opened the bridge to traffic.

The association campaigns for redwoods roads; conducts publicity and advertising to bring tourists, vacationists, and prospective settlers into the Redwood Empire; urges transportation companies and tour agencies to promulgate redwoods attractions; broadens the appeal of the region to prolong stopovers of tourists—'imported transient cash customers'; gives cooperative support to airport projects, harbors, fairs, rodeos, fiestas.

Established in 1920, it has a long record of serving redwoods visitors. Its maps and travel promotion folders are among the most informative and satisfactory to be had; different ones cover air travel, special events, attractions and accommodations, and scenic and recreational features. A magazine is published, *Redwood Empire News,* which editorially has urged reform of sub-standard wayside places: 'If improperly treated, the visitors will angrily leave the Empire, knock the Empire to people they meet.'

Today with about fifteen thousand members, the Save-the-Redwoods League, formally organized in 1919, has been responsible for putting large acreages of redwoods forever out of danger except from natural hazards and the natural death that will eventually come even to them generations hence.

The league, at its formation, announced several main

purposes: to purchase, by means of private subscriptions and state and county bond issues, redwood groves, especially the finest ones along the highways; to establish a national redwoods park; to encourage purchase by the state of cut-over areas for reforestation; to study the use of second-growth trees for timber.

A national park is not specifically included in today's five main objects: to rescue the redwoods from destruction, to establish parks and reservations, to purchase groves, to pre-serve roadside trees, to support reforestation and conserva-tion. The league publishes, at ten cents a copy, four illus-trated booklets: *A Living Link in History, Redwoods of the Past, The Story Told by a Fallen Redwood,* and *Trees, Shrubs and Flowers of the Redwood Region.*

Inherent in the league's memorial grove project is the idea of simplicity and dignity. A horseback traveler through the Santa Cruz redwoods in 1912 had his enjoyment considerably marred by such signs on the biggest trees as 'Dedicated to the Los Angeles Produce Exchange by the San Francisco Dairy and Fruit Exchange.' or 'Dedicated to the Reading Commandery No. 42, Knights Templars of Pennsylvania.' Said he, 'I can never enjoy these spots dedicated to Masons and butter-men.' Such extreme use of a great forest for superficial obeisances has been succeeded by a designation practice of complete good taste. Yet a visitor still feels, in the atmosphere of the redwoods, that the sight of someone's name thus perpetuated is an intrusion. He inescapably feels exploited, as though his visit to the trees is perforce an homage. There is placed upon every tree a proprietary flavor.

At the time of the dedication of the Bull Creek-Dyerville Forest of ten thousand acres in 1931, the league's president, Dr. John C. Merriam, said:

'There has never been a movement with greater appeal and finer support than that directed toward saving of the redwoods. . . . Our preservation of these groves we recognize as not merely the saving of a natural feature such as only centuries upon centuries could produce. We see it as the continuation of one of the splendid aspects of creation in the world of living things.'

THE LADY OR THE TIGER?

Said Padre Pedro Font, three months before the Declaration of Independence was signed: '. . . A few trees called redwood, a tree that is certainly beautiful; and I believe it is very useful for its timber, for it is very straight and tall.'

Said a present-day lumber official: 'The bloodthirsty fairy tales assembled by the Brothers Grimm have scared the daylights out of more people than have reports of lumbering "waste," but the margin is slim. The "waste" topic is coming up fast. It's a subject that professional deplorers beat like a drum.'

Said that redwoods dweller previously quoted: 'You can't kill a redwood.'

Said a United States forester: 'Conditions in the region are extremely favorable for intensive timber-growing as a definite part of a permanent timber business.'

Said Madison Grant in an article on saving the redwoods: 'A highway was planned through the redwoods to carry visitors to see the trees, and then arrangements were made to have the timber removed.'

Fatalistically said John Muir, in reference to the Lord's previous protection of the trees: 'He cannot save them from the sawmill.'

Said a nineteenth-century individualist: 'The American citizen knows no dearer privilege than to cut down a tree.'

The Honorable Abbott Kinney, at a California forest conservation meeting in 1893, suggested the planting of Tasmanian blue gum trees—the lofty peppermints—in the burned-over redwood district. It would be trading, without discomfiture, one tall forest for another, for the blue gum, said he, 'often exceeds four hundred feet in height.'

In 1946, in a mortgage foreclosure, thousands of living trees went on the block in one of the saddest spectacles since slaves were described by an auctioneer; but those whom it would have made sad weren't present. Up for auction was the Mendosoma Redwood Tract, which lies amidst Sonoma County's old stumps, one of which, undismayingly sprouting, had been observed with grief by Robert Louis Stevenson. The county wanted only its delinquent taxes of $10.50 an acre on 21,549 acres of trees that somehow, in the midst of settlement, had continued to exist. Since it was only a hundred-mile haul to San Francisco, the tract was desirable for the sawyers of planks—but why not equally so for recreation? For one no less than the other here was a bargain—the land was estimated at twice the assessed valuation of $20.20 an acre, which plus Sonoma County's much-wanted taxes added up to a price of a dime under $51 an acre. Seventy-five men came to Santa Rosa to bid, all lumbermen, all after the forest for logging operations. But was their presence more deplorable than the absence of representatives of the public domain and of philanthropic givers of groves? The auction incident is one of alarm. It touches upon the functioning sincerity of redwoods guardianship, making it suspect of being academic, raising the question whether too much save-the-redwoods melancholy is little more than the pathos of a poem.

Such is a quick cross-section of lady-or-the-tiger testimony and evidence. The whole record at least supports the opinion that, though the redwoods are not enough saved for practical vigilance to be relaxed, much has been and is being removed of the heavy fate that once hung over their lofty heads.

LAVA REGION

LAVA DESERT

By Joaquin Miller

Go ye and look upon that land,
That far vast land that few behold,
And none beholding understand—
That old, old land which men call new,
That land as old as time is old . . .

How broken plunged the steep descent;
How barren! Desolate, and rent
By earthquake's shock, the land lay dead,
With dust and ashes on its head,
The fiery rain of red volcanoes . . .

The very devastation gleamed.
All burnt and black, and rent and seamed,
And torn with thunder-stroke, and strown
With cinders, lo! the dead earth lay
As waiting for the judgment day . . .

Then stunted sage on either hand,
All loud with odors, spread the land.
A dull-eyed rattlesnake that lay
All loathsome, yellow-skinned, and slept
Coiled tight as pine-knot, in the sun,
With flat head through the center run . . .

Some low-built junipers at last,
The last that o'er the desert looked,
Thick-boughed, and black as shapes of hell,
Where dumb owls sat with bent bills hooked
Beneath their wings awaiting night,
Rose up, then faded from the sight . . .

The vastness of that voiceless plain,
Its awful solitudes remain
Thenceforth for aye a part of you,
And you are of the favored few,
For you have learned your littleness. . . .

19

TWO HIGH MOUNTAINS

MT. LASSEN

A VOLCANO may not shoot any straighter than a scared artilleryman. All things considered, the forest lookout house on Mt. Lassen stood the 1914 bombardment of that reawakened volcano remarkably well. After 68 eruptions the windows and roof were wrecked, after 72 eruptions just the framework was left, after 192 eruptions there was nothing. Nobody was in the cabin, but if there had been the occupant would have had a fair chance of getting out and down the mountainside before boulders and rocks were hurled around too dangerously.

Seventy-two of the eruptions occured between May 20 and October 20, 1914. These made a crater 500 feet wide, 800 feet long, and 200 feet deep. A rather impressive excavation, but man with modern machinery could have done almost as well in five months' time.

When the mountain began to belch smoke and throw out lava, the inhabitants down below at the margins of the peak's base did not crouch in awe and terror, then jump in their Model T's and head for Red Bluff. The almost

157

immediate instinct of forest ranger Harvey Abbey was to go and investigate. B. F. Loomis had his mind on taking good pictures and not on hightailing it off. Parties were organized to get up close enough to see what the spectacular exhibits were all about. Curiosity in such matters is stronger than fear. This was the first time since the white settlement of the United States that living man had seen one of his own mountains turn into an active volcano; in certain western regions he was used to seing plenty of lava, but it was all associated with a prehistoric period.

As it turned out, the 1914 activities were but preliminary fireworks. The next year, on May 22nd, at half-past four in the afternoon, there was an eruption of tremendous size and force. At Lassen Park are contemporary photographs show-ing the spectacle—one taken six miles away, one forty miles away at Red Bluff, where it interrupted a fair, and one fifty miles away. It wasn't hard for the camera lens to catch the explosion at such distances, for the great roily funnel of smoke rose six miles into the air, three times as high as the mountain itself. Volcanic dust fell on Reno one hundred miles away.

There was this black mushroom pouring out magnificently from a white smokestack, and there were also horizontal blasts of gases and of rocks that leveled everything in their path down Lassen's east slope. The mud currents tore out trees and carried upon their terrible buoyancy rocks that weighed upward of twenty tons. Meadowlands eighteen miles away were reached by the colossal litter. Seven square miles of forest were inundated. Five million feet of timber were devastated. Thousands of great pines were uprooted or snapped off.

Mt. Lassen, though a considerable distance down into California, is more properly a part of the Cascades than of the Sierras. It is the southern outpost of the former range, the southern terminus of the 'Pacific Circle of Fire,' wherein are 'untold thousands of extinct volcanoes,' as well as some dormant ones which might flare up again just as Lassen did. Lassen Peak, about 5000 years old, is the remnant of Mt. Tehama, which was about 15,000 feet high.

A total of 298 eruptions were observed before Lassen recovered from whatever tremendous cathartic had troubled it. The average length was 2½ hours. The last one occurred in February, 1921; and while this seems to have been the dying gasp of the fiery Cascades, in the park museum is a statement gravely pointing out that there is no sure method of predicting possible future activity.

If those in the close neighborhood of the mountain were not scared out of their britches, there was a lot of fearful interest far off over the nation. Congress, which is itself very sensitive to matters of alarm, got all excited and made Mt. Lassen, together with 124 square miles round about it, into a national park. A few years previous President Taft had made it merely a national monument. The fine new status was achieved in 1916, whereupon, as if it had all been a political demonstration for effects now secured, the mountain quieted down except for two minor explosions.

I have been through Lassen Park four times and have climbed the peak once. It has a charm and a fascination which can scarcely be explained by the visual-aid eruption history in the park museum, much less by the concessions indifferently run by private individuals and the campground indifferently run by the park management.

People who do a lot of camping with their own tents and galley equipment, without benefit of cabins, will find the park an informal, inexpensive place to spend a vacation. The fine, smooth roads rising to lofty elevations afford especially enjoyable motoring. Chipmunks, almost more than anywhere else, dart across the pavement with their tails up at right angles, running as smoothly as if mounted on wheels. At one small lake you can feed the trout.

When not in the car, you can allot some time to the museum, hear the inevitable lectures, fish, hike, and climb the mountain. It is definitely one of the easiest of the major peaks. There is a good trail running up, with switchbacks to the summit. A paved highway lifts you a long way in your automobile before you have to start lifting yourself.

It is a poor man's and a lazy man's mountain.

MT. SHASTA

The immediate precincts of Shasta are unkempt, unpatrolled, even considerably unknown to government officials. Most of the high mountains which people climb are in national parks; Shasta is not.

With a stop to pick up a gunnysack full of big 14-inch pinecones and a visit to a ghost town back in the hills from Redding, we had come in one day from Lassen to Shasta. At Lassen for two days and nights we had camped among numerous other tents. At that time Congress was disposed to save some money on the Interior Department, and the campers were made to feel the pinch, a little unduly, we thought. There wasn't enough wood and no evident place to get it. We went through the barrier of a closed road and found bark and limbs in plenty, with which we filled the luggage compartment and became the envy of our less-fueled neighbors. With our tent fronting toward the snow peak, we were able to give it a lot of meditative looking one day before we climbed it, and one day afterward. It was a good aesthetics experiment—the change wrought in our appreciation. A professor ought to assign it to a graduate student sometime.

Each bivouacking saved us the $6 cost of an auto court. So, reaching Shasta with a $12 sleeping fund, we put up in the town's best motel, to which we brought our Lassen dust and Lassen soreness. The hot water of our deluxe accommodations cleansed us of the one, and relieved us of the other to such a degree that, though by now it was late afternoon, we drove as far as the road went up Shasta, and then climbed a considerable elevation before approaching night turned us back.

The next morning we went to the United States forest office to get information on the other side of the mountain. Our Shell and Texaco maps showed a road coming through from McCloud on that side, traversing high up the whole east base. As we drew up in front of the forestry office an energetic official went briskly by us, greeted us in buoyant friendship, and entered the establishment. We went in shortly thereafter, expecting on the basis of this sidewalk good morning with its true Kiwanian fervor to receive superb attention.

It wasn't that way at all. Our official did not deign to receive us. We would ask the girl at the counter a question; she would go into his sanctum and ask him, then return to tell us. The girl became quite active in carrying on this liaison, because our inquiries were somewhat perplexing. Finally we were assured that the road from McCloud on the east slope was passable. So we set out to take it.

It was a memorable drive, even if it did end abortively. We met two men in a car, two indignant men. The road didn't go through at all, they said. We drove on a distance and put up a warning sign on a tree near the road, then turned back, went through Scott Valley, saw the long fences made out of lava rock, passed little Shasta, and so on to Yreka.

We did not feel aggrieved at our official friend; he merely added some more evidence of the fact that the Government of the United States more or less let the mountain get along by itself, without knowing or doing very much about it. In truth we hoped the Park Service would never come, and that this particular forester or one like him would continue to represent that function of the government, for we liked

Shasta unkempt, unsupervised. It made this western heap of earth fit into West Virginia's appealing motto: *Montani Semper Liberi.*

If there had been any prospect of gold on top of Shasta, the Forty-Niners would have climbed it quick enough. Otherwise, they had neither the time nor the desire. So the mountain had been a familiar white man's sight for five years before someone went up it—a Yreka storekeeper, J. D. Pierce.

At that, the white man did better than the red one. There is no record, no tradition in the tribes, that the Indians dwelling for untold centuries in the precincts of the great white dome had ever climbed to its summit.

Pierce went up all by himself on a September day in 1854. Apparently he told no one beforehand that he was going. When he returned and reported it, his fellow townsmen declared it was impossible.

He said all right, he would lead a party up to show them. Accepting his challenge were an unlucky thirteen, six of whom, sure enough, lost their horses. But all finally reached the top, to be convinced that Pierce had been there before them—not only the first white man to ascend that 14,161 foot mountain but probably the first human being to do so.

Dr. G. F. Hearn had brought along a Roach's thermometer, with which he recorded the temperature every five minutes. On the following page is the hourly record on that September day from timberline to the top.

How many times the mountain has now been climbed in a little less than a hundred years, there are no statistics to tell, but the total could not be expected to be impressive (The climbing months are July, August, and September). An allure which many have felt but to which few have actually responded is to stay all night on the top so as to see the sunrise. The first man to attempt this, and to be amply re-

6:00 A. M. ....61°
7:00 (first snow) ...58°
8:00 ....52°
9:00 ....58°
10:00 ....58°
(But a quarter of an hour before it had been 61°, and a quarter of an hour later it was 46°)

11:00 ....60°
12:00 noon ....50°
1:00 P. M. ....50°
1:15 ....44°
1:20 ....70°
(At Hot Springs, the water of which had a temperature of 180°.)
1:30 (summit) .....36°

warded, was N. C. Mayhew. In the summer of 1859, with two or three companions, he was a witness, from nearly three miles up, of the rising sun—and what he remembered most was the mountain's shadow stretching from the mountain itself clear to where the ocean met the redwoods shore.

The climbers carried up blankets, wood, and coffee. They drank the latter as warm as they wanted it with the help of the hot springs, near which they camped. At last came dawn and sunup and that long shadow. As the sun pushed above the horizon's rim, the east was all aglow. But to the west the lofty peak cast a shadow of intense gloom, of midnight darkness. Its edges were sharply defined as the light swept past the mountain north and south. To the men it was an unforgettable sight—this dark band extending limitlessly over the mountains and forests and canyons, with their own three images somewhere out upon the green waves.

Some time between 1856 and 1859, Joaquin Miller, the future poet, guided a party of missionaries high up Shasta's slopes, taking two of them to the summit. For three years, from the age of seventeen to twenty, he could look up from whatever he was doing and have his eyes filled with the tremendous mountain. As a cook in a mining camp, as a hired hand on Mountain Joe's ranch on McCloud River, as a squaw man for two years, as a forty-day volunteer in the 'Pitt River Expedition,' he lived in sight of Shasta. The only time he was shut off from a view of the great peak was while in jail at Yreka.

The missionaries were solemn, self-important-looking men, garmented in black, spectacled and beaver-hatted. As Miller wrote of the trip later he had anything but pleasant memories of it; the mountain itself could not take away the taste of these devout climbers who paid him in tracts, sermons, and prayers. He found them 'the most sour, selfish, and ungrateful wretches on earth.'

Though they ultimately paid him in such insubstantial coinage, they let him work and wait on them as though he would be handsomely rewarded. He bore on his shoulders all the toils, took on his breast all the dangers. He looked after their horses. He spread their blankets for them and then served as a sentinel while they slept. 'But,' he wrote, 'I led them to the summit—two of them only—panting, blowing, groaning at every step.'

The others gave up the struggle somewhere short of the top and sat down on blocks of ice to rest, and as they sat there they merely nursed their aching flesh without taking in, or taking in with only a sluggish and unkindled gaze, the glory of the view. The successful pair didn't do much looking either. 'What to them was the far faint line of the sea to the west, [the Klamath lakes] like snow drifts a hundred miles away to the east?' They had been to the summit, they had said a prayer, they had given themselves something special to discuss, to report, to write about.

Their stay on the summit was brief. The future poet was looking at the black and unbroken forest toward the sea and the faint edge of the latter where it met the land, at the silver winding rivers south over into the Sacramento Valley, and eastward across the sagebrush plains to Pit River Valley, and northward across a brown basin to the Siskiyous —looking to the uttermost limits of the outspreading world as Moses looked from Nebo.

But hastily the devout men he had led up here muttered something that may have been a prayer, 'hurriedly drew some tracts from their pockets . . . then turned as if afraid to stay, and retraced their steps.' The future poet took his eyes away from scanning twenty-five million acres of forest, valley, ranges, and plains to see these tracts fluttering at his feet, lifted up and blown upon the snow, upon that summit area bigger itself than an emigrant's donation claim, a mile and a half across.

What did he do? Merely follow the pair as they quickly quitted the summit, leaving the tracts there in their miserable presumption for God himself to read?

No. He was strangely, fiercely moved to do something first. 'I drew my bowie-knife, drove it through the open, fluttering leaves, and pinned them to the snow, then turned to descend the mountain, with a chuckle of delight.'

In September, 1870, Clarence King, the noted geologist, took with him three men—S. F. Emmons, and Fred and Albert Clark—and spent two nights on the summit of Shasta. Like Mayhew, they not only carried up blankets but fuel. The party bivouacked the first night on the rim of the summit crater, sheltered somewhat by being on the lee side of a mass of rocks. They built a small campfire and huddled closely around it, the two Clarks blanketed together, King and Emmons each with a sleeping bag.

King, finding that the rocks underneath had a way of shoving up into his ribs and under his shoulderblades, arose a little after midnight. A black firmament was full of stars. Every breath of wind or whisper of sound seemed 'frozen.' The rising moon lighted up ridge and gorge and glacier and crag to produce a scene 'of arctic terribleness.' The light showed him to be above the clouds, which had a cold-gray upper surface like that of a frozen ocean. He went back to his sleeping bag and for the rest of the night enjoyed a slumber that was deep and dreamless.

Next morning he carefully studied the view. North he could see incredibly far into Oregon—clear on to the Three Sisters and Mt. Jefferson.

Northeast and east his eyes took in great flatnesses marked with lava chains, burned-out volcanoes, and Goose and Klamath Lakes. Farther still, at an immense distance, he identified bare lava hills and the Nevada desert.

Southeast, he noted smooth, chaparralled mountain spurs and beyond them the green and canyoned Sierras, with Lassen towering up eighty miles away.

South, the Sacramento canyon opened a view of the California plain, bright and brown and backed up in vanishing perspective by Coast range peaks.

West, in semicircle, stretched ridges, peaks, and canyon walls 'as wild and tumultuous as an ocean storm,' blue-billowed and indistinguishable except for some Siskiyou heights and a segment of the Klamath River trough. King did not comment on the far-stretching Shasta shadow, but this absence of detail could have been an effect of it.

Night approached, with mighty gusts of wind which beat upon the crags like an ocean surf. The men camped near the hot springs. There they built a lava pen two and a half feet high, chinking it with pebbles, and banking sand against it. The continuing wind—howling, merciless, cold—blew their coffee into spray before it reached their lips from the cups. It seemed to swoop down vertically to scatter the sticks of the fire among their legs and upon their coats and blankets. It blew down stones from the enclosing walls as they slept, and pelted them with the chinking pebbles and the banking sand.

The naturalist John Muir was compelled by a storm to spend a night on the summit in April, 1875. He and a guide were without blankets and without wood. As the storm increased, they went to the hot springs and tried to keep from freezing to death by lying in the mud there. The heat below blistered them; the cold wind numbed them above in instant refrigeration. Each temperature had to be taken in its excess. Each had to be quickly alternated, for human flesh could not stand one or the other long. The hot springs transmitted an unbearable heat to the mud, which could not warm the freezing wind or be cooled by it. The extremities of heat and cold made the night one of agony for the two men.

One Fourth of July a fitting celebration was worked out by two groups of mountain climbers. One group was to climb Mt. Hood, the other Mt. Shasta. At a prearranged moment both were to set off red fire, great quantities of it. This would not only be a suitable and exciting spectacle for thousands of inhabitants down below, but it would have scientific value—it would determine whether the curvature of the earth bulged up enough in the intervening two hundred and fifty miles to shut off the view of those great heights from each other. Unfortunately, a fog on the summit of Shasta interfered with both purposes.

There is also an account of a forest fire in the trees and chaparral of the slopes. Some men fled to the closest stream, and there, as every kind of animal and bird and reptile came, they beheld a repetition of the gathering at the Ark.

Mt. Shasta's greatest recreational value is a long-distance one. Thousands upon thousands receive refreshment from it who may never have been in its immediate precincts. With its eternal snow, it looms up boldly from a hundred miles around.

20

SEARCHERS FOR THE LOST

————

THE BLUE BUCKET MINE

A<small>T THE</small> Snake River emigrant crossing in 1845 if Steve Meek hadn't lured two hundred covered wagons from the well-known Oregon Trail to follow him up the unknown Malheur River, there never would have been a Blue Bucket Mine to be lost so long.

A smooth, broad highway—Route 20—goes along the Malheur now. If you have ever traveled that thoroughfare, you may have been within a mile of the Blue Bucket Mine, or five miles, or ten. Certainly you were not more than forty miles away from it.

Many others have been as close to, or closer, without coming upon the old campsite where it had been possible to stoop and pick up nuggets as agates might be picked up from a strewn ocean beach. In that wagon train of 1845 were two hundred men, yet not one of them could later go back to it, and no others looking for it have been able to retrace the precise route of the bewildered emigrants through the desolate region of the Malheur headwaters.

One afternoon the Blue Bucket Mine was discovered. The

next morning it was left behind. Then it vanished from human sight and has stayed vanished for over a hundred years.

The two hundred deluded wagons that trailed in a long line after Steve Meek are known in history as the 'Lost Train.' Meek had never been over the route himself prior to that trip, which was to prove a grim honeymoon for his bride of four months. He barely escaped hanging from a gibbet made of three uplifted wagon tongues. Finally allowing him to live but repudiating him as guide, the emigrants took to piloting themselves, with even more confusion than Meek had occasioned.

In their wanderings they came to a swift stream divided from the Malheur by a ridge. The water, as rapid as in a millrace, flowed southwest, while the main river flowed east, but headwater creeks in the tortuous defiles could easily be hurrying off toward any point of the compass. At a little past noon a stop was made for the rest of the day to bury a man who had died enroute. While several dug the grave, the rest went about their camp duties.

The Helm outfit was a blue ensemble—blue wagonbeds, blue ox-yokes, and blue camp utensils, including three or four buckets. While Mrs. Helm did the family washing, some of her brood of seven played in the gravel and at the shallow edges of the stream. These young and all-unknowing prospectors found numerous small pebbles at the river margin, like gleaming tubers in the grassroots. They picked up the pretty rocks and put them in one of the blue buckets, till it became very heavy to lift.

After the funeral some of the emigrants attempted to fish, but the rapid current swept hook and bait downstream in a twinkling. Used to catching catfish in sluggish creeks, the anglers sought sinkers. Three men, one of them a blacksmith, tried pounding the yellow pebbles flat upon a wagon tire; they proved soft enough to be hammered out for fishing purposes.

It didn't dawn on a single one of the travelers what these extra-heavy, malleable rocks might be. The time was three years before Sutter's Mill, and the emigrants of 1845 were not looking for gold. They were not looking for anything in this godforsaken country. All that they wanted was to get away from the sufferings of Meek's Cut-off and, by the Lord's mercy, find their way safely to Oregon City.

The next morning the blue bucket was emptied and put in its accustomed place in the Helm wagon. Each fishline, with its extemporized sinker, was thrown among odds and ends wherever such things were kept by the particular owner. Steve Meek finally fled to save his neck. In so doing he guided the party right after all, for the others followed fast in his tracks to the Deschutes River. There seems to have been much wear on fishing lines in three years of Oregon pioneering, so that by 1848, when the emigrants realized ever so ruefully that the sinkers had been gold, not a single one could be produced.

Such are the ingredients of the favorite version: small hands gathering up the nuggets, mamma washing, the unimaginative fishermen, and the blue bucket—'it is essential that the pail shall be blue in a narrative that owes so much of its vitality to a name.'

In addition to a wide assortment of minor versions, there are two other main ones, not necessarily any truer for being more commonplace.

The first says that one of the seven Herron boys, while out looking for strayed cattle, picked up two good-sized lumps from a bouldered streambed. Back at camp no one could tell what the metal was, 'and no one thought of its being gold.' The two pieces were hammered together into a saucer-shaped disk, which the boy later threw into the Herron tool chest. His son said seventy-five years later that the tool chest had a secret drawer wherein the gold was hidden. 'No one but members of the family ever knew what became of it.'

The second variation is to the effect that Sol Tetherow, wagon-train captain, gathered up some fine specimens and put them in a blue bucket. At the Deschutes River crossing the Tetherow wagonbox was used as a ferry, upset in the boiling current, and the blue bucket, nuggets and all, went to the bottom.

These three accounts have one thing in common—in each case the evidence manages to get lost. No actual nugget was anywhere around by the time people began to look excitedly for the Blue Bucket Mine. But there was plenty of testimony —and why should reliable, Godfearing emigrants perjure themselves? A good many persons can be hauled in two hundred covered wagons and pulled by nearly a thousand oxen, and all of these who said anything whatever upon the subject said the Blue Bucket discovery was a fact. All but one, W. A. Goulder, later of Boise, a Meek's Cut-off pioneer who hadn't known anything or heard anything about it at the time and was always 'just a little bit skeptical.'

The first return expedition to the Malheur River—to the little stream, the grave, the golden pebbles—was organized as early as 1849. In that year of the Forty-Niners, when the whole planet was aware of gold and the digging of gold, a great waking-up came to the erstwhile unconcerned emigrants. The Meek's Cut-off travelers, once with so little consciousness of the precious metal as not to recognize a litter of nuggets half the size of coffee berries, now remembered vividly and coveted strongly. Four years after the event, those men of 1845 racked their brains to recall the identical spot.

It might be expected that such a grim trail could be retraced without much trouble. Two hundred wagons, each drawn by from four to six oxen, ought to have left a record of their passage through any kind of country. But those who returned were to see that the record was segmentary, not continuous. The road at times was still worn a foot deep where the wagons had been rough-locked down the hills. Then there were long windswept stretches of sandy or gritty or alkali places where the wagon tracks had been faint and transitory, and rocky places where there had been no tracks at all. Over the grave at the creek and over the other nineteen graves along the way, fires had been built. From these the ashes would have long since been blown away, but there should have remained charred sticks or bare spots or surely some observable relics of the sepulchres, but the successful concealment from the Indians had become a perpetual concealment from everybody. Big campfires had been made in the sagebrush, using sage for fuel, which, even after four years, ought to have left circular areas of low bushes amidst tall ones. And there ought to have been a lane of low bushes where oxen and wagons had gone. But this was not found to be so in either case. A sameness had come back to the vast sagefields.

All those burned places at the graves and campsites, all those long avenues trampled out by beast and vehicle, had been restored to their original monotony by strong-scented bushes so quickly maturing, so precociously aging, that in four years' time their stalks could be as big and gnarled as those growing for generations. This earliest party of searchers could not be sure of the old route for long distances. They never found a stream that fitted the description of the little one which hurried like a millrace. They finally had to return home unsuccessful.

About six years later, one of the seven Herron boys tried to find his way back to where, as recited in the second Blue Bucket version, his brother had picked up the two large nuggets. Maybe he was rummaging in the old tool chest and came upon the secret drawer still containing the flattened-out gold. Whatever it was that caused his excitement, he set out hopefully with four companions to return to the locality which by then had become, all up and down the Pacific Coast, the subject of 'many flying reports and legendary tales.' But the Indians were uncooperative, killing two of the men.

Also turned back by hostile Indians was a seven-man expedition of 1857, headed by Dr. James McBride, a veteran of Meek's Cut-off. This was the third party to include someone who had been present at the discovery of gold in 1845—convincing evidence that it was a reality and not something imagined by a whole wagon train. Dr. McBride was so certain himself of its existence that he started out the next year with twenty-five men. This time they duly reached the upper Malheur country, but it did them little good. After thirteen years some of the steep hillsides still had foot-deep wheeltracks upon them, but vitally important portions of the stern thoroughfare over which Dr. McBride had driven a covered wagon could not now be identified, and the Blue Bucket Mine eluded this quest as completely as it had the first.

In 1861, four California miners—David Littlefield and Henry Griffin, with their two partners—came to Portland on their way to Oro Fino. One day on the streets they saw a soapbox orator holding forth to a considerable audience. The Californians joined the listening crowd.

The man—J. L. Adams—was telling about the Blue Bucket Mine of emigrant story. He said, in fact, that he had been one of those who had followed Steve Meek in 1845. The four Californians didn't miss a word as this persuasive individual proclaimed that he could lead a party right to the spot where gold could be picked up in bucketfuls. He summoned three witnesses to declare that he, Adams, had been present at the discovery of the Blue Bucket Mine there on the small, swift creek somewhere in the region of the Malheur headwaters. The witnesses spoke with authority because they had been there too.

The California quartette, who had been souring on Oro Fino anyway, were in the proper frame of mind for a more likely undertaking, and this sounded good. They eagerly questioned Mr. Adams, who seemed as authentic in private discourse as he had oratorically. He repeated that with his own eyes he had seen the gulch where the golden pebbles lay so thick, and he could find it again without difficulty. The need was for a company big enough to protect themselves from the Indians. He would be willing to guide such a company to this place where fortunes could be picked up from the surface of the ground.

The result was an expedition of sixty-one men, including Adams and his three supporters, and the four Californians. They went to the Deschutes River, thence pushed up Crooked River to its headwaters. Soon they came into a dry region and began to suffer for drinking water, just as the emigrants had sixteen years before. And there was another parallel. Adams, like Steve Meek, showed that he knew little or nothing of the country.

They wandered about for weeks and finally reached the sources of the Malheur. They cursed Adams, just as the original travelers had cursed Meek. The angry searchers scared confessions out of the three witnesses—who had not been with Adams at all in 1845, and had never set eyes upon the so-called Blue Bucket Mine.

Adams, for his part, even after all this stood his ground unabashed, a rather magnificently brazen fellow. Yet he might really have been present in 1845, for there is a bare mention of an Adams as a member of the Meek's Cut-off migration. As to his not knowing the country, who could be familiar with such a trackless land, which wouldn't keep its tracks, wherein the returned traveler was as bewildered as the stranger?

Without wilting, he looked his complaining followers in the eyes and told them in the old positive manner that if they would quiet down he could easily lead them to the swift little stream and its nuggety margins. So, notwithstanding the strong shock received from the witnesses, they continued to follow him. They followed him until they came into the region of poison alkali water.

There they balked. They said turn north. He said go on. They prevailed. And though they went their direction and not his, they still insisted that he find the Blue Bucket Mine, threatening him with death if he failed. He tried to point out how unreasonable it was not to go where he said, yet to hold him accountable. They refused to listen to such an outlandish attempt to shift responsibility onto them. Adams looked into the barrels of two or three pistols and perforce accepted the terms.

Finally he was given three days and an alternative at the end of them—produce the Blue Bucket or get a noose around his neck. A whole platoon of the expedition were farmers who had left growing crops to join the treasure hunt. The expansive Adams back there on the Portland soapbox had made wheat and hay and potatoes seem mighty small in comparison with the riches they could expect from their shares of the nugget harvest. Now they not only thought of their wasted crops but of the hardships they had endured, and all for nothing. These agriculturists were the bitterest against Adams.

The four Californians, and a number of others, were more tolerant of their guide's failure to lead them to the golden pebbles. They were used to the disappointments of mining life, and had no crops.

When the third day arrived and sunset brought no Blue Bucket Mine, the farmer element was in favor of executing Adams at once. The Californians successfully argued for a postponement until morning. He was guarded through the night, and the next day a miner's tribunal, with a duly impaneled jury, was organized to try him. The trial lasted all day. In the evening the case was given to the jury, who deliberated it by a separate campfire on and on into the night. Not until ten o'clock the next morning, after some clarifying sleep, did they reach a verdict—a stiff one when it did come. Adams was guilty; he was to be separated from the rest of the company and marooned in the wilderness with nothing but the clothes on his back; each member was privileged to shoot him on sight; and, in crowning humility, he had to sign a confession of perjury.

Poor Adams, obedient to the sentence, moved away by himself, out of sight and, ergo, out of reach of an authorized bullet. But the compassionate Californians smuggled food to him in the darkness. He traveled roughly parallel to the path of the expedition until it broke up into two parts. The lugubrious farmers headed due west, back to their neglected fields. The still-cheerful California group struck out north towards the Oregon Trail.

The latter test-panned the dirt of every little stream they came to. Five days after breaking away they crossed over a divide, and upon a small Powder River tributary, just above where it enters the lava hills, Henry Griffin sank a hole three feet deep. Ever hear of Powder River? Of Auburn? Well, they were a bunch of the richest gulches on the whole round earth. And that was the way they were found.

Did Adams get rich? Nobody knows. History is indeed reticent. He was chronicled in detail while being harassed by querulous treasure-hunters, but when, as a left-handed result of his blandishments, the party located one of the principal gold regions of America, obscurity wraps him round.

It is possible, however, to follow him a little farther before he is entirely lost to sight.

He did not continue on with his forbearing friends, the

Californians. The farmers went back in two contingents, fourteen one day and five the next, and Adams apparently made his peace with one group or the other; either that or he traveled west alone, for on his way home he discovered along the John Day River the bountiful gravel that eventually was to yield a total of fifteen million dollars. At this point, even as the amazing Adams triumphs, he vanishes from the records of history.

Thus the Blue Bucket Mine, while itself eluding the searchers, was the cause of two fabulous discoveries.

There were two more expeditions to the Malheur in 1861 —each involving about threescore persons and both heavily made up of husbandmen turned adventurers. A good deal of agricultural neglect was due that year to the Blue Bucket and the effect of its haunting mystery upon toilers in the fields.

In 1862, a certain Moses Splawn ran into a party of farmers headed by Tom Turner. Splawn wanted some men to go with him to a place where a Bannock Indian claimed he had picked up, when a boy, chunks of yellow metal such as he had seen palefaces work out of the gravel. Splawn bargained with Turner to look for the Blue Bucket on condition that if it were not found Turner and his party would go with him to the Bannock Indian's place, which was Boise Basin.

Thus was a third big goldfield discovered as a by-product of exploring for the Blue Bucket. The next year there was to be a fourth. Twenty-nine Boise-Basiners left the riches there to search for the emigrant mine. They didn't find it, but what they did discover resulted in the Owyhee mines— Boonville, Ruby City, Silver City, and other famous camps.

Finally the original guide, Steve Meek himself, organized an expedition of thirty men. This was in 1868, twenty-three years after he had led the two hundred wagons over the cut-off which made his name a reproach and a byword. There are no details of what he found or what he did, beyond a scornful reference to the enterprise as a wild-goose chase.

In 1891 a newspaper in the present-day ghost town of Harney City announced that the long-lost Blue Bucket Mine had been discovered not many miles away in the Peter Mortimer Canyon.

An old prospector by the name of White had gone about the matter in a businesslike way. He started in at Snake River to retrace Meek's Cut-off, going west in the same direction as the wagon train, instead of contrary to the route as all the other searchers had done. He located one of the twenty graves—that of a woman who had died one full travel day and part of another before the migration reached the place where the nuggets were picked up. It took him six months to find this grave; from it he made a careful examination westward. He learned from aged emigrants who had been young men at the time, that on September 16 and 17, 1845, eighty wagons traveled all night, a distance of twenty-five miles, to reach at daybreak a stream 'winding its way through a level valley,' which might have been the Blue Bucket creek. They stayed there until two o'clock the next afternoon. Then they moved on only six miles to another stream named by them 'Sandy,' flowing northwest without trees but very grassy; and this also might have been the watercourse that had so long excited the imaginations of men.

The old prospector decided that the Peter Mortimer Canyon (not far from the present Route 20) was the place. After spending some time in that lonely ravine, he dispatched a horseman to California. This man had instructions to change mounts and ride a hundred miles a day. A short time later White himself packed his things and started south.

The rider ahead made the mistake of talking. At one of

the stopping points he said that his boss had panned out $3.25 to a pan from a number of pans, and had sent for friends in California. The man to whom this was told hardly let the southbound horseman out of sight until he started north to Harney City. Soon a rush for the Peter Mortimer Canyon began. Gold was discovered there, sure enough, and everywhere people said this was the Blue Bucket Mine. Men on horseback rode races for the first claims. Notices were written and pasted on stones.

While White and his rider were gone, the hills and ravines filled with men. In the spreading excitement wagonloads of prospectors came daily into Harney City. Wild rumors were afloat of great banks of gold dust being found. Paying claims were staked out on Rattlesnake Creek, Soldier Creek, Coffee Pot Creek. The boom continued all winter and then the placers pinched out, and there wasn't enough left for even the Chinese to make pay. Yet there had been enough and more than enough to make Mr. White rich, if he could only have muzzled his talkative rider.

Had the mystery finally been solved? A drawback was the absence of water. These dry creeks, Rattlesnake and the others, not one of them could really be the live, refreshing stream where lay the nuggets half as big as coffee berries and thicker than acorns under the oaks. Not one of these empty, parched, and melancholy channels could be the Blue Bucket stream, because the latter still had a swift, full flow of water near the end of the dry season in mid-September.

The Blue Bucket Mine was still to be found, and still is to this day—and, if you will listen, you may be able to go right to it.

First you must have faith that there was a Blue Bucket Mine. Said a wise Oregon editor in 1919: 'The mystery of the Blue Bucket is unsolved. Perhaps there was such a mine; perhaps not. There are still living men who believed it once, and some of them acted on their belief. A few believe it yet.'

You can expect it to be very hard to identify the stream, whose hiding place nature has guarded so well for over a hundred years. The grandson of one of the emigrant discoverers said that by 1902 he had personally investigated at least forty versions of the location of the mine. One description put the creek 'among abrupt hills, in a narrow and steep gulch.' Another says it flowed through level plains. A third, as remembered by a pioneer who was then a boy of fourteen, placed it 'somewhat along the rim of Harney Valley, with hills to the northward and the level stretch of desert to the south.'

The rim of Harney Valley is not far from Route 20. Coming from Boise and Ontario on the east, you travel a mile a minute over the paved Meek's Cut-off of today, going in ten minutes as far as those two hundred wagons followed Steve Meek in a whole long day. Don't descend from the heights where the great Harney Valley is outspread before you; turn to your right on any graveled road of your choice and go as far as you can, and then become a wayfarer in that vast remoteness which somewhere encloses the Blue Bucket.

Coming from the west, go along Route 20 eleven miles past Burns. Pick out your turning-off point, to the left in this case, maybe into the sideroad leading into old Harney City, with Rattlesnake Creek beyond, but remember Rattlesnake Creek isn't the one. If you keep going you'll soon have to walk, and remember that while civilization seems close in any wilderness with a strip of pavement through it, it is very far away when there is only a trail behind you bearing none but your own tracks upon it, and only the pathless hills and ravines ahead. As you trudge on in fatigue and thirst, the water in the Blue Bucket stream will fill your vision more than the nuggets, but once you have had a good drink there the nuggets will come back into their proper perspective.

One of the Meek Cut-off veterans left a 'leather-bound memorandum book, with maps and diagrams showing the water courses'; but don't depend upon still finding this somewhere, and anyway his son, having this information, couldn't locate the Blue Bucket. Something better to keep in mind is that the emigrants certified that the Three Sisters, two-mile-high snow peaks of the Cascades, 'bore generally westward when the find was made.' These mountain spires are a mighty big landmark; and the region from which they lie generally westward is 'big enough, indeed, to engage the minute attention of an army of prospectors for a century or so.' Yes, it could be a hundred-year quest. It has been, in fact.

SOMEWHERE IN THE SISKIYOUS

The second week after arriving in San Francisco in July, 1860, George Gibson of Jacksonville, Oregon, unexpectedly received a three-pound Wells Fargo express package from his hometown. He unwrapped it to find a piece of very red rock. With it was a note from a Jacksonville friend, Harvey Miller, asking him to be good enough to have it assayed.

He took it at once to the well-known firm of Justh, Hunter & Company.

When he went back for the report, Mr. Justh eagerly wanted to know the history of the specimen. Then he handed Gibson the assay certificate—seventy per cent quicksilver.

"The richest cinnabar I have ever seen," said Mr. Justh. "Nothing like it was ever brought here from New Almaden."

Gibson, knowing nothing about this extraordinary fragment of stone, returned to Jacksonville in August and immediately learned that Harvey Miller didn't know anything about it either. The rock belonged to R. S. Jewett, the Rogue River ferryman, a dozen miles from town. They went to Jewett, and were horrified to find that he too knew nothing about it.

The richest piece of cinnabar ever found on the Pacific Coast was like a picture without a caption.

Jewett, all a-tremble with the assay report in his hand, voiced his vast expectations. Incalculable wealth lay hidden in the hills and ledges where that rock came from.

"And where did it come from?" asked Gibson.

"I don't know,' said the ferryman.

The rock—untreasured, just kept—had been around the place for two years. It was a six-pounder to start with. He still had the other half. It was in a box on the living-room corner shelf. In 1858 a fifty-year-old Rogue River Indian had been allowed to live as a hanger-on and odd-job man at Jewett's house at the ferry. Only a mile away had been the rancheria of his particular Rogue River tribe before their sad, decadent days, and to stay thus close to the old *illahe* and to wander at times into the uninhabited hills seemed to satisfy his strongly lingering homesickness.

One day, after a week or so in the mountains, he returned with the six-pound rock. Jewett at that time didn't have the least idea what it was. But it was a curious-looking piece, and to throw it away would have offended the giver. So he put it in a box with some other finds he had gathered. A traveler, looking at the collection while he waited for his own supper and for his horse to be fed, pronounced it cinnabar—might be very valuable. Jewett then asked Miller to send it to Gibson.

And here they were, the three of them, standing and talking on the ferry, in a lull between horsemen and wagons and burro pack trains. Three pairs of eyes swept the blue heights roundabout, covetously. The river came to them from the southeast through a great wedge of rich, outspread valley twenty-five miles wide, with every acre plowed or grazed and known and owned; and in its tameness there was assuredly no ledge of vermilion rock. But elsewhere there was a hemming-in by the spurs of three high elevations—the Cascades, the Coast range, the Siskiyous—and these tiers of dreamy, uprising ridges held many things which the white man seeth not. Somewhere out there, not more than twenty-five miles away . . .

They formed themselves into the quicksilver mining firm of Jewett, Gibson & Miller and shook hands upon it. And they made a pact of secrecy.

The Indian was no longer around. He had been removed with the rest of the Rogue River tribe to the Grand Ronde Reservation. Their first business was to get him back—borrow him for a while from an amiable government. Gibson knew the superintendent of Indian affairs. Jewett knew the Indian. So Gibson wrote a leter to the superintendent, and Jewett took it and an extra horse. In due time the ferryman returned and the redman rode by his side.

On the way Jewett had not told him what he was coming back for and the Indian hadn't asked. Meanwhile Gibson and Miller had gone home to Jacksonville to wait for a report that Jewett had obtained the secret of the rock's location and of about a million dollars' worth of the same. They allowed ample time for the trip and a few days more, and yet there was no report. Nearly a month went by, making their suspense an agony.

Jewett had not reported because he had no report to give. The Indian would not tell where the rock came from.

Three days or so after reaching home, while Jewett and the Indian sat in front of the fireplace, the former took in his lap the remaining half of the cinnabar chunk and began to pick at it with his knifeblade in an offhand manner. The Indian disdained to show any interest.

Then he threw it into the blaze. Thereupon the Indian ran off in a panic. Jewett ran after him and tried to get him to come back. The ferryman realized that something in

connection with the rock in the fire—not the rock itself—
had a mysterious influence upon the Indian. The man for
some reason was in mortal fear of that piece of ore when
it was in the fireplace. He came back and sat on the steps
only after Jewett showed him that the rock had been raked
out of the coals before the heat could affect it. For a week
afterward he went about in an unbreakable Indian silence
and during that week he slept a mile away at the old tribal
rancheria.

Such was the bad news the Jacksonville partners finally
received. Wasted was the money they had invested in bring-
ing this mute savage back to the ferry; gone were their
dreams of thousands of flasks of mercury at fifty dollars a
flask. It was a great shock to have an untalkative and oddly
acting Indian stand in the way of everything.

Though it was unlawful to give an Indian whiskey, they
were sparing of the law in this case. They brought him to
Jacksonville and made him drunk but he was as obdurately
silent in that condition as when sober. What was it that
frightened him? What sealed his lips? What was the strange
effect the rock in the fire had that it didn't have in a box
or on a shelf or in Jewett's lap?

The two Jacksonville partners dejectedly stayed home.
The ferryman as dejectedly went back to the ferry with the
keeper of the million-dollar secret, who was the only one
of the four not cast-down; in his stoical way he was happy
because of his trip to Jacksonville.

Finally, of his own free will, he became communicative.
He called Jewett to the riverbank one afternoon and there,
while the swift current went by, he told the ferryman about
the cinnabar—told about it up to a certain point.

Before the time of the whites, when the Rogues were
planning a raid against their Klamath foes, a Rogue warrior
returned from the hills. Everybody looked at him in wonder

and admiration. He had been gone two days. His face was painted with the strangest red they had ever seen.

He told the chief he had killed a deer and was cooking some of the venison. He had built his fire upon a ledge of red stone. While his meat was getting done, he amused himself hammering a piece of the rock against a larger surface. A fragment fell into the fire. During his meal he noticed the brilliant particles of this burnt lump. He raked these out and examined them after they had cooled. His fingers were agreeably colored. So he smeared his face and hands.

He said, though, that after he had daubed himself there was a slippery taste in his mouth. And otherwise he felt ill. But to this statement little attention was paid. The chief and the warriors were only interested in the wonderful red paint and how to get plenty of it. He told them the ledge was nearly a day's chase from the rancheria. The chief ordered him to lead them there.

One who looked upon the splendidly reddened warrior, and listened with envy in his heart to the plans for all the braves to be similarly blessed, was a Klamath slave.

The chief said they would go to the 'paint rock,' put on the newly discovered, most gorgeous war coloring, dance and feast, and then make their raid against the Klamaths.

It was a big ledge. A great fire was built. Masses of the bright-red rock were broken off from the protruding shelf and cast upon the large bed of coals. The warriors daubed their faces and bodies all over with the vermilion glory; they likewise reddened their horses. Thereafter they feasted; next they danced till the moon set at midnight; then they went to their blankets. At dawn they would refresh the paint and go upon the warpath against the Klamaths. The slave was to keep the fires bright.

They went to their blankets but not to sleep. Their teeth shook but not from the cold. Their gums were afflicted but not with boils. It was not oil or grease or slippery elm which caused the slicky, nauseous taste in their mouths.

The Klamath slave, the bringer of wood, had been denied the new paint in his ignominy. His work in keeping up the fires exposed him but slightly to the effects of the roasting ore. The next morning he took in the scene, and his hostile heart so recently envious now rejoiced. He saw the salivating and sickened Rogue River braves. He saw their horses unfit for service. He sped from the camp. By nightfall he was across the Siskiyous, where some Klamaths lived. On the morning of the second day a hundred Klamaths followed the slave. They headed for the Rogue River rancheria, there to await the disabled homecomers.

As expected, the Rogues returned on weak and suffering animals, themselves groaning in agony and writhing in pain. They were as helpless as infants. The Klamaths crept upon them and attacked. It was a massacre rather than a battle while it lasted, but it lasted very briefly. Another tribe of Rogues living on the upper river had seen the Klamaths on the march, and had hurried to the rancheria to warn their brothers. They found the butchery just starting and put an end to it. The Klamaths fled from the ground.

The Indian who had discovered the paint rock was put to death. The same fate awaited any tribesman ever venturing near the accursed red ledge. The place was forbidden by Tomaniwos to the approach of mortals. The torture which their bodies had suffered was a warning and a sign. If they made another attempt to visit the spot, Tomaniwos would surely cause them all to die.

And from that day forward no warrior would go within miles of the sinister paint rock, or tell its whereabouts.

The old curse had not been lifted against telling. The Indian whom Jewett, Gibson & Miller had brought from the reservation at so much trouble and expense, was still bound to secrecy and would be, like every Rogue River

tribesman, till the end of his days. He could reveal where
he had secured the six-pound rock, but no more than that.
When the Rogues made their mournful return home after
the terrible war dance, some warrior had brought the rock
along as far as the river and dropped it there. He had found
it years afterward and given it to the ferryman—it was
harmless to handle when cold.

Jewett heard all this by the riverside while the swift current went by on its long journey to the sea; he told it to
his partners at Jacksonville.

The Indian was forthwith returned to the reservation. En
route, the ferryman was inspired to get the forbidden secret
obliquely—if the old Rogue were to give him the slave's
whereabouts, the slave would tell him. The Klamath doubtless knew equally well where the paint rock was. He would
scorn the Rogue embargo and promptly, for a fee, lead the
three white men to the place.

"Slave dead in battle," said the Indian.

The firm of Jewett, Gibson & Miller even yet did not
surrender all hope. Wouldn't there be one direction which
the Indians had not gone to hunt or never gone in warfare
against the whites? And wouldn't the pioneers remember?
The voluble oldtimers did remember, but too well and too
inconsistently. Their various answers would have had the
Indians not hunting or not fighting in practically every
direction.

The rancheria was a mile from the ferry. The red ledge
was nearly a day's chase from there, about twenty-five miles.
Therefore the country to be explored would have a circumference of roughly a hundred and fifty miles, from which
could be subtracted the outward wide rim of the valley
wedge, together with the pastured foothills—say, forty miles.
The examined strip ought to be ten miles wide, to cover
distance allowances. The gross area to be searched would
therefore be twelve hundred square miles, which, however,

could be reduced by half. The Indian slave was supposed to have gone across the Siskiyous; a spur was meant, for even this fast runner could not have crossed the whole range in the time stated. So the northern part could be eliminated, as could be the Upper Applegate portion of the Siskiyous west of the valley.

The details of the actual explorations of Jewett, Gibson, and Miller are not on record, but it is known that they never found the ledge from which came the richest specimen of cinnabar ever seen in a leading San Francisco assay office. Fourteen years later there was a quicksilver mining stampede to the Rogue River, but the activity died out without any prospector's digging his pick into that ledge of unparalleled ore.

Addendum—In 1945 there were thirty-five quicksilver mines and prospects within a twenty-five-mile radius of the old Jewett ferry. Only four of these were in the 'B' production class—51 to 1000 flasks; most were in the 'D' class, with no production; not one was in the 'A' class—over 1000 flasks. Can it be believed that the extensive ledge where the rich Rogue specimen came from would have had a lesser status? It is still there somewhere, twenty-five miles from the old ferry in the blue dreamy hills.

21

MODOC LAVA BEDS

THE lava beds, perpetually re-
mindful of Captain Jack, seem to contain action like a film,
to hold sound like a record, ready to flash the movements of
a slim-hipped Indian, ready to play back the boom of howitzers reverberating in the crags. These and Tule Lake in
front of them are today serene, singularly so upon a summer
Sabbath, with a drowsy aspect of remoteness, of solitude, of
the past. The quietude is enhanced in its effect on the visitor
by seeming to be a cessation of forces in tremendous turmoil.

Tule Lake has been greatly drained down from its dignity
as a sagebrush sea in the period when emigrant trains of
covered wagons went beside it. The white man has had
much skill and enormous zest for making seas into lakes,
lakes into ponds, ponds into alkali flats where a rancher's
plane might land. This once gracious focus of the life of
man and beast and fish and bird was discovered by Jesse
Applegate in 1846 and called Modoc Lake. Now reduced
to a width of a little more than two miles and a length of
a little less than three, it formerly spread out in its farthest
reaches eleven miles both ways. A town, many smiling farm-
steads, paved highways, and a segment of the Great Northern
Railroads are now within the old shorelines.

Near the southeast corner of the original water area there jutted out a long, lofty ridge still called the peninsula. At the base, for a distance of two city blocks along its vertical walls, extending from the ground up the surface so high it would take a ladder to reach them, are ancient carvings or petroglyphs, so durably chiseled that a camera can catch their details. Memory of old Modoc squaws handed down to old squaws cannot go back to the time when these numerous and varied scratchings were not upon the peninsula's cliffs.

This rock tapestry is now part of the Lava Beds National Monument, which has built a woven-wire fence, high and stout, all along the front of it to prevent the chipping-off of hieroglyphic slabs for souvenirs, some of which already took place before the wall was protected. Lighter patches without gravures show where choice figures have probably been lifted away.

The scribes of these prehistoric markings had already come and gone when, according to one theorist, a bunch of adventurous Welshmen showed up from God knows where and founded the Modoc nation. (Their white blood, though heavily diluted, would of course explain why Captain Jack was so smart—yet why was the tincture in his veins so much more effective than all the pure quantities in the veins of the bluecoats and volunteers?) The leader of the Welshmen was a Lloyd George sort of fellow by the name of Madoc. The *a* understandably got changed in the course of time to *o,* which joined with the other *o* to fall very agreeably upon the ears. All a lot of nonsense, say the ethnologists, who ask quite pertinently why the Modoc language happens to be so much like that of the adjacent Klamaths.

In the Modoc marriage system it was the custom to give young squaws to old bucks and often, by reciprocal necessity, old squaws to young bucks. This was caused by the high cost of the young ones—fifty horses. Nobody but an old man could afford such a price. So the ponyless young man took an old woman; her he had while his blood was hot, but she helped to make him successful. In time he had fifty horses to spare, so he bought a young wife whose blood was hot; by then his own was getting cold. Thus from generation to generation the blood temperatures alternated, but at least it suited the young women enough not to want the price lowered. Polygamy was allowed. A wealthy man might be willing to stand the expense of three—one to keep house, one to hunt, one to dig roots. Captain Jack had only two; he was thirty-six but his old wife looked very old indeed, while his young wife seemed but a girl.

Another feature of the Tule Lake region was and is a remarkable river. Due east from its southern part, in Captain Jack's time, was Clear Lake. The stream connected the two lakes in an eccentric way and with a great prodigality of ditching. If it had flowed out of the western end of Clear Lake into the eastern end of Tule Lake and had flowed straight, it would have needed to be just five miles long; in one place indeed it could have almost made it in four. Instead, it left Clear Lake at the northeast corner and entered Tule Lake at the north end, and wandered all over the landscape getting there. It made a big loop roughly like a horseshoe. Sometimes in its journeying it disappeared and dipped underground, to play hide-and-seek with a Modoc riding beside it. It fooled around that way until its length was seventy-five miles, perhaps the best example among rivers of the longest distance between two points. Such an erratic, inefficient stream was properly called Lost River. But Captain Jack and his people loved it. In its superfluous seventy miles how much valley it made, how much grass it moistened into ever-fresh verdure, what fat roots it grew, what abundance of game and fish it furnished! He kept begging the Great White Father to give it to the Modocs, but some of those 'white mans' in covered wagons were also excellent judges of real estate and there was nothing in the

Homestead Law against picking out your 640 acres along a river, and still farther along its narrow richness, and along it yet another mile. In this manner even Lost River would soon be exhausted.

But the most unusual part of the Tule Lake area remains practically unchanged today—a tract of about 45,000 acres known as the Lava Beds, lying south of the lake. It is surfaced with billowy slag, fissured with trenches sometimes a hundred feet deep, and underlaid with three hundred caves and tunnels. Its passages and tubes, its pyramids and ridges, its depressions and cracks and chasms make it a volcanic wilderness.

At the time of the Modoc War, a Yreka man rather imaginatively told of the 'Ben Wright Cave' there, containing fifteen acres of open space underground, with an everflowing spring bubbling up and with a number of entrances and exits just big enough for a man to crawl through and the main opening no bigger than a common window. Consider the demoralizing effect on bluecoats and volunteers of having such a great subterranean Indian armory described with flourishes at night around a sagebrush campfire.

Another man said, more responsibly, 'It is supposed their retreat furnishes no water excepting that produced by storms.' With spring came exhaustion of these winter cisterns, as will be seen.

The Lava Beds as a perfect Indian battleground were described by Jesse Applegate:

> An Indian . . . from the top of one of these stone pyramids . . . can, without undue haste, load and shoot a common muzzle-loading rifle ten times before a man can scramble over the rocks and chasms between the slain and the slayer. If at this terrible expense of life a force dislodges him from his cover, he has only to drop into and follow some subterranean passage with which he is familiar, to gain another ambush from whence it will cost ten more lives to dislodge him, and so on *ad infinitum*.

An Indian could see a white man coming at a distance of five miles without himself being seen; as the intruder approached within shooting distance, he could draw a sure and steady bead on the latter without exposing so much as a square inch of himself.

In the lava fields were small meadows of rich bunch-grass, which the settlers' cattle reached with difficulty over long circuitous trails through the rocks. There, even during the war, the animals grazed, and were picked off by accurate marksmen for warrior beef.

The Lava Beds, so sinister for aliens, so great a refuge for the Modocs, held in their sterile breast nurture for the oldest living things in America. In areas some distance from the Indian stronghold were and still are groves of arthritic junipers more aged than the petroglyphs down at the peninsula. A botanical scholar claims that this tree in its supreme longevity is older than the redwoods, older even than the sequoias by perhaps a century. So tenaciously does it cling to life in the arid soil, so little is required to feed its immortality, that with no more than a single strip of bark connecting it to the nourishing earth it goes on reproducing berries and green, juicy boughs and delicious odors.

The Lava Beds National Monument lies just south of the Oregon border. The government has built trails through the battlefields and marked and legended the places. There are no concessions. He who stays all night, sleeps in his own tent, and the memory of it will be remarkably pleasant and lasting. The campgrounds—and it is quite possible he will be the only one there—look out at a distance over all the country where the Modocs fought. Nearby is a lava butte named after sub-chief Sconchin, eloquent in pow-wows, the Webster of the Modocs. As likely as not a wind will come up in the night and blow down the tent, which probably will not have been put up very securely, since the mantle soil is too shallow on top of the lava and too non-glutinous to hold the pegs very well, and the anchorages on loose rocks are few and far off—not as it was and is down at the stronghold. But the collapsed tent will only be a disguised opportunity to gaze at the battlefield deep in the night under the stars, and imagine that it is 1873, and Captain Jack is down there in his cave, the small sagebrush fire has burned into ashes, his three-year-old daughter is sound asleep, and there is no noise except the low but cadenced tramp upon stone of the moccasined sentinels.

Tule Lake, the peninsula, Lost River, the Lava Beds— the stage. Ben Wright and Captain Jack—the principals in a two-act drama. Time—1852 and 1873.

BEN WRIGHT

All the water in the original Tule Lake would not have been enough to wash the blood from Ben Wright's hands. He was born of Quaker parents, but what a terrible distance in his frontier manhood he traveled from that gentle faith.

Wright and his men, in the guise of friendship, in 1852 went to a Modoc camp for the purposes of killing all the adult male Indians. Out of fifty braves only two escaped, but these two were mighty important—Sconchin, later to become sub-chief in the Modoc War, and Curley-Headed Doctor, the principal medicine man. Among the forty-eight slain was Captain Jack's father. And the son saw it all. He was a boy fifteen years old, and there was planted in his heart an indignation that was never extinguished.

So much for Ben Wright. He is important mainly for what he inspired, rather than what he did.

CAPTAIN JACK

God is nowise snobbish in the wayward manner he deposits in mortals the seeds of greatness. Captain Jack was very much a nobody by inherited status, not being descended from a long line of chiefs. Some of his Modoc associates worked as domestic servants in Yreka households.

Yet as this one lay an infant in a tule cradle in the Lava Beds, Tomaniwos touched him with his wand—the first and last time he ever did so to a Modoc baby—and thereby dispensed a capacity and a destiny the telling of which would for generations be upon the lips of men.

Captain Jack's people, the Modocs, occupied a country just south of the Klamaths. The two nations were neighbors in a region of lakes and sage and tules and mountain rims; in both cases dark eyes looked up from canoes and from the backs of ponies to see the towering whiteness of Shasta. Yet between the Modocs and the Klamaths there was no love lost, and when put together on the Klamath Reservation in Oregon, there was trouble.

The Modocs split fence rails. The Klamaths came and removed them. Captain Jack asked redress of the Indian agent. On the third trip the latter lost his temper. "You black sonofabitch with your complaints," he said, "get out of here!"

The next day Captain Jack and a band of the Modocs packed up, left the reservation, and went back to Lost River, to their old haunts around Tule Lake and the Lava Beds.

This leavetaking was in 1870. Captain Jack and his secessionists lived a delightful life till September, 1872. They frequently visited Yreka, where captive and not very disconsolate Pit River squaws were traded to white men. Captain Jack's own sister, 'Queen Mary,' joined up with half a dozen miners and frontiersmen during a ten-year period, each one glad to get her, it is said, and gladder to let her go. Some of the Modoc men, working as Yreka house servants, usefully learned paleface ways.

Captain Jack in his association with the whites disdained to learn English beyond a few trade words, and did not speak Chinook jargon, thus barriering himself in dignity behind his own language.

He shrewdly traded on the friendship of several prominent Yreka citizens. On visits to the Klamath Reservation he boasted that these Yrekans gave him passes to travel about as he pleased. Did he stop to realize what a melancholy thing was liberty only upon a white man's passport?

Finally, in November, 1872, James Jackson of the United States cavalry was ordered to put Captain Jack and his band back upon the Klamath Reservation. The attempt to do this resulted in the killing of a soldier and a warrior.

Captain Jack remained sullen and silent in his tent until the shooting started. Then he rushed out to lead his tribesmen. They headed for their stronghold in the Lava Beds. On their way they killed more than a dozen settlers.

The Modoc War had started.

The volcanic region of their refuge had rocky caves, and canyons a hundred feet deep, and a sunken basin for their horses and cattle. It had grassy places for their stock to graze upon, and various small cisterns for water. Indians and ponies, and cattle for beef, could live there in complete concealment, for the wild surface would reveal nothing.

In this refuge four miles wide and seven miles long, the Indians had natural breastworks, which could be quickly heightened and extended by piling up loose lava chunks. The paths, in many places, were already tunnels in which a man could walk without his head showing; the walls in the lower places could be built up. Thus travel from Captain Jack's cave to Sconchin's on the other side of a ledge, and from point to point everywhere in the stronghold, could go on in safety from white snipers. It was probably the most perfect natural fortification to be found on earth. It is all there today, informingly marked, for anyone to see. Lieutenant Tom Wright spoke from experience when he said, "The match to the Modoc stronghold's never been built and never will be. I'm telling you, it's the most impregnable fortress in the world."

For their war budget this nation had seven hundred dollars, plus confiscated provisions worth perhaps $3000. They also had rifles and a good supply of ammunition (bows they used mainly when silence was of the essence). So prepared, fifty fighting men took their horses and went into the Lava Beds to make a vast amount of newspaper reading for the rest of America. Here are introduced some of the leading characters in the drama to be enacted:

Captain Jack—'In natural sagacity, diplomatic ability, genius, this savage was more than a match for them all.' Another writer said that there was 'something grand in his desperate obstinacy.' Into his cave (it was the biggest; a 'medicine flag' waved in front of it all the time he was there, and the cave itself can be seen today) he took a family consisting of his old wife, his young and favorite wife, Lizzie, an eighteen-year-old daughter and a three-year-old daughter, and Queen Mary, who certainly ought to have been able to give him good advice on the tactics of the white man.

Sconchin—Though a brother of old Chief Sconchin, his place had been little more than that of a common man until he became Captain Jack's sub-chief. He was fifty years old and very wrinkled, had a height of five feet nine, and was the Modocs' principal orator.

Scarface Charley—Captain Jack's actual second in command in military action. He had a big basso voice which soldiers once heard like a trumpet three or four miles away across the Lava Beds. The whites had killed his father in 1847.

Boston Charley—A tobacco chewer, twenty-five years old, with an expressionless face.

Bogus Charley—So called because he was the tribe's joke-man, the representative of Modoc humor.

Black Jim—Captain Jack's half-brother and, like him, dark-complexioned. Toward the last he and Captain Jack quarreled in the Lava Beds.

Hooker Jim—He said that Captain Jack got mad at him for something he couldn't understand. His family of eleven was the largest in the Lava Beds.

Shacknasty Jim—Chief of the Hot Creek band of Modocs. He had a family of ten and his lodge was an exhibit of awful housekeeping—hence his name.

Curley Headed Doctor—Medicine man of the Modocs.

The Modocs attacked an ammunition wagon train on December 21, 1872. Whereupon, four hundred soldiers, regulars and volunteers, closed in on, or thought they were going to close in on, Captain Jack's fifty fighting men. The latter didn't have a chance. So imagined a volunteer captain on Thursday night before the battle.

"I won't be able to restrain my men," said he. "Why, if I'd let 'em, they'd eat the Modocs up now."

Replied Fairchild, local settler and captain of the California volunteers, who had hunted cattle in the Lava Beds, "They won't be a bit hard to keep back when the Modocs open fire."

On the same evening, Private Bill remarked, "Say, Jim, are you goin' to eat your Modoc sirloin tomorrow raw or cooked?"

Jim replied, "Bill, gol-darn it, I don't like the idea of facing them red devils."

Who was to be right, Bill or Jim?

Reveille the next morning was at four. By daylight the troops were at the edge of the Lava Beds, ready to enter. But as they climbed they moved into a fog, gray, thick, opaque. The canyons and the fissures and the basins were all smoothed over with vapors; what was in them nobody could see. They caught sight of no Indian, and from out of the fog there came no sound. The howitzers could not be set up because there was no target to aim them at.

The fog lifted briefly around five o'clock in the afternoon.

The pale winter sun was about to dip down behind Shasta. The soldiers, who had been fighting a sightless, soundless battle for ten hours, now received the concentrated fire of the Modocs. Bugles sounded. The Indians knew the import of those notes floating out over the Lava Beds; they meant retreat. Nine whites were killed and thirty wounded. Next day the Indians went out and picked up almost a fresh rifle apiece—Henrys, Remingtons, Spencers, Ballards. Said Shacknasty Jim, "Have plenty volunteer hats."

There was an armistice while the White Father at Washington and a lot of lesser white fathers considered what to do. Heap big talk seemed to be the answer. The 'peace mans' consisted of A. B. Meacham, General E. R. S. Canby, the Reverend E. Thomas, and L. S. Dyar, agent of the Klamath Reservation.

Messengers were sent to Captain Jack's stronghold to open the way to a conference. These were Captain Jack's old friend Steele from Yreka, Fairchild, Frank Riddle, and Riddle's squaw, Winema. Quite uninvited, Bill Dadd, reporter for the Sacramento *Record,* went along. The party spent the night in the Lava Beds as Captain Jack's guests. Steele pointed out the futility of resistance. Said the Modoc chief, "Kill with bullets don't hurt much; starved to death hurt a heap." Bitterly he recalled Ben Wright. Nevertheless, Steele reported, when the messengers got back, that the Modocs had agreed upon matters more than Fairchild understood them to have done. There was a dispute, so the envoys had to return to find out just what the Modocs *had* said. This time Riddle and Fairchild begged to be excused. But not Bill Dadd, who was to become the top correspondent of the Modoc War, though the New York *Herald* and the London *Illustrated News* were among the publications represented.

Dadd went back with Steel and Winema. The Indians were now in bad temper to the point that their lives were in danger from the more hotheaded tribesmen. They spent the night once again, Winema in Captain Jack's own cave (after all, she was his cousin). During the night, whenever Steele or Bill Dadd waked up, he saw he was being guarded by Scarface Charley or Queen Mary or Captain Jack himself.

Finally, on April 11th, Riddle and Winema acted as interpreters at a conference of Meacham, General Canby, Reverend Thomas, and agent Dyar with Captain Jack and his leaders. The day was cloudy and chill. A small sagebrush fire was built. Captain Jack impatiently waited. Peace commissioners and Indians had agreed to come unarmed, but Meacham and Dyar had derringers in their pockets, and clothes bulges showed that every Indian wore a pistol.

The upshot was that Captain Jack killed General Canby, Boston Charley killed preacher Thomas, and Sconchin tried to kill Meacham, who made poor use of his derringer but survived many wounds and an abortive effort to scalp him. Dyar and Riddle fled; Winema ducked flat upon the ground.

Captain Jack put on General Canby's hat and belted the army sword around his slender waist. Back in the Lava Beds he knew that the worst was now to be expected. "Soldier mans come, all right," he said.

But they did not come right away. The troops could not go forth against the Modocs until they gave General Canby and the Reverend Thomas a fine funeral, with eight commissioned officers as pallbearers for the general, and eight sergeants for the preacher.

Ten days after the massacre the soldiers went forth—ten of them for every warrior—to take the stronghold which the Modocs had now held four months.

The impregnability of the lava fastnesses had inspired a lot of armchair strategy. The army had experimented with and then given up the idea of putting mortar-boats on Tule Lake to shell the Indians at a distance. There were other suggestions. Put the bluecoats and volunteers in steel armor.

Send bloodhounds in. Burn sulphur in the caves (an especially impractical expedient under the circumstances).

The battle was started by setting up mortars two hundred yards from the lakeshore and one-thousand yards from Captain Jack's lair. One was shot off every fifteen minutes through the night to keep him and his warriors awake.

For two days the attack went on, with five whites killed and a dozen wounded. The soldiers had learned also to build breastworks, small ones to hold half a dozen men, where two slept while four did sentinel duty around the clock. The Indians, who had previously concealed themselves, now lifted taunting heads above the lava rims, daring the cowardly soldiers to do the same. Water was getting scarce; warriors took risks to get it from the lake. The troops captured a frantic squaw on the way for a drink.

On the third morning, the troops moved in on the famous stronghold. When they arrived, the Modocs had vanished. The soldiers saw in the lava a fissure which led from the caverns back toward the hills. By this route the Modocs had left during the night. The First Cavalry captured no more than the medicine flag, which was floating in front of Captain Jack's cave on a four-foot staff planted in loose stones. This war banner was made of mink-skins and hawks' feathers.

The Indians had left the stronghold but not the Lava Beds. They fell upon a pack train. They fired on some Warm Springs Indians—allies of the whites—as these were digging a grave. They went down to Tule Lake to get water and contemptuously bathed in the lake while the astonished soldiers watched.

Three days went by and then four more, and all the time the Lava Beds exhaled a sickening stench of rotting bodies—white ones, not red. Then for two days the Indians no longer were seen going to the lake for water. Had they left the Lava Beds? Two friendly squaws made a reconnaissance.

They saw no Modocs. Eighty-five men were sent out to make sure there weren't any. Noon came without an Indian or a fresh sign of one. The men rested and ate their rations.

The Lava Beds are quiet, especially so at midday. Suddenly there came a volley that shattered the silence. Of the eighty-five soldiers sitting there so relaxed and unsuspecting, several, almost as in a drill, fell back or forward dead. Officers were struck instantly lifeless and motionless in their bright uniforms upon the rusty-red lava. Others writhed and cried out from the bullets in their bodies. Of the living, half fled and did not stop until they reached camp. The rest found two small basins and one large one in the rocks, but these proved to be traps. As night came on, the hiders in these terrible places heard a loud voice, the voice of Scarface Charley, "All you mans what ain't dead better go home. Don't want to kill you all in one day."

The Sacramento *Record*'s Bill Dadd and other correspondents told the dismal news to the people, who cried out at this perpetuation of Modoc havoc, "Whipped again! Whipped again!"

The army was inactive for over a week, but not the Modocs, who captured a wagon train. Two squaws were again sent into the Lava Beds, whence had come no sign of life and wherein at last there was indeed none. The next sight of the Modocs was at Sorass Lake, where an army camp was attacked, with five bluecoats killed and seven wounded. The attackers were led by Captain Jack in the uniform of General Canby.

But with the timely return of an absent detachment, the Modocs were pursued three miles into the woods. Their flight continued toward Pit River. It was Captain Jack's first setback in the Modoc War, and, small as it was, it marked the turning point in his fortunes.

Half of his warriors deserted him. Useless to continue, they said. It was a stormy conference.

"We no fight for you no more," said Bogus Charley.

"Everything good, you brave," said Captain Jack. "Dark cloud come, you run."

Lack of water, not the soldiers, had routed him out of the Lava Beds. Disloyalty, not the soldiers, now made him a fugitive, with two dozen warriors.

On May 27th, after the war had gone on nearly half a year, the main body of Modocs gave themselves up. Soldier jubilation was distinctly lessened at Captain Jack's not being among them. Bogus Charley, with an eye to saving his own hide, offered to lead the soldiers to the chief. With him went Shacknasty Jim, Steamboat Frank, Hooker Jim, all in uniforms, all with army rifles, all mounted on good horses. At length they rode up to a makeshift wickiup where sat the man they had come to betray.

"What for you come?" he demanded. "Go before I forget you Modocs and kill you dead."

They reported back. Troops went forth to get him, led by the traitor scouts. Boston Charley and some others surrendered. For half a plug of the colonel's tobacco Charley bargained to go get the fugitive chief. He was allowed to leave, and the colonel waited hopefully. He didn't know that a detachment of his bluecoats had captured a tobacco-chewing Indian and wouldn't believe him when he spat much amber and claimed he was on duty for the colonel.

Scarface Charley, he of the loud voice talking low now, delivered himself up, accompanied by Sconchin and three others. They said that Captain Jack would probably surrender in the morning.

Dr. T. T. Cabiniss went unarmed with Queen Mary to induce Captain Jack to yield at once. They came to a small lava field; in the midst of it, on a rock, sat the chief. A faded army blanket was around him like a shawl. His face was buried in his hands. To the white men he looked lonelier than his lonely surroundings.

He listened sullenly to his sister's plea. He said he would give himself up in the morning.

Next day, in a canyoned region, the Warm Springs scouts saw where a man had leaped from rock to rock to keep from making footprints in the earth. They found a trail twenty or thirty yards off where several persons had stepped in the tracks of one. A scout raised his head and sniffed 'as if to gain news from the passing wind.' He said he knew the Modocs were around, though up to that time none had been seen. Sure enough, the next moment one leaped from behind a large boulder in the canyon rim, and fled below out of sight. Another Indian appeared, looked hurriedly around, and also vanished. In three minutes the first one showed up again, and a scout called out in Chinook jargon, "Come here; no hurt you."

The Indian approached the scout, who dropped his own guns to shake hands. It was Captain Jack's surrender messenger, and the chief himself came out of the canyon in about fifteen minutes and shook hands all around (as the paleface powwowers had taught him to do the first thing in strained situations). Soon appeared five squaws and seven children with the Modoc baggage.

Captain Jack no longer wore anything that belonged to General Canby. He had on a dirty shirt and soiled, ragged cavalry pantaloons of knee length. At once he asked and was given permission to put on clean clothes. Lizzie unpacked his bundles and he changed from head to foot.

He and Lizzie rode together on a spotted cayuse to the house of a settler. Thence all went in three large wagons, with two wagons to carry their baggage, to the military prison camp on Tule Lake, not far from the Lava Beds. Battery G marched beside the wagons. Forty Warm Springs scouts walked behind them, with songs and warwhoops.

There was no other music, none of fife or drum, but this Indian yelling gave to the scene a tone of sadness.

Everybody was at camp, soldiers and citizens, to see the Modocs brought in. From them came the cry, "Where is Captain Jack? Where is Captain Jack?"

But they did not catch a glimpse of him. He had too much dignity for that. Wrapped in a blanket he sat crouched in a corner of the wagon which he occupied with his lieutenants.

At the prison camp the chief was chained to Sconchin, and Boston Charley to One-Eyed Mose. In the tented stockade the men were placed on one side, the squaws on the other, with one notable exception: Lizzie was allowed to sit beside the chief, to lay her head upon his breast, and their three-year-old daughter had the run of the place.

The surrendered Modocs, including those who had deserted previously, numbered fifty fighting men and boys, fifty women, and sixty children—deaths from soldiers' bullets had been practically nil, while they had killed sixty-five of the enemy, and wounded sixty-three. That enemy, toward the last, had numbered 1056—twenty to one, yet not they but thirst and treachery had defeated the Modoc chief.

In Captain Jack the soldiers saw a slender man of about 145 pounds, five feet, ten inches tall, with small hands, small feet, thin arms, thirty-six years old and looking younger. In his fresh cavalry pantaloons his hips were as slender as a cowboy's. His face, for all he had been through, was round and boyish; his hair, parted in the middle when combed, now fell unkempt over his forehead and some old trimming had cut it across above his eyes. These eyes, bright and glittering (but soon to have dark lines and crow's-feet under them from confinement), were perhaps his most distinctive feature, at times as meditative as a poet's but oftener watchful and darting.

Wrote the Yreka *Union* correspondent, who was present

at the capture: 'Never, not even in repose, has his face a pleasant look. Place him among a thousand Indians, and he would be thought the chief by any observing stranger. Those who have seen him marvel not that he is the leader of the Modocs. Though in chains and on the brink of eternity, he is yet feared and respected by the Indians about him.'

At first the military intended to hang Captain Jack and the other ringleaders right there at Tule Lake in sight of their Lava Beds. Not so thought the compassionate White Father in Washington. Accordingly, some days later, all the Modocs were hauled in wagons to the Klamath Reservation.

The main prisoners were Captain Jack and Sconchin (still chained together), Black Jim (not yet fully reconciled with his famous half-brother), and Boston Charley (the tobacco chewer, at least with the advantage of having more of it to chew now). Their offense was not the gallant war they had fought, but killing the 'peace mans'.

The trial began on July 5th, and made a Roman holiday in the newspapers for a matter of three months. Bill Dadd of the *Record* did not get away to return to Sacramento till October 10th. (On that day his stage was robbed near Red Bluff. The bandits took $4500 from the five Chinese passengers. From Bill Dadd they took forty cents.)

Only six Indians were tried, all in chains before the resplendent judges—Captain Jack, Sconchin, Black Jim, Boston Charley, Slolux, and Barncho. The latter pair were finally sent to prison instead of the gallows because they were 'just common men' taking orders to do their bad deeds. Unfettered and unguarded, the perfidious four, whom the whites called scouts but whom the chief now hated as traitors, were on hand as witnesses—Bogus Charley, Hooker Jim, Steamboat Frank, Shacknasty Jim.

Captain Jack resented being hobbled like a horse. (The

chain that connected his right ankle with Sconchin's left had about a dozen links.) He wanted to talk with the Great White Father himself, but was patiently told that this benevolent parent had millions of children and couldn't come to see all of them when they got into trouble. He suggested that Scarface Charley (also unchained and not up for trial) be substituted for him. He later proposed another proxy. To the white chaplain's propagandizing of the beauties of heaven he replied, "Preacher mans say where Jack go is nice place. You go, me not. Me give preacher mans twenty-five ponies."

When told that death was no farther off than the next day, he asked to see that traitorous pair, Bogus Charley and Hooker Jim. Said General Wheaton, "I will give you an opportunity to see them but advise you not to spend your last moments in an altercation with them." Wrote Bill Dadd:

> About 5:00 P. M. the wives and the children of the condemned men were admitted to the guard house to take leave of their husbands and fathers. Such a scene we never hope to witness again. They clung round the necks of the prisoners, filling the air with their lamentations. The cries of the women could be heard far away, and soon other squaws came flocking around, asking with blanched faces if Captain Jack was to be killed tomorrow. For hours the wailing and moaning was kept up, and not until the poor creatures were removed was the dismal sound hushed, and to the clamor of grief succeeded the silence of despair.

Came a quarter to ten the next morning. An October haze softened the ruggedness of the distant mountains, the somberness of the pines. A wagon was ready. In it were four coffins. The four Modocs climbed in, three of them dressed in old blue army blouses and trousers but Captain Jack wearing a bright checkered shirt, a red undershirt, and a blanket over his shoulders. They sat upon the coffins during the short journey to the gallows, which they looked at intently as they approached. About a thousand people watched them, every move they made, every expression on their faces.

The white officers who had fought so badly received the ones who had fought so well. The former had on splendid uniforms, and the breaths they breathed were of long duration. The latter were more poorly clothed than privates on fatigue duty, and their breaths would mix in a matter of minutes with the soft winds coming from the mountains and shaking the foliage of the pines.

At the scaffold their chains were removed. Boston Charley took a chew of tobacco. He and Black Jim went up first. Captain Jack next. Sconchin last. All ascended with firm step. Boston Charley took another chew of tobacco as he walked up. The four sat down as calmly as four speakers upon a platform.

The execution orders were read, a business which consumed twelve minutes. General Wheaton had reminded Captain Jack that quarreling with the traitors was not the best way to spend his last moments. Was this a better way? All through it the doomed men sat unmoved.

By now little indeed was left of their time on earth. Yet more of it must needs be taken up hearing a prayer. This did not visibly affect them either. Boston Charley had the solace of his tobacco cud.

The executioner trimmed Captain Jack's hair, then put on the hangman's black cap. No longer, forever, could he see the rugged mountains, the somber pines. But could he and did he still behold the Lava Beds where the goodness of life had been spent, where, as he lay in a tule cradle, Tomaniwos had touched him with the wand of genius?

Black caps were put on the three others. The hangman took several minutes more to cut off parts of the caps and adjust the nooses

Then quickly the Modocs were hanging in the air, and the thousand people down below saw them in silhouette against the blue sky and the far blue mountain range. 'Sconchin died hard; Jack instantly—all like men.'

The bodies were cut down and buried. But, according to the half-breed son of Riddle and Winema, the corpse of Captain Jack was dug up from an unguarded grave the following night by ghouls, carried to Yreka for embalming, and later exhibited to the public at ten cents a person.

It was a great day for the journalists of 1873 in their efforts to get vivid accounts to their papers first, because the telegraph was a long way off from this wilderness scene. The San Francisco *Chronicle* man, with two Eastern correspondents, hired a four-horse spring wagon to race forth from the gallows bearing them and their dispatches. Men on horseback were ready to dart off across the sagebrush at the last gasps of the Modocs. Some papers heralded the use of carrier pigeons, mostly to scare their rivals, but had the birds been trained 'there is no doubt that they would have outdistanced the horse courier, and the telegraph also.' The Associated Press was ahead of all others by twenty minutes.

The remaining Modocs were taken to the Quapaw Agency in Indian Territory, where Scarface Charley and then Bogus Charley became chiefs. In 1909 the exiles were allowed to return to the Klamath Reservation. By 1914 only four of the Lava Bed warriors were still alive. All of Captain Jack's noted lieutenants were in their graves.

A considerable literature sprang up about Captain Jack and the Modoc War, with caustic attention to the paleface soldiers, especially the volunteers. The latter came in for two especially notable pieces.

Said the Yreka *Union* on January 4, 1873: 'Governor Booth of California refuses to call out volunteers. . . . He says he has hundreds of applications for *commissions* from people in the Siskiyou area but no applications for *privates*.'

Said the Portland *Bulletin* a week or so later, of General Miller of the Oregon militia:

> There is only one argument against the effectiveness of the General and that is this: *he is bitterly opposed to the killing of an Indian.* While in the Indian service at Grande Ronde he acquired the habit of letting Indians live for indefinite periods, as mere matter of policy, since dead Indians could not conveniently draw Government annuities.
>
> If Captain Jack will not come out of his cave, why waft hard words at him? It will only disturb his temper. The General's best strategy will be to get him upon a Government voucher somehow, and his fate is sealed. It was never intended that men should fight—especially militia men. Like the curl in a pig's tail, they are intended for ornament, not use.

The Modoc War fared much better with the poets than contemporary events usually do. Rhymers throughout the land 'trained their lyric pens' on Captain Jack and his exciting deeds. The poetry was 'grave, gay, sarcastic, tear-provoking,' and the newspapers of 1873 printed a lot of it. Following are verses from two fair samples: the second with two prose parentheses to the effect that "white man he make too much bombshell and telegraphy dispatch".

Lava-Linden

In Klamath, when the sun was low,
The lava beds held Mr. Lo,
Who dared to fight and wouldn't go,
    For all the Peace Commissioners.

In truth it was a gallant sight,
To see a thousand men of might,
With guns and cannons day and night,
    Fight fifty dirty Indians.

For every foot of lava bed
They threw a pound of hissing lead,
A ton for every Modoc head,
    In three days roaring battery. . . .

Captain Jack of the Lava Beds

I'm Captain Jack of the Lava Beds
I'm 'cock of the walk' and Chief of the Reds;
I kin 'lift the har' and scalp the heads
    Of the whole United States Army.

I'm Captain Jack of the Modoc braves
And 'cock of the walk' to the lava caves;
When I catches 'em out, their heads I shave—
    The heads of the braves of the army. . . .

About two months after Captain Jack's death he gave a communication from the great beyond. The Yreka *Union* explained that the spirit of Captain Jack spoke 'through the instrumentality of Mrs. J. H. Conunt while in a trance,' as follows: ' "Me come back to make speak through your great talking paper. Me want to tell the Great Father he got bad children out on the plains—bad children there—and they make bad injuns badder. Soon there be big war—big war; cost the Great Father much wampum, many warriors. He better look to it; he better take care of his bad children. Me Captain Jack." '

22

REPORT OF THE BOTANIST

DAVID DOUGLAS AND THE BIG CONES

Wʜᴀᴛ Dᴀᴠɪᴅ Dᴏᴜɢʟᴀs, Scottish botanist, saw in the Indian's tobacco pouch made him very covetous. The native, whom he encountered in July, 1825, on the River Multnomak (the Willamette), carried in his buckskin poke the seeds 'of a remarkably large Pine.' The botanist treated the Indian to a smoke and thus made him amenable to questions. Then he learned that these pine seeds had come from the mountains about two degrees to the south, in the country of the 'Umpqua Indians.' Jean Baptiste McKay, Hudson's Bay trapper, was going in that direction for beaver skins. Douglas asked him to bring back a dozen cones, a bag of seeds, a few twigs, and some of the gum.

The trapper said he would, but it was late in the fall and the cones were almost completely gone. When he returned on February 20th to Fort Vancouver, he brought Douglas only one cone. But he said he had given 'strictest orders to his Indian friends' to be on the alert for the next crop.

By this time the botanist had learned that the source of the interesting cones were trees from 170 to 220 feet high and from 20 to 25 feet around, which produced 'a quantity of saccharine substance, used for seasoning the same way sugar is by civilized nations'; that the cones reached a length of 16 inches and a girth of 10 inches; and that the seeds were collected at the end of summer, dried, pounded, and made into a cake considered a great dainty.

In the fall, when Douglas got back to Fort Vancouver, he found that McKay had already left for the Umpqua country. He talked with Dr. John McLoughlin, who said another party would leave in a few days under A. R. Mc-Leod. Douglas was told that each individual on this trip had 'to restrict himself to the least possible quantity of encumbrances.' He bought a new gun for two pounds, packed up a tent, two blankets, two extra shirts—a linen one and a flannel one—a small copper kettle, six quires of paper, and some trifles and tobacco for presents.

In time the McLeod party joined McKay, from whom the botanist bought the skin of a large she-grizzly, paying one of his blankets, described as small and old, and a little of his tobacco (he was one of the world's famous botanists but he was also a Scotsman). He wanted the bearskin for an under-robe 'to lie upon, as the cold dew of the grass is very pre-judicial to my health.'

In the middle of October, 1826, Douglas went up the Umpqua River to a place at Sugar Pine Mountains near present Roseburg, where he thought he recognized the country that had been described to him by the Indian of the tobacco pouch. On October 26th, a cold, cloudy day, he walked out from camp. He met an Indian who lost no time in string-ing his bow. Douglas simply laid his gun down on the ground at his feet. Then he waved the Indian forward. The Umpqua came slowly and cautiously, but obeyed Douglas and laid his bow and quiver of arrows beside the new Hudson's Bay rifle of the botanist.

The Scotsman apparently had no extra pipe. He lit up his own and gave the Indian a smoke. Then he made a rough sketch of the pine tree with the big cones. The native pointed to the hills fifteen or twenty miles to the south. Douglas started thither, the Indian with him, and about noon he reached his 'long-wished-for pines,' some of them over two hundred feet high. The great cones hung from the points of the branches 'like sugar-loaves in a grocer's shop.'

The cones on the dead and fallen trees wouldn't do for Douglas, and those on standing trees grew only on the loftiest branches. He couldn't climb the tree. He couldn't cut it down. So he tried shooting the cones down with his bright, new gun. How many times he shot he didn't say, or how many times he missed. But three big cones fell. All the noise brought Indians.

They were painted bucks, with fierce painted countenances. They were armed with bows, spears, and flint knives. Douglas explained to them that he was merely getting some of the big pine cones that hung so high above. The Indians seemed to consider this all right but he noticed some significant actions. One of the Umpquas was stringing his bow. Another was sharpening his flint knife. Douglas, not believing he needed 'further testimony of their intentions,' and seeing he had no chance to take to his heels, stepped back five paces, held his cocked gun in his right hand and his pistol in the left, and faced them in silence and with outward calm.

In this belligerent attitude he stared them down at last. The leader gave a sign that they wanted a smoke, but Douglas said they would have to get him some cones first. While they were gone he picked up the three he had shot down and moved off as fast as he could. The Indian who had come with him hurried away too, but Douglas got rid of him before reaching camp.

David Douglas' discovery was the now-famous sugar pine (though the Douglas fir is the one which bears his name down to posterity). Aside from the remarkably large cones of this tree, it produces a peculiar kind of manna. If the great bole is wounded by fire or by ax, then the sap leaks out to make kernels or beads of sugar. This sugar has a laxative quality, so that the Indians, though liking its taste, know better than to eat too much. Bears are notably fond of sweets, but they curiously never seem to eat the saccharine exuded by the sugar pine.

JOE KNOWLES, NAKED IN THE WILDERNESS

The place—the Siskiyou Mountains of southern Oregon and northern California in the Klamath and Siskiyou National Forests. The time—July and August, 1914. The person— Joe Knowles, artist and nature-man, who claimed to know the woods better than any other civilized human. The proposition—that Joe Knowles should spend a month naked and without so much as a pocket knife in the wild and remote Siskiyous, and eat the while, and sleep not too uncomfortably, and come out clothed.

Professor T. T. Waterman of the Anthropology Department of the University of California was to see that the experiment was properly carried out, at the same time remaining always far enough off not to interfere with Knowles in any way, or give him the slightest succor, as daily the two receded farther and farther 'from the haunts of man.'

The starting point was to be at Indian Creek on Monday, July 18th—in as complete a wilderness as could be found. For a month Knowles was prepared to wring existence from the wilds with his bare hands and with such weapons as he could fashion out of sticks and stones. He expected to put on weight and gain health during the ordeal. Before starting out he lovingly stroked a cedar tree; upon this, he said, he would depend more than upon any other plant in the woods. From its bark he could strip 'long ribbons, light and strong,' that would serve him in many ways.

At his base camp were reporters, who sent out dispatches aimed at working up the Pacific Coast public into preliminary curiosity and excitement. Joe Knowles obligingly stated: 'It is barely possible that I shall have a hand-to-hand conflict with some of the wild animals. If I do, it will be worth telling about. I have heard of a gray timber she-wolf with cubs in the mountains where I am going, and I would like nothing so well as to get that wolf and use her hide for a coat.'

He told the newspapermen, and the newspapermen told several million readers, that he expected to send messages out of the wilderness. How? Simple enough. Scratch them on the gray-and-brown fungus growths on tree trunks.

He further said:

> I will show that I'm as good as the stone-age man. And nature has spread the same table for me as for him. . . . Now, I'm going to tell you what I'll do for the first two days or so. I shall strip to the skin. Professor Waterman will go over my entire body to be sure I have concealed nothing. If I have my way, I shall speak to no human being for at least thirty days. I shall eat a good meal before I leave. I shall get out of sight as quickly as my legs will carry me. Then I shall begin first of all to look about for a place to sleep and something for my feet. Out of cedar bark I can make a fairly good pair of sandals. I shall make them on me and there they will stay until either worn out or I secure a deer or other animal with which to make real moccasins. This bark sandal I make on me with my feet under water, and the part up the legs will be of braided bark like a basket. They are not durable, however, and will not be comfortable on my feet.

(The author went through the region of the Joe Knowles experiment in June, 1948, from the Oregon side over the tops of the Siskiyous down Indian Creek into California. The country is still the utmost in the way of wilderness. Knowles surely needed moccasins immediately, for the ground is rocky and full of dry and spiky limbs and thickets of harsh brush.)

Knowles didn't start till July 21st. Then he disappeared into the forest. July 23rd and July 24th passed and the 'forest was silent as to his presence.' On July 25th he was located and spoken to, but he didn't reply. Three men camping on Grizzly Creek sighted him. He waved a string of fish 'and looked happy.'

Then there was found a message which he had written on July 24th, and left twenty yards off the trail at the foot of a large cedar tree, about a third of a mile from camp. A secret sign, previously agreed upon, directed the men to the cache. The message was not scratched upon fungus but was scrawled in charcoal upon three slabs of the bleached rind of dry-rotted fir. The items were numbered from one to five. One said: 'Slept before open fire the first night. Ten miles Indian Creek.' The next three items dealt with the embarrassing presence of prospectors. He said he had seen five 'and one has seen me' (this was before the three at whom he had waved the fish). The fifth item read: 'This will be the very hardest week. It is hell. You will hear from me Saturday. Joe.'

On July 27th came word that he was ranging up and down Indian Creek. (Along that creek, in June, 1948, the author failed to find anything wild to eat except a few green and unformed hazelnuts.) Then came the finding of a second note, written on bark broken in two places, in the forks of an old tree. It said in part: 'My fourth day—I have done nothing so far but exist. I have eaten fish that I caught with my hands, and a few berries, and it has taken all my time. . . . I have no clothing yet. I keep a fire all night and sleep part of the day in the sun. I am about ten miles from you on what I call Hedgehog Mountain. The underbrush is like the quills of a hedgehog's back; they have left their trademark on my legs and body. . . . Joe.'

A third message was found along the trail, and with it a pair of discarded wilderness shoes. An examination showed how they had been made. Slabs of wood for soles had been trimmed with a stone knife to the size of his feet. Rope of marsh-grass served as thongs to fasten them on. Knowles had no instrument for punching holes in the sole wood, so the binding cords had to go around and under the whole sandal. The grass would not have lasted ten minutes of rough walking unless something had been done to protect it from wear, and what he did was to braid two sticks skillfully into it, and to dig out grooves in the soles for the cord to rest in. His message said:

> My seventh day— No one can live in this country alone for seven days and seven nights without seeing wild game. I have seen one bear and seven deer, but have caught nothing except fish and a few squirrels.
> I am having trouble with my feet. . . . I have made several pairs of bark moccasins, but they only last a day. I have now a pair with heavy wood bottoms and twisted grass tops that will stand the rough footing. I am weaving a blanket out of fine grass and when this is finished I can let my fire go out in the night. I have kept a fire every night so far and have slept days in the sun. . . .
> I shall try to get a deer or a bear. I could make good use of one of their skins these cold nights. I am eating fish, squirrels, and hazelnuts that are not ripe. The fish are plentiful and not hard to catch and I have eaten more of them than any other thing.

In his next message he told about finding the carcass of a buck deer which had been killed by a cougar and afterward visited by a bear. He was glad to get the part of the skin left behind.

He told later how he caught trout in swift Indian Creek.

He wove a series of nets out of willow withes and set them in waterfalls. Then he went upstream with a pole to scare out the fish, which darted downstream into his nets. He also made a casting line out of cedar bark. This, when wet, became tough and pliable. The hook he fashioned from the wishbone of a woodpecker, and the fly from partridge feathers.

It was decided to terminate his wilderness stay at the end of a month, on the basis that if he could manage thirty days in the wild, primitive Siskiyous he could live just about anywhere in the world just about as long as he pleased.

A heavy beard was on his face when he came out. He had been unable to find a Siskiyou stone sharp enough to shave with. When he went in he had weighed 202 pounds. When he returned he weighed 181½ pounds, but he scoffed at the idea that he was weak from exposure.

23

NECROLOGY

DEAD RIVER

ONLY SIXTY-FIVE miles of the ancient channel of Big Blue River have been traced out, but Argonauts took therefrom in gold dust over three and a half million a mile, making it about the richest streambed in recorded geography.

Fully two-thirds of the discovered distance has been eaten away by rivers running athwart Big Blue with their canyons, like broad breaks in a mighty dam. This notched segment has produced a quarter of a billion of wealth. Since the river could scarcely have failed to be two hundred miles long in its mountain part, there is probably a billion dollars of gold dust in that unknown remainder running somewhere loftily along the western side of the Sierras, like an irrigation flume along a hillside, two hundred and fifty times magnified, fifty times elevated.

Let the remaining length of Big Blue River be found, and there indeed will be the mother lode. But don't rush off too quickly to find it. Even the sixty-five miles of it observable to expert and scientific eyes are without vestiges for the ordinary person unable to trace out the river's ancient bed athwart the ridges where it is cut up by living streams entering at right angles. Not even trained observers have been able to follow Big Blue up from where the sixty-five-mile length stops. The rest may be underneath modern streams; it may be below great lava inundations.

The known part starts at Little Grizzly, California, not far south of the Oregon border in Sierra County, and disappears at Forest Hill south-southwest in Placer County, all the while running parallel with the main ridge of the Sierras and about thirty miles from it—truly a gigantic flume along a gigantic hillside. Some think the Big Blue River has been traced to near Placerville, which would make the total located distance one hundred and ten miles. The sixty-five-mile length is, however, the segment generally accepted.

The elevation at Little Grizzly is just a little less than a mile above sea level; at Forest Hill it is just a little more than half a mile. The average fall of Big Blue River, therefore, was thirty-three feet a mile, and a river seems to be pretty much standing on its head when it drops that much. The Sacramento has an average fall of five feet to the mile.

The traveler up the western side of the northern Sierras today would see no signs of a dead river, and the traveler in the old days saw no signs of one. How, then, was it found?

Big Blue River flowed roughly north and south, parallel with the backbone of the Sierra upthrust. The rivers and creeks of today flow down the sides of the mountain range, roughly from east to west. They either had to be dammed up by the Big Blue River bed when they met it, or they had to flow over it and eventually erode deep canyons through it. In the course of many centuries they did the latter. Then, in the early 1850's, the miners came and prospected along these living streams—Canyon Creek, Goodyear's Creek, North Fork of the Yuba, Rock Creek, Oregon Ravine, Wet Ravine, and Middle Yuba, to name the important ones.

Miners in 1853 went up Oregon Creek. At a certain point, or, rather, in a certain section about a half mile wide, the stream was rich in gold. The abundance of the dust and the size of its particles got better and better as the prospectors approached that point. Then, as they went excitedly above the spot, the riches almost abruptly departed from the gravel. The streams became practically no good at all farther up.

Other miners ascended the Middle Yuba, and the same phenomenon occurred. About thirty miles short of the main Sierra backbone the gold would get better, then get mighty good, and then peter out.

Others along other streams had the same thing happen to them. The rich areas would always be about thirty miles short of the Sierra ridge, nearly in line.

At the paydirt sections, ravines would extend from the stream up the ridge. The beds of these ravines would be very rich, the dirt, where the descent was not too steep, being a foot or two deep over the slate rock. The miners kept taking out dust as they neared the summit of the ridge. But here the shallow rock bed of the ravine suddenly disappeared.

The miners, however, kept digging around, and eventually found that the main body of the hill was composed of gravel which had a peculiar blue color, and that right there in front of them, five feet thick and a half-mile wide from east to west, was a stratum startlingly rich in gold.

The case was identical along the other streams. Miners would put in a tunnel to follow the rich vein north. In due course they would break through and find themselves face to face with another outfit, which had been tunneling south from the next stream beyond. Back in the 'sixties, those going from Monticello to Excelsior regularly used a tunnel of the 'fifties that penetrated the ridge; it was a mile through. It saved the hikers from climbing six hundred feet to the top of the ridge and traveling a distance of two miles. Forest City and Alleghany were similarly connected by a tunnel, which became choked and closed in the late 'sixties.

The blue lead went north and south across all the ridges, which were but three to six miles apart. The great vein was from two hundred to one thousand feet below the ridge top, too much cover to be removed; hence the tunnels.

While the very rich layer was five feet thick, the whole auriferous deposit varied from one hundred to three hundred feet deep. Blueish-gray was the 'predominant color.' The material was 'almost exclusively quartz.' On the basis of an average thickness of two hundred feet and a width of half a mile, there must have been five billion cubic yards of quartz, and quartz is the mother of gold. In live rivers quartz forms 'only a small portion of the gravel.' Where did all the quartz of the Big Blue River come from? Clean out every known quartz vein in California and it wouldn't equal the immense quantity held in the abandoned bed of the Big Blue.

The pebbles were all waterworn. Ground smooth likewise were the big boulders, and they were not scattered about as if tumbled down from the bank. They had been brought from the north by some swift and mighty current—and one which fell thirty-three feet to the mile, and was a half-mile to a mile wide, could move such loads.

This bed of a prehistoric river had 'banks, bars, eddies, ripples, rapids, falls, with little gold in the rapids and much of it in the eddies.' The richest places yielded up to fifty dollars a cubic yard.

But how could a riverbed fill up with gravel that sometimes reached a depth of three hundred feet? Well, when a river is given an unnatural load to carry, this can happen. Take the Yuba, for instance. As a result of mining operations along this river, its bed was raised as much as seventy feet above the natural one of 1853.

Back in 1868 a writer asked: 'But why did the Big Blue River die, and leave nothing but its gravel and its gold to tell the story of its existence and its greatness?'

Probably the upheaval of the Sierras provides the answer. After that geological event many streams would have started down the mountainside. Instead of flowing into the Big Blue and continuing on south with it, these streams with their floods would tend to flow across it—particularly after volcanoes had broken over and poured lava down into the river, bridging it. The new streams, however, couldn't keep on flowing west, right on to the sea, without running square into the mountain barrier of the Coast range. So another north-to-south river was formed farther west—the Sacramento. It was only about one-fourth as large, and carried perhaps less than one-fourth the water of the Big Blue. One river died, the other was born.

The Big Blue was nearer the size of the Columbia than of the Sacramento. Some have speculated on the possibility that it *was* the Columbia. Where the latter turns west at Wallula—old Fort Walla Walla—it *could* have kept on flowing south. Its old bed, from Wallula, just north of the Oregon border in Washington, to Little Grizzly, not far south of the Oregon border in California, *could* be covered up with lava.

There are fourteen evidences that the Big Blue was a mighty river: long course; nearly uniform width, from a half mile to a mile; nearly straight route; bends with eddies on inner side; quartz probably brought from northern region now covered with lava; waterworn gravel; flat stones pointing downstream; strata of coarse and fine gravel; uniform descending grade; coarse particles of gold evenly distributed over a wide channel, as could be done only by a strong current; an immense quantity of gold, which required ages to be scattered through a deposit 330 feet deep; water worn driftwood; trunks of trees with butts upstream; and finally, tributary brooks.

There are other dead rivers in California. The deposits left by them, most of all by the Big Blue, formed the gold belt of the Sierras, producing more treasure 'than any other region upon the globe.' Find the rest of the Big Blue and there ought to be a billion dollars for somebody.

DEAD LAKES

If the Red Sea should dry up, would ruts of chariot wheels show across it—where the Israelites went and where Pharaoh's captains followed and were engulfed?

Whether the roadway would still be there, deep and plain to be seen after so many centuries, is a speculation caused by wagon tracks being preserved almost without change for nearly a century across the bottom of an American sea that is not so big as the Red Sea but yet pretty large.

Goose Lake is an extensive body of water that straddles the line between Oregon and California. In the two states it covers many square miles, shimmering under the desert sun or rolling in sizable waves under the desert winds.

In 1926, after twoscore increasingly dry seasons, the long southern end of the lake went dry—and there across it was a wagon road, deep-worn, mysterious, startling! It was as vividly marked as if a train of heavy vehicles had passed that way during the night, coming from nowhere and going nowhere, for the road faded and ended some distance short of where the two opposite shores had been. Whence and when and how had the disconcerting thoroughfare come? In the memory of the oldest inhabitant there had never been a time when several feet of water had not covered the long level stretch where wondering eyes now beheld the parallel marks of many wheels.

"It's the Red Sea business all over again," said one oldtimer. "Indians might have been after them, as bad as Pharaoh was."

What was indeed perplexing to the local residents, looked much more logical when examined in the light of history and desert weather.

One variation of the Oregon and California emigrant route—the Applegate Trail—went through southern Oregon. It is assumed that between 1849 and 1859, when thousands of covered wagons were coming to the Pacific Coast, Goose Lake was dry at the southern end just as it became again in 1926. This wide tongue of temporarily dry land was in the direct route of the wagon trains—and all the pioneers who had made the journey were dead by 1926. They had left no written account. Why should they?—for them it was not a notable experience, simply some travel across the end of a desert lake.

Emigrants quit coming, and it was a good many years before settlers established themselves sparsely in the arid region. By that time the lake had filled up, and remained full. Water became several feet deep over the road. But at the bottom there was no wash. The liquid depths lay over it calmly, without eroding effect.

In the shallows near the shore, on the other hand, agitation of the water erased the two ends of the road. And where it came to the lake from across the desert, and left the lake at the other side, all marks of it were destroyed by the wind and weather.

That the southern end of Goose Lake could have been dry in the decade from 1849 to 1859, when hundreds of covered wagons rolled across the dusty miles, and have been brimming full of water for the next seventy years, when settlement was taking place, is shown to have been possible by such scanty rainfall records as have been kept.

Records of the military posts show a precipitation of 100 inches a year from 1866 to 1870; and in such a wet period the lake could have filled up to high enough levels to deposit preserving depths over the emigrant roadway. From 1870 to 1900 the average rainfall was only 20 to 25 inches a year. From 1900 there was a slight decrease of precipitation till 1910, after which it seldom exceeded 20 inches annually.

Finally, in 1926, the southern end dried up completely—and there across it were the deep parallel ruts, as if but recently made.

Uncovering of the long-inundated segment of the old Applegate Trail made dramatic the low water in Goose Lake. This shallowing-up, often to the point of vanishing, has happened to many lakes in the lava country.

Abert Lake in south-central Oregon is one of the biggest inland seas in the state. Yet a tall man can almost wade across it. It is thirty miles long, but only six feet deep in its deepest place.

Silver Lake, where many fossils have been found, used to have a water surface of twenty square miles. Now it is entirely dry, and on windy days its alkali bed is blown across the highway.

Many years ago, great Malheur Lake receded so much that thousands of acres of its bed were left high and dry. This rich land was coveted both by homesteader and cattle-man, and there was an immense amount of litigation over it. It was claimed that a cowboy in the night had dug a little trench in the sand with his high bootheel. The rushing-out water did the rest, draining Malheur Lake into Harney Lake, which was close by and lower, thus creating the land wanted by the cattlemen.

24

SOME PLACE NAMES

CALIFORNIA

CALIFORNIA might have been named after the Roman matron Calpurnia, the wife of Julius Caesar. That is one of the ingenious or absurd or preposterous guesses about it.

There are several others: the Catalan word *californo,* signifying a hot oven; *cal y forno,* the first a Spanish word meaning lime and the second a Catalan word meaning furnace and so amounting to 'lime-kiln'; *colofon,* Spanish word for resin, presumably called out by the Spaniards upon seeing the yellow beady accumulations of pitch on the boles of pine trees; *calida fornax,* two Latin words signifying 'hot furnace'; *cala,* a Spanish word for cove, and *fornix,* a Latin word for arch, supposedly applying to a vaulted cove where Cortes and his men landed. The reference to heat in three of these terms was either to the hot climate or to the hot baths of the Indians.

Such etymological speculations had been going on for some time when, in 1862, Edward Everett Hale, one of the theorists about Oregon's name, made an important discovery relating to *California*. He ran across the word in an old Spanish novel, *Las sergas de Esplandian* (The Exploits of Esplandian). This may have been printed as early as 1498, certainly as early as 1508. In it Hale came upon these statements: '. . . Know ye that at the right hand of the Indies there is an island named California, very close to that part of the Terrestrial Paradise, which was inhabited by black women, without a single man among them, and that they lived in the manner of Amazona. . . . In this island, named California, there are many griffins.'

Well, Hale had found it, and it is no wonder that in his pride he should tell about the discovery in the *Proceedings* of the American Antiquarian Society and in the *Atlantic Monthly*. But where had the novelist picked up the word, three and a half centuries before Hale saw it?

That question started off another series of speculations. Some thought that the author of *Las Sergas de Esplandian* got it from the Greek words *kalos* ('beautiful') and *ornis* ('bird') the beautiful bird being a griffin; or from *kalos* and *phornia*, meaning 'beautiful woman' or 'fertile land' or 'moonshine' or, if you please, adultery.

Some thought its source was from the Arabic *khalifat*, meaning 'province,' and without much difficulty becoming Spanish *califon* for a 'large province,' and easily going on from there to become *California*. Others cited the possibility of the *Chanson de Roland*'s being the famous piece from which the old Spanish romancer took it. This French epic poem dates back to the eleventh century, and was therefore old enough and familiar enough in 1498 for a writer to be acquainted with the line, '*E cil d'Affrike e cil de Califerne*' ('And those of Africa and those of Califerne').

Cortes never wrote the word *California*. In a diary of Ulloa's voyage of 1539 it is used once. The plural, *Californias*, was the more common form in the early centuries. *Las Islas*

Californias referred to both the lower and upper sections, and the latter became *California Septentrional, California del Norte, Nueva California, California Superior, Alta California.*

Samuel Brannan might have confused the etymologists if they hadn't smelled a dead herring. He fixed up a word as Barnum did a giant. He came forth with *Calistoga,* which had a deceitful aura of age and mystery. The son-of-a-gun had synthesized it out of California and Saratoga.

YUBA CITY

On a quiet Sunday morning when Yuba City consisted of only three little houses and was known as Yuba Dam, a stranger rode into the place. In front of the first cabin stood a man, of whom the visitor politely inquired,

"My friend, what village is this?"

"Yuby Dam."

The stranger, shocked at such rude profanity, put spurs to his horse. At the door of the next cabin was a woman sweeping the steps and threshold. He asked,

"Madam, will you please tell me the name of this village?"

"Yuby Dam."

Now nothing less than horrified, he hurried on to come next to a little boy playing by himself in the street. From the innocent lips of this lad he should be able to get the information withheld in the other cases with such ungracious blasphemy. He reined up and spoke to the boy,

"My son, what is this place called?"

"Yuby Dam."

"Heavens!" exclaimed the astounded stranger as he galloped out of the town. "What a place is this where even the women and children swear—and on Sunday too!"

OREGON

Ouragon was first used in 1765 in a letter from Major Robert Rogers to King George the Third of England. Jonathan

Carver, in 1788, employed it in a book, spelled as we spell it today. Seen there by William Cullen Bryant, the eighteen-year-old poet, it pleased his sensitive ear and fitted in with the meter of his *Thanatopsis*. So he wrote at first, '. . . the continuous woods, that veil Oregon,' later changing it to '. . . the continuous woods, where rolls the Oregon.' All three of these early terminologists—Rogers, Carver, Bryant —used it to designate the Columbia River.

Where the name *Oregon* came from, where Rogers got it, nobody knows to this day. Speculations have been popping up for over a hundred years and still its origin is a mystery. We do not even know for sure the language the word belongs to, whether Spanish, Indian, French, Portuguese, Chinese, or Greek. Following are fifteen of the guesses about it:

1. Edward Everett, the famous orator, said in 1829, 'Mr. Miner . . . was inclined to think it a Mohegan word, & . . . signified *regal* or *princely*.'

2. An anonymous investigator found it to be an Algonquin word—*wau-re-gon*—meaning 'beautiful water.'

3. George H. Himes, Oregon historian, explained excathedrally that it was an Indian word signifying a 'high ridge.'

4. Charles Wilkins thought it well might be the Shoshone word *oyer-un-gon*, meaning a 'storehouse.' Said he: 'Pronounced quickly, as by the Indians, the sound reaches the ear as *Orrengen, Oregon,* etc. When first hearing the word used it sounded to me as *Or-e-gun*.'

5. An authority of unknown identity also favored a Shoshone expression of two words, *ogwa* and *pe-on*, referring to the 'River of the West.'

6. Hall J. Kelly, New England schoolmaster and first Oregon booster, declared more than a century ago that the word had a Chinese source, tracing it to 'a large river called *Orjon* in Chinese Tartary.'

7. Kelly, after he made a trip to Oregon, changed his opinion and stated that the word was of Portuguese derivation from *orejun,* a 'fort.' He thought the name appropriate because the Columbia River entrance was 'well fortified by nature.'

8. Another theory is that early discoverers found an abundance of wild marjoram—scientifically called *Origanum*—hence the name. The trouble is that this plant did not grow at all thick where the explorers landed.

9. In 1899, a newspaper writer announced a French origin, explaining that the French-Canadians, who called a type of oblong wooden dish an *oregon,* applied the name to the land because it looked like a dish.

10. A popular conjecture of early days was that the name came from the Spanish word *orejon,* variously translated as 'a pull of the ear,' 'long ear,' or 'lop ear.' Spaniards presumably encountered an Indian tribe with fascinatingly enormous lobes, wherefore, very naturally they called the land *La Tierra de Los Orejons.* It is a fact that in California in the days of Forty-Nine the Oregon gold miners were sometimes called 'Lop-ears.' A variation is that *Oregon* did not apply to people but to rabbits.

11. In 1603, Martin d'Aguilar noted a stream near the latitude of the present Columbia, and on some old maps this river was designated as *Rio d'Aguilar.* One writer considered it not improbable that this got changed around to *Oregon.* The Indians pronounced McLoughlin's name as *Macubah.* Tongues that could do that, could also make *Oregon* out of *Aguilar.*

12. Joaquin Miller declared that *Oregon* was derived from the Spanish phrase *oye-el-agua,* 'hear the water.' Some other writers did not take much stock in this theory, inclining to ridicule it as farfetched and fanciful. The famous poet admitted he had no authority in particular: 'Alas, what evidence have I further than that written on the face of the

waters and heard in the clouds from the stupendous steeps?'

13. Another Spanish word put forward is *huracan*.

14. One writer said it was all very simple. Some Spaniards from Aragon, one of the Spanish kingdoms, gave the name to Oregon because of the similarity in many ways of the two countries, just as freebooter Drake called it New Albion.

15. The various explanations, some of them rather wild, as to how Oregon got its name, caused a wag in 1890 to come forth soberly with the authority of an old Dutch tar, gray-haired and of weatherbeaten face at the time of the interview:

"Boys, do you know I christened Oregon?"

"How so?"

"Well, you see, way down in the early days of the century, on one of my many trips around the globe, we experienced a terrible gale and had to run into what is now the bay of Yaquina, where we anchored. It rained and kept on raining and we hallooed in despair to each other in Dutch —'O Regen, O Regen!'—which means 'rain.' The Indians heard us and kept on repeating 'Oregon,' and in a council adopted this as the name of their country."

CRATER LAKE

In 1853 a party of Californians went into the southern Cascade range in search of the famed Lost Cabin and its gold. A party of Oregon prospectors followed them to get in on the find. One of the Oregonians was riding along on muleback eight thousand feet above the level of the sea when, lo! in a miracle of sudden vision there was a sea before him. So little was he expecting anything of the sort that he might have tumbled forward over a two-thousand-foot precipice into it, if it hadn't been for the mule. The animal thrust his forefeet forward and put on the brakes at the brink of almost perpendicular walls which went down to a lake with water as blue as the sky. The others came up to gaze in wonder. They rolled some boulders down, failed to spot an outlet, and got busy at once with the naming. The offhand nomenclature included Lake Majesty, Mysterious Lake, Sunken Lake, and Deep Blue Lake, the last being the one they chose.

Sixteen years later it was rechristened. In 1869 a party went from Jacksonville up to the rim and named it Crater Lake—an excellent choice, for it lies at the bottom of the caldera of an extinct volcano called Mount Mazama, which was about the size of Shasta. The lake's surface is more than a mile above sea level, 6177 feet, and the highest point of the rim is 8156 feet, making the inner walls at that place almost 2000 feet of precipice, while the submerged portion is at least equally deep.

Nobody has ever found an outlet. There has been much speculation about an invisible one. Some authorities think there is none. The lake's drainage area is little bigger than itself; rains and snows almost entirely feed it, and evaporation just about cancels this out.

The walls for the main part go right down into the deep water without beaches; salamanders were originally the principal life about the steep edges. There were no fish. W. G. Steel started out from Rogue River in 1888 with six hundred fingerlings to stock the lake; by the time he arrived he had thirty-seven to let loose in the blue water. These survived and multiplied. Crater Lake has been in a national park since 1902.

NEVADA

Nevada took its name in no exciting way, but merely from the mountains in front of it. Motions were not lacking in legislative meetings to give to it a less obvious name and a less beautiful one. Suggested terminologies included Humboldt, Washoe, Esmeralda, Sierra Plata. A waggish newspaper editor suggested it be called the State of Buena Vista, and that the seal contain a tree shading two miners, working their claim with a deck of cards.

WINNEMUCCA

This Nevada town is named after the most noted Paiute chief, but that doesn't quite settle the matter. Where did the chief get it, for it is not an Indian word? Old Chief Winnemucca's other name was Poito; Young Chief Winnemucca's other one was Numaga. The Indian meaning of Winnemucca was reportedly 'bread giver,' wherein there might be a clue.

The word is pure Irish, and an actual Celtic origin is not at all impossible, if one may speculate only a little outrageously, along with the zestful Hibernian author of an old book on the early Irish of the Far West.

Some sailors deserted from Captain Drake's crew while the old freebooter was on the California coast in the summer of 1579; others were sent out to catch them, but they in turn escaped into the back country and contentedly stayed escaped, and were denounced to the devil. Yet if they were by way of being Irish seamen (and Drake buccaneered on Erin's shores), it is more likely that the boys went to the Indian girls than the devil. Mayhap one of them ended up as the happy squaw man of the Paiute chief's daughter. Perhaps a half-breed son later found his way across the Sierras, remembering and cherishing a word taught him by his white father, even proudly proclaiming it as his name. The resourcefulness of his white blood, especially the Irish blood in him, could have given him the reputation of being a good bread giver.

Old Chief Winnemucca was at Humboldt Lake when the first emigrants passed through on their way to California. "My white brothers," he exclaimed, "my long-looked-for white brothers have come at last!" Was this, as it sounds, based on an expectation handed down from white fore-bears?

Anyhow, Winnemucca is an Irish, not an Indian name.

IDAHO

Joaquin Miller, one of the confident speculators about the name of Oregon, sounded off even more loudly and emphatically concerning the origin of Idaho, where in early days he had gone with one lawbook and two six-shooters to be an attorney. He said the name came from the Indian word *i-dah-ho*, 'sunrise mountains,' the source of dawn, 'a sort of Mecca in the sky' whereto every Indian lifted his face the moment he got up in the morning. Each tribe had a Mount *I-dah-ho*. The Shastas called it *Pou-dah-ho*, the Klamaths *Num-dah-ho*, the Modocs *Lo-dah*. The *dah*, which was heavily accented, was the root word, signifying 'Lo, light!'

According to the poet, he and a squaw man, Colonel William Craig, were on their way together through the yet-nameless land to the new gold discovery on Salmon River. At the edge of Camas Prairie the dawn came up on the black-and-white mountain ahead of them. Whereupon their Indian guide looked back, pointed to the bursting light, and shouted, *"I-dah-ho!"*

"That," said Colonel Craig, "shall be the name of the new mines."

'Alas,' wrote Joaquin, who did a good deal of alas-ing, 'alas for the soft Indian name! The swift-speeched miners clipped it short to *Idao*. And, compromising between this contraction and the two-*h* original, the territory was called *Idaho*.

This explanation sounded nice and reasonable, but the poetical Joaquin was always being tripped up by sober-speeched, practical men. This trip took place in 1861, they reminded him. How then was it, they asked, that there had been on the Columbia River a steamboat with *Idaho* painted boldly on it a good eighteen months before the sunrise christening at Camas Prairie? If the poet replied to the query, there is no record of what he said.

George B. Walker, one of the first gold-hunters at Pierce City, said that the name definitely came from the steamboat *Idaho,* and that he was the one responsible. While the region was still part of Washington, three candidates for Congress were guests at his cabin. From them he got the promise that whoever was elected would favor a separate territory, because Olympia was so far away. The name, he told them, should be Idaho, just as it was on the steamboat.

When Congress duly concerned itself with creating the new territory, the first bill called the country *Idaho,* but two other names came before the committee, *Shoshone* and *Montana.* The bill was about to pass with the latter when Senator Wilson of Massachusetts proposed an amendment to change it back to *Idaho,* as originally proposed. *Montana,* said he, was no name at all, while *Idaho* had a meaning: 'Gem of the Mountains' (now generally accepted).

But where did the steamboat get the name?

25

WE THE PEOPLE

TERRITORY OF HONEY LAKE VALLEY

Twenty freemen (they were certainly that) met at Isaac Roop's cabin where Susanville, California, now is. Though numbering only a score, they declared themselves to be coming together in mass convention. Their business was to organize a territory of the United States of America. This in due time would become a state, with a star in the flag, and, by the bald-headed Elijah, having two senators the same as New York.

The center of this new commonwealth was to be Honey Lake. It is marked now as dry-in-summer on some maps and as simply dry on others. Its alkali bed has been no good for farming or grassland; it stretches out barren over a considerable territory, and often shines in a wettish way as though it actually contained water. Route 395, northwest of Reno, for a distance runs beside it.

In emigrant times the covered wagons passed about three miles west, without seeing this shallow sea twenty miles long and sixteen wide. The view of it was mostly shut off by the hills, so that homesteading desires were little aroused by its broad margins of clover, blue-joint, red-top, and bunch-grass.

Now the time was April, 1856. The Honey Lakers felt that politically they were neither flesh, fowl, nor good red herring. They were across the mountains from the rest of California. Mormon Utah might formally claim them, but its theocratic dominion was hardly aware of their existence. So, with Peter Lassen in the chair and Roop as secretary, the twenty very solemnly resolved: 'Inasmuch as Honey Lake Valley is not within the limits of California, the same is declared a new territory . . . the said territory to be called Nataqua.' This name had in it a gallant implication; it was an Indian word for woman. The enterprise was also called the Territory of Roop, after the cabin's owner, and the Territory of Honey Lake.

This declaration of independence wasn't exactly the way matters looked to California. The state believed that Honey Lake Valley was in its Plumas County, to which it pretty much left the enforcement of state sovereignty. The latter had a very amiable administration. The county seat was high up in the Sierras. H. J. Bradley, owner of the Quincy Hotel, had a small shake building at the rear which he let the county use rent-free for a courthouse. Two men, running for assessor, secured a tie vote; the matter was decided by a game of seven-up. In winter the mail, at twenty-five cents a letter, was brought in by Whiting & Company's dog team. Such a county government could hardly have been expected to bear down heavily on the rebellious Honey Lakers. They were only 35 miles away as the eagle flies, but to this day if you want to get from one place to the other by road you have to travel 120 miles by one route and over 80 miles by the other.

The twenty freemen were very strategically located to reach out for independence.

The territory, in its generous reaches, was to be 240 miles

long and 155 miles wide, an area of 37,200 square miles. Six hundred people in the valleys of Carson, Eagle, and Washoe were taken in, all unbeknownst, by the Honey Lakers. But the settlers down there were a tame, allegiant breed. Many of them were Mormons, strong in the habits of obedience, and governed by Orson Hyde, one of the twelve apostles. If they hadn't been called back to defend Zion, there might have developed, under the eastern shadows of the Sierras, a second Salt Lake City instead of a Reno, with wives still being the core and the center of the place but in multiplicity and acquiescence instead of severance.

Contemporary references to the event were singularly calm. Historians had great sport, in later years, quoting the grandiose and ungrammatical documents of the twenty commonwealth-makers. At the time the ridicule included such derisive phrases as 'a crack-brained enterprise,' 'an abortive movement,' and 'a political fiasco,' but the main effect of the publicity was favorable. It brought in more settlers—stockmen, miners, homeseekers. The presumptious wildcat government of Nataqua looked to them stable enough to risk developing land under its laws. During the next half-dozen years there were duly recorded under Nataqua authority no less than 299 claims.

In the late summer of 1857, ending more than a year which Nataqua had enjoyed practically without interference, the Plumas County officials bestirred themselves from their mountain retreat to give the true law to the outlaw community. They set up the frontier beyond the Sierras as Honey Lake Township.

A great comedown for the Honey Lakers—from a sovereign territory half as big as Illinois to a township. But in one way they liked Plumas County's action fine. They liked it not because they had any intention of complying, but because it gave them another chance to meet in indignant mass convention. They were not a little lonely on their mile-square claims in the valley, and these assemblies were welcome breaks in the monotony of their lives. And the more there was to get mad about, the more recreational were the meetings.

They met and said: 'Resolved the citizens of Honey Lake Valley in Mass Meeting assembled that we consider the action of the Board of Supervisors of Plumas County an unwarrantable assumption of power.'

Two months later they met again, with Peter Lassen in the chair, as he had been that very first time. Judge James M. Crane, who wanted to be the new territory's delegate to Congress, was on hand to make a long speech (the Shasta *Courier* remarked than any mere mortal man having to listen to him an hour would be in a fit state of mind to do any desperate deed). The assembly of citizens resolved that it was the unanimous opinion of the inhabitants of Honey Lake Valley that they were not living in California. They appointed a committee to ask the California legislature to give up its real or supposed claim. They declared that they would resist with all the power at their command any attempt to coerce them under the subjection and jurisdiction of California.

The proclamations this time did not set well with the California papers. The Shasta *Courier* said they smelled of war and had a decided odor of treason.

Soon after the meeting there was an Indian scare, whereupon the Honey Lakers went squealing to California for help—which was disgustedly rebuked by the California editors to whom it seemed amazing that men of such sturdy independence and self-reliance should solicit outside protection.

Meanwhile Isaac Roop, Peter Lassen, and three other Honey Lakers met with the settlers of Carson Valley, now minus most of the original Mormons; and Judge Crane was duly chosen delegate to Washington, from where in Feb, ruary, 1858, he sent a report that a bill to organize the new territory would assuredly pass both houses of Congress. President Buchanan was counted on. But the proposition, wherein the Territory of Nataqua became part of the Territory of Nevada, did not in the upshot get approval. Utah had accepted Alexander Cummings as governor in place of Brigham Young, and under these improved circumstances Congress designated the inhabitants of Carson Valley and the Honey Lakers as part of Utah.

The settlers did not see it that way. So they established a provisional government, which in 1861 was to become the Territory of Nevada. Isaac Roop, who had been in on the independence business from the beginning, was elected governor.

Of this action the Salt Lake *Mountaineer* spoke in its most satirical vein:

> We publish elsewhere Nevada's Declaration of Independence. . . . Poor souls! how much they have been abused. Their vigilance committees have not been indicted and arraigned as banded murderers. The gibbets in their dismal groves remain unnoticed and unknown. Renegades of many lands, their vices have not drawn upon them even the contempt of the nation.
> There is something to be regretted in their arrangements. They have not provided offices for much more than half the citizens, red and white included. That should not be so. Each of the three or four hundred who are citizens of that majestic Sovereign Territory ought to have an office. Instead of forty they should have about four hundred . . . members in the assembly, and then each would have been his own representative. . . . But do not be afraid, sister Nevada. We shall not contest your right to a divorce . . . and in the meantime would suggest the propriety of your becoming an independent nation at once.

Nevada Territory organized the Honey Lakers into Roop County. California's Plumas County again undertook to exercise control. The result was the Sage Brush War, which went from injunctions and warrants to revolvers and rifles.

The Roop County judge issued an injunction to restrain the Plumas County justice-of-the-peace from functioning. This gentleman refused and was promptly fined $100. Whereupon came an order from the mountain fastness of Quincy by Judge Hogan of Plumas County restraining the Roop County judge, who had enjoined the Plumas squire from exercising any jurisdiction whatever in Honey Lake Valley; eke the Roop County sheriff. When these two refused to obey, Judge Hogan issued warrants for their arrest, which the Plumas sheriff, bristling with pistols, executed and started with his prisoners on the long, roundabout way to the Plumas jail at Quincy.

With this journey seventy-five or a hundred Honey Lakers proceeded to interfere, gathering preventively at the old Isaac Roop cabin, which thus became Fort Defiance. A deputation of less headstrong citizens prevailed upon the Plumas sheriff, still hellbent upon doing his duty, to suspend arresting operations until the governors of Nevada and California could be consulted. The California governor was Leland Stanford; the acting Nevada one was Orion Clemens, Mark Twain's brother.

The upshot was a survey to determine the disputed boundary lines by engineers' instruments instead of by resolution. The lines, as eventually determined, put the Honey Lakers right back in California, where they had said all the time they didn't belong. But they won a victory after all, albeit a limited one. Plumas jurisdiction ceased, and a new county, Lassen, was formed right close to home—with the county seat where the Roop cabin was. Thereupon the independent, recessionist spirit of the Honey Lakers seems to have settled into a permanent calm.

The names of eighteen of the twenty original framers of the constitution and laws of Nataqua are now merely records;

practically all else about them has passed away. Not so with the two leaders. Isaac Roop found fame as the first governor of Nevada. But Peter Lassen, the Danish blacksmith, gained a greater immortality. He had a high mountain named after him.

JOHN BROWN'S WIDOW

At 135 Main Street in Red Bluff, California, is a small house. Architecturally it has little distinction. As a symbol it is even more important than the house of William B. Ide, the Bear Flag leader, two miles away. Chief of Police Walter Williams lives there now. You will be told, "It was the house of John Brown's widow."

Mary Anne Day, 'a large, silent girl,' was the daughter of a Pennsylvania backwoods blacksmith. She was sixteen when she came to the John Brown household, a sister of his housekeeper. At that age, a little less than a year after John Brown's first wife, Dianthe, had died, Mary Anne married him—this 'big-boned reticent girl, with heavy, competent hands'—and became the stepmother of his five living children.

This was in 1833. It was not until 1859, in December, that *Frank Leslie's Weekly* published four vivid pictures—'Mrs. Brown Escorted to Her Husband in Jail,' 'John Brown's Ride to His Execution,' 'John Brown Ascending the Scaffold,' 'Execution of John Brown.'

In the twenty-six years between these two events she had become the mother of thirteen children, yet in all this giving of life how little survival of it there had been—seven had died in childhood, and two had been killed in early manhood at Harper's Ferry.

Mrs. John Brown received much tender public attention and sympathy. But such things are transitory. What happened to her, how she fared, soon ceased to be a matter of solicitude or even knowledge. She and her family for some time lived an obscure life, while from the throats of hundreds of thousands of soldiers and civilians came the song "John Brown's body lies a-mouldering in the grave . . ."

In 1864 Mrs. Brown prepared to leave for California with two daughters and with her son Salmon, who had declined to join his father at Harper's Ferry. They went across the plains in covered wagons, reaching Red Bluff in the fall of 1864.

The Red Bluff *Independent* ran an item on October 3rd, in which it picked her out for special mention: 'A large emigrant train from the east, by the plains across, arrived in town this forenoon. Among the members were the wife, son, and three daughters of John Brown, the hero of Harper's Ferry and the frightener of the great state of Virginia. With her are several men and a cow. The train gives evidence of settling in Tehama County.'

She was then only forty-eight years old, but how much her memory encompassed, how much her 'heavy competent hands' had done. Salmon secured for her and his two sisters (not three, as the newspaper had said) a small cabin on the outskirts of town. He himself settled with wife and children near Corning and began raising sheep.

During the winter Mrs. Brown and her daughters had a hard time making the barest kind of living. They served as nurses and did anything they could to earn enough for their necessities. Helpful neighbors gave calico parties for them.

The spring of the next year, 1865, in the closing period of the Civil War, the State of California began to consider the gift of a home to her. Said the Sacramento *Union* in April, 'If every man, woman, and child in California who has hummed *John Brown* will throw in a dime, his family will have a home.'

The small home on Main Street was the one obtained. John Brown's widow received a certificate of title to it on July 6, 1868. Thereafter she was never allowed to suffer the deprivations and poverty she had previously known. Her daughters married. In 1882 she made a trip back to North Elba—where, near a great boulder, John Brown's body lay a-mouldering in the grave.

GEORGE WASHINGTON

It is said a postage stamp served as model for the equestrian statue of George Washington which now stands in the rotunda of the Idaho capitol, and which for two-thirds of a century stood in the capitol grounds. Of heroic size, it is one of the most remarkable pieces of folk sculpture in America. An Idaho miner carved it by hand, with only crude tools, out of a yellow pine tree.

The sculptor was Charles Ostner, a German emigrant who had come to the United States at the age of eighteen. He was thirty-four when he traveled in 1862 from California to the Idaho gold mines. After working in the mines for some time, he went back to California and brought his family to Idaho. He took up ranching in Garden Valley, about forty miles from Boise, and also continued to carry on some mining. In the winter of 1864-65 he had to travel twelve miles for food and supplies.

That postage stamp is the enigma in his motivation. Had he no other pictures of George Washington?—there were many in the history books. But if he read no history, how then did he come to be so filled with admiration for the Father of His country? What started him to meditating upon the force of this tremendous personality in the development of the United States? Did Washington become a hero to him while he was a boy in Germany? Did the first president become synonymous with freedom, and dignity of man, and opportunity?

For four years, in his cabin in the hills, he carved out portions of the great statue. The horse and rider were worked out fractionally and put together in Boise. He often labored into the night, and darkness in any case came early in the winter. A small son, from six to ten years old while the statue was being made, frequently had to hold a tallow candle for his father to see by; the son remembered later that this duty was somewhat like turning a grindstone, done reluctantly and protestingly.

In 1869 the work was completed. The smoothing-up itself was a big task—scraping with glass and then sandpapering all over. Next the statue was painted with gilt paint, and later covered with gold leaf.

Ostner presented it to the Territory of Idaho as a gift, but the legislature, nevertheless, voted him $2500. Some members wanted to give him $7000, but since the territory was poor and the times were bad they finally made it the smaller sum.

There is an old contemporary sketch of the ceremonies of unveiling the statue and dedicating it to the pioneers of Idaho. This was one of the big occasions of the early days. There was much patriotic bunting and many white shirt-fronts. The speaker is shown throwing out his gesturing left arm in a way decidedly similar to the pointing right arm of Washington.

The horse with arched neck is pulling against the taut reins; his right foreleg is highstepping; his tail is semi-elevated. The sculptor would perhaps have done better to use an ordinary Idaho horse for a model, instead of copying the one on the postage stamp. Washington is in military garb but bareheaded. His left hand pulls the reins, causing the familiar fourfold response in artistic horses—arched neck, opened mouth, raised foreleg, lifted tail. Washington's right arm is pointed off in a sweep which, in the Boise of 1869, encompassed a little frontier settlement of rude frame houses.

By the time the statue became the property of the state, Ostner, then forty-one years old, had moved with his family to Boise. He died there in 1914 at the age of eighty-six. As a miner, farmer, later as a merchant, he had made a living for himself, his wife, and six children (the boy who grudgingly held the tallow candle became a cowboy). This folk sculptor lived and worked and earned a livelihood very much the same as other Idahoans—the difference, a tremendous one, being the employment of his spare time.

But his talents were untrained and, as often happens in such cases, unsustained. Though he painted several large canvases, the one statue seemed largely to satisfy his creative urge; and the conspicuous honor it received, that of becoming almost a living thing for generation upon generation of the people of a whole commonwealth—seemed to dull any further desire for fame.

The statue of yellow pine stood out in the statehouse grounds for more than a half-century, in all weather. Thousands looked at it and halted in front of it and looked some more, and their appreciation was increased by knowing it had been made by an Idaho miner with cunning hands and with a spirit of the United States in his heart which he could thus transmit to them.

Often these passersby 'might have seen an old man seated on a bench in the capitol grounds, his eyes fixed on . . . the great American, but few perhaps knew that in this bent figure they beheld the man whose hands had transformed a block of Idaho wood into the image before him.'

U. S. GRANT'S SEVEN IDAHO GOVERNORS

The six-horse stagecoach set down a passenger in Boise. It was late in the fall of 1870. The stranger looked up the street. He saw the sign of the Overland Hotel. He saw the sign of Oldham & Taylor's Saloon. He was tired, dusty, and travel-stained. But it was to the saloon he went first, not the hotel. The barkeeper and the patrons looked at the stranger as he entered, but no faster or more fully than he looked at them.

He stepped up to the bar and said, in a sweeping statement to all present, "Is there a sonofabitch here who will take a drink with the governor of Idaho?"

What a propitious beginning that was for Governor Thomas W. Bennett. In three days he knew every citizen in Boise. In three weeks he knew everyone in southern Idaho. His popularity was unbounded. Ulysses Simpson Grant, bungler of patronage as of other things, had in his fifth try picked a winner.

In the summer of 1870, Congress had made things difficult for the President by putting a stop to the territorial legislature's considerate way of doubling its governor's salary. The pay had been $5000 a year, half from Uncle Sam, half from Idaho. Now it was back to $2500, all federal. Outsiders—carpet-baggers, the people called them—were the only ones Grant wanted for the job, and Idaho seemed a long way off with no more than $208 fresh every month after one got there.

Andrew Johnson's appointee had stayed on into Grant's presidency for over a year. His term would be up on April 30, 1870. Then he was to leave, notwithstanding the fact that two-thirds of the people petitioned for him to stay. In March of 1870 Grant began making appointments. He was still making them six years later. The succession was somewhat as follows.

No. 1—Samuel Bard was the first. As one Idaho historian succinctly put it, 'He never came.' He was a New Yorker.

No. 2—Nine weeks later A. H. Conner was appointed. The same laconic historian said, 'Failed to show up.' He was a good Republican of Indianapolis.

No. 3—It was seven months before anything more was done about Idaho. Then Gilman Marston of New Hampshire was appointed. Stated our historian, as admirable in his variety as in his brevity, 'Never put in an appearance.'

No. 4—Thomas W. Bowen was appointed three months after Marston. Grant had now been President for two years, and our historian thinks he may have become a little desperate and insisted on 'the next appointee's at least seeing the territory.' Bowen did see it—for a week or ten days. Then he climbed into the six-horse stagecoach and went from Idaho's capital in a cloud of alkali dust, presumably back to Arkansas, where he had been a district judge.

No. 5—Thomas W. Bennett, the aforementioned gentleman of the saloon debut. He came and stayed out his term with conviviality, yet in that cheerful head was an acute intelligence, and he handled the affairs of the territory with wisdom, energy, and honesty. He was so popular that he mistakenly thought he could beat an old pioneer in the race for Congress, though Idaho was Democratic. In a speech at Silver City he had a good time ridiculing his opponent, who challenged him to a duel.

"Do you think he means it?" he asked a mutual friend.

"Sure he does, and he's a dead shot."

"Then I guess I'll square it," said the governor, and they became good friends.

He had been mayor of Richmond, Indiana, before he came to Boise. He went back, to be elected mayor almost continuously until he died a number of years later.

No. 6—Forty-one-year-old David P. Thompson of Oregon was appointed in March, 1875. At the age of eighteen he had walked the two thousand miles across the plains behind a herd of sheep. The Idaho Congressman, in despair of ever getting a local person into the office, was glad to have at least a man from an adjacent state. There is a terse mention by our historian, 'He duly qualified and that was about the only official duty he performed outside of two or three short visits.' Grant let Thompson go after a year; the rumors of benefits from his public-land surveying were a little too much for an administration which by then had become sensitive about such matters. He afterward became twice mayor of Portland, Harrison's minister to Turkey, and a president or director of seventeen national banks. So his little Idaho interim didn't hurt him any.

No. 7—Mason Brayman, given the office in the summer of 1876, was the last of the Grant appointees. During all the absentee business, Ned Curtis, territorial secretary, had carried on, and Idaho would have liked to have him for governor in name as well as in fact. But Curtis returned to being just secretary, and Governor Brayman came out from Wisconsin. The people wished he hadn't. He had been a Civil War Officer; he was still military-minded, and two ensuing Indian wars just suited his predilections: as commander-in-chief of the militia he ordered and proclaimed with zest. He was just the opposite of Governor Bennett, very unpopular. Said another historian, not our sententious one: 'Governor Brayman could not get used to western ways, and was in more or less trouble with the citizens of the territory all the time he was here.'

26

SQUAW MEN

———————

JOAQUIN MILLER

After Joaquin Miller had become a famous poet, he looked back in zestful and rather proud retrospect and told of his experience with two coquettish Indian girls at the time he was living with one of the Shasta tribes.

He was detailed, along with the two Indian virgins, to gather pinenuts for winter food. The cones hadn't fallen to the ground; they hung far out of reach up in the trees. The Indians had no ladders, so the trees were prodigally cut down. The young white man was the chopper. From the fallen boughs the Indian maidens harvested the small, rich seeds.

He worked a while, got warm and a little fatigued, and threw down the ax.

One of the girls picked it up and fled through the pine woods with it. He pursued her some distance and, because his legs were faster or she deliberately slowed up, overtook her. She threw down the ax and then fell supinely upon it. There was only one way for him to claim it.

They walked back to the area of their chopping and gathering, and diligently resumed work.

After he had felled several more trees, young Miller wiped his sweating forehead and threw the ax to the ground again. Before he could sit down on a fallen tree trunk for a rest, the second girl stooped, picked up the ax, and darted away with it. This seductive pattern was something he hadn't counted on. As he briefly hesitated he saw upon the first girl's face no look of reproachful detention, but rather one of encouragement, at least one of natural expectancy. When he caught up with the second fugitive, she protected the ax in exactly the same way as the first, and he needs must reclaim it in exactly the same way.

The poet in 1857 began living with an Indian woman in the McCloud region. Whether one of these two, by evidencing a special charm during the trial by ax, became his squaw wife, he never said. But in a pioneer's scrapbook there is a record of Miller's wilderness domesticity:

> One day he met on the trail a sojourner, dressed and equipped in full aboriginal outfit, who proved to be Miller. . . . When asked what he was doing in that remoteness with such an equipment, Miller told him to come with him and he would find out. So they footed it among the ranges until they found where an Indian village nestled on Pitt River. One of its tepees was Miller's house, and waiting to greet its lord was a tidy Indian girl in charge. This homekeeper provided them a good dinner and made the world pleasant around her. She was no doubt the heroine of his later verse.

The poet's 'later verse' indeed had special recollection of her; there are the following lines:

> *I love*
> *A forest maiden; she is mine;*
> *And on Sierra's slopes of pine . . .*
> *A solitary lodge is set*
> *Within a fringe of watered firs;*

And there my wigwam fires burn,
Fed by a round, brown, patient hand,
That small brown faithful hand of hers
That never rests till my return . . .
She is not over tall or fair;
Her breasts are curtained by her hair,
And sometimes through the silken fringe,
I see her bosom's wealth like wine
Burst through in luscious ruddy tinge—
And all its wealth and worth are mine.

A realistic pioneer historian says that the poet's claim of having married the daughter of a Modoc chief is entirely false, for his tepee was not within a hundred miles of the Modocs. He actually lived with a McCloud squaw named Sutatot. After his irresponsible departure, she married a frontiersman by the name of Jim Brock, had several half-breed children, and became well known in the Shasta country as Amanda Brock.

In 1898, while Miller was on his way across the Sierras from Redding to Alturas, he and his companion stopped at a mountain eating house. He joshed with the woman who ran the place, and the banter was about Amanda. While he could write in tender and poetic retrospect of his squaw bride in *Life Amongst the Modocs,* here in the rudeness of actuality he left with the proprietess a lecherous message, coarsely laughing as he did so. He explained to his companion: "Mrs. Brock, the mother of Cali-Shasta, lives in a canyon near here, and I sent word to her that I was coming back to enjoy my old age with her."

Amanda Brock died ten years after this event, in the summer of 1908, at the age of seventy-five; her grave is in an Indian burial ground on McCloud River.

In his own highly romanticised account of his life amongst the Modocs, Miller is vague and obscure and elliptical when referring to his red-skinned bride, cleverly achieving the literary effect of a delicate and hallowed reserve. Their halfbreed daughter was called Cali-Shasta, 'because she was born . . . under the shadows of Mount Shasta.' Miller received credit for taking her to San Francisco and educating her, after deserting her as a child. A San Francisco paper said she had her mother's dark eyes, and was black-haired like her mother and clear-complexioned like her father. Her city schoolmates thought she was a Spanish girl.

The main responsibility actually fell upon Ina Coolbrith, the poet, who was the girl's foster-mother for seven years. Cali-Shasta became the wife of a young man who worked for Wells Fargo & Company in San Francisco, but the marriage failed because, somewhere along the line, she had picked up an uncontrollable appetite for drink. Then she went to live with her father in Oakland, at 'The Hights' (as Miller always spelled it), where she soon died.

Some squaw men have been guilty of a strongly implied attitude that marriage fulfillment is not so satisfying with an Indian woman as with a white one. Joaquin Miller was one of these. He spoke of Minnie Myrtle, his white wife, as his first Saxon woman. It was as though his experiences with at least two, perhaps three Indian girls scarcely counted against his chastity. Nevertheless, after he had found fame in London and with his outlandish garb had pleased the utmost in what was Saxon—the duchesses—and after he was separated from Minnie Myrtle, he did go back to the Shasta region to look for and find his halfbreed daughter, then about thirteen years old. Was he moved by some nostalgia for the girl's mother, some memory of delights not smothered by Saxon wedlock?

WINEMA'S HUSBAND

"The Modoc girl won't make me forget her," declared Frank Riddle, Shasta region frontiersman, as he strengthened his fidelity by holding a package of letters and a photograph of a fair-haired girl back in Kentucky.

Riddle and his partner lived on Bogus Creek, twenty miles east of Yreka. In 1862 some Modocs camped a few days below Riddle's cabin. After work, he and his partner visited with the Indians. Among them was the Modoc chief, Se-cot, and his daughter Winema, whom Riddle understood to be no more than fifteen, but who was as ripe as Pocahontas had been when she inspired the love of Captain John Smith. Winema was really about twenty, which among the Indians meant being somewhat of an old maid (although her son, long afterward, claimed she was fifteen at the time), and Riddle himself was thirty. He had been away twelve years from the Kentucky girl he was making himself remember.

At the period of this visit Riddle could not talk Modoc and Winema could not talk English. Just the same, after the Indians had gone, Riddle confessed to his partner, "I've got an a-goneness in my heart."

A squaw man, living some distance off, came to the cabin. He was married to Winema's cousin, and he had brought a message from Winema, saying, "She's left the chief's camp. She's at my lodge now. She wants you to visit her."

With the letters and the portrait from Kentucky he had fortified himself against the winsomeness of the Modoc maiden—or so, at least, he had tried to do and thought he had done. "I'll go," he promised the squaw man, "just for the fun of the thing."

He put on the clean shirt that was special for such occasions as going to Yreka. "Be careful, Riddle," admonished his partner, who accompanied him.

As he walked and looked up at the serene heights of Shasta white as wool, the face of the Kentucky girl went with him reproachfully. Once he halted, half-inclined to go back.

"Come on," urged his practical partner. "If you don't like the girl, you needn't take her, that's all."

At the lodge Winema was humming a low tune, '*Ka-mis-no-stin-to,*' a Modoc love song. He couldn't understand the words but the melody brought plainly to him a libretto of affection. She was dressed to the utmost in Modoc finery, making him feel uncouth fixed up in only his clean shirt. The squaw man, Winema's cousin-in-law, interpreted their conversation. This, by the end of the evening, had become interesting, provocative, snaring.

As he went home, with Shasta's pure snows high up under the moon and the stars, he felt the accusing look of the face in the portrait.

Yet Riddle made more visits. He picked up a number of Modoc words and Winema picked up some English ones. Thus, with love to stimulate and hasten their linguistics, he became able to tell her without an interpreter what was in his heart in spite of all his fortifying.

When he began to speak there was a final reminder of his Kentucky vows; he seemed to hear the Southern tones of the white girl. He faltered, hesitated, trembled. But before that evening was over he had proposed marriage, and she accepted.

But she made a condition—he must give a present to her father, the chief. It was a reproach among the Modocs for a girl to marry someone who didn't think enough of her to give gifts to other people. Riddle promised. That was practically the extent of the marriage ceremony. Forthwith she gathered up her few personal things and went back with him to his cabin.

This place on Bogus Creek became clean and considerably transformed by her good housekeeping. She put away the dress and habits of a squaw and learned white people's cooking from Riddle. One glorious part of her was let alone

—her dark-brown hair falling down thick over the shawl upon her shoulders.

Chief Se-cot was not pleased at the marriage, or appeased by the six ponies Riddle duly sent him as a dowry-in-reverse. But when the young people visited him in the summer he became reconciled; he liked his paleface son-in-law and found him competent with a gun and upon the trail. He gave Riddle back the ponies.

In 1863 was born their son Charka, otherwise known as Jeff C. Riddle. He associated to some extent with white boys his own age at Yreka and at other settlements, but spent most of his time, and preferred to spend it, with his grandfather, the old chief. When time came for him to love a woman, the Indian half of him was dominant. He married Manda, the daughter of sub-chief Sconchin of the Modocs, who had died on the scaffold with Captain Jack; by her he had five children.

In 1868 Riddle and Winema sold their place on Bogus Creek and moved farther into the wilderness. By now she was widely known as 'Toby' among the whites, though still as Winema among the Indians. In their association they had become completely bilingual. Riddle could talk Modoc as well as she, and she English as well as he, though with an accent somewhat different from that of Kentucky. Winema was Captain Jack's cousin, and served with her husband as interpreter during the Modoc War. Finally, seventeen years after the war, she was granted a government pension of $25 a month.

27

HEATHEN CHINEE

—————

THE SIX COMPANIES served the growing West well, if in their own fashion. They provided raw material of the human variety; they were Chinese, and dealt in their own kind. In 1876 the Ning Yung Company brought to San Francisco 75,000 coolies; the Hop Wo, 34,-000; the Kong Chow, 15,000; the Yung Wo, 12,000; the Sam Yup, 11,000; and the Tan Wo, 4300. The Six Companies passed as benevolent organizations, but with an iron hand each one reached forth and controlled the pigtail who had wandered to Trinidad among the redwoods, or to the high slopes of Shasta, or along the lavas of the Snake, or wherever it might be. No less than a devout Catholic looked for spiritual guidance to Rome, the imported coolie looked for all guidance to the San Francisco headquarters of the Six Companies. Woe to him if he broke a company rule or got too big for his baggy trousers. Swiftly and mysteriously he would be cashiered.

This kind of tight and ruthless control from San Francisco made possible such things as the Oregon and California Railroad strike in 1883. Upon a certain day in January, upon a certain hour, three thousand coolies laid down their tools. Contractors tried to coax, to compromise, and finally to starve them to terms. The Chinese bosses smiled their bland smiles and said there had never been an unsuccessful strike of Chinamen on the Pacific Coast.

But these strong heathen brotherhoods were weak against the race prejudice of the Anti-Chinese & Workingmen's Association and the Order of Caucasians, a pair of Ku Klux Klans working secretly 'to pursue and injure' the Asiatics, and the whites who employed them, 'each and everyone forever.' In Chico on a March evening in 1877 four Chinese were killed in cold blood. The next night a number of notices were mailed after eight o'clock to Chico citizens: 'Get rid of your Chinese help within fifteen days or suffer the consequences—Committee.' A $3000 reward for the killers was offered by the people of Chico, the governor, and the Six Companies. Less than three weeks later the grand jury at the county seat at Oroville indicted fourteen 'Committeemen' for arson or murder, and they were later sentenced to a total of two centuries in prison. Half were members of both secret organizations, whose real leaders escaped punishment to instigate many more outrages at other times and in other places.

The power and long life of the anti-Oriental groups was demonstrated seventeen years later at Grants Pass, Oregon. A bomb was thrown by 'parties unknown' in front of a Chinese wash-house. The determined mayor and council, unable through the local sheriff and marshal to uncover the criminals, brought in a Pinkerton detective. This man put in forty-five days 'at the ferret business' and produced plenty of evidence, as well as a bill for $485.45. The town recorder, backed by a paper with one hundred and forty signatures, refused to sign the warrant.

The harried yellow man found anything but a brother in the redman who was very much his brother in adversity. One of the sayings of the day was that even a wild Indian despised a pigtail. A cage of monkeys passing through Reno was being watched by a Paiute when a white bystander asked him if he knew what they were. "Me know," he said, "China papooses." Though the Jacksonville, Oregon, sheriff was 'China tax collector,' he sometimes had a celestial deputy do the actual taking. In the sheriff's office a Rogue River buck saw the big pile of gold dust the taxes made. Thinking it a good idea, he got a big book and started out. 'The Chinese were deathly afraid of an Indian. So he had no trouble gathering his poll tax. He was having a fine time when the authorities learned what he was up to, and arrested him.' It was characteristic of Chinese-Indian relationships for the former to be at the little end of the deal. At least once it was the other way. John of Oroville in 1856 was making a right good thing out of violating a stern government *don't*—he was selling liquor to the Indians.

The seemingly instinctive hostility of the Indian tribes resulted in a number of tragedies. The greatest of these was the slaughter of fifty Chinese by the Shoshones in southern Idaho in 1866. Only a boy of this whole Asiatic train coming up from Winnemucca escaped. He said his people offered no resistance and begged for mercy, crying out: "Me bellee good Chinaman; me no fightee!" But the savages seemed especially to fancy the scalps with long pigtails. Travelers passing that way a little later saw a shocking sight. The dead, queue-less bodies were strewn along the trail for six miles.

Representative of another group of the oppressed who had no use for the Chinese was Tony Imri, Japanese second cook at the Depot Hotel, Ashland, Oregon. On a fair June evening in 1895, after hearing about a Japanese victory over the Chinese in the Mongolian War, he aroused the fighting spirit in his own breast with several drinks, 'formed a Japanese cohort all by himself,' and invaded Chinatown, where he fired off his pistol promiscuously. A celestial commotion resulted, together with Tony's own prompt arrest by Marshal Smith and a five-day jail sentence by Recorder Berry.

28

NOT FULLY DOCUMENTED

―――――

CHINESE BRIDE

ALMOND-EYED and enameled, Ah Toy had recently come to the remote Idaho town of Warren with Wing Lee, Hang Ki, Ah Lin, and Shun Wo. She was seventeen, and, notwithstanding she was the delectable chattel of the four Chinese miners, still retained an unsoiled freshness of look.

Rough and profane Charlie Beamis was a Warren gambler and the principal Warren saloonkeeper.

Ah Toy was one of the six thousand prostitutes brought from China to the United States after 1852 by the Hip Ye Tong Company and other slave syndicates. The four miners had purchased her in San Francisco at the regular price of $40, and had carried her with them to Warren in 1872, at a time when the town had a white population of four hundred and a Chinese population of twelve hundred. The latter had come to the exhausted placers to rework the tailings of the rich gravel days.

Of her owners, Shun Wo was the handsomest, the ablest,

the most imperious. It wasn't long before he bought his partners out. She would have preferred to be the exclusive property of any one of the others, but hers perforce was the complaisance of a slave.

Ah Toy wore her hair plainly in plaits like a schoolgirl, not with it arranged at the back of her head into rings and knots, ribboned and shiningly waxed and held by gold bodkins. Shun Wo did not want the other Chinese to think he was married to her.

A leader of men is easily recognizable across the barriers of race. Shun Wo and Charlie Beamis came to be on somewhat more equal terms with each other than ordinarily existed between Oriental and Saxon. In a dispute over a card game, a gambler threatened to shoot Charlie's eye out if he didn't do what was wanted. The saloonkeeper not taking the ultimatum seriously and not complying, was shot. The bullet hit the bone at the corner of his left eye, then glanced and plowed deeply along the side of his head. He was not blinded, but the wound laid him up painfully and helplessly in bed for several weeks.

The nature of Beamis' calling and the manner of his injury combined to put him beyond the compassion of the white women of Warren and quite beyond their ministrations. So Shun Wo announced that Ah Toy would nurse him. He not only led the girl into the wounded man's room, but he led her there with a new and convenient name. "I bling Plolly," he said.

Charlie's left eye was bandaged. He felt very miserable, and for several days did not pay much attention with the other. Then he noticed that Ah Toy seemed less enameled than during the few times he had observed her in public with Shun Wo. She was stripped of most of her Chinese artifice as she waited upon him. Clean and fresh, and with her hair in two plaits, she seemed indeed like a schoolgirl.

The deliciousness of her services grew upon him. If she

were absent only a few minutes it appeared to be a long time. "Polly," he would call.

"I come, Mlister Bleamis."

She had a mincing gait. He inquired if her feet had been bound. She explained that the low-caste women brought to America were mostly from the big-footed river people of Canton, but she and the other girls had rounded soles to their shoes so they could imitate the bound-footed gait of the genteel ladies. She showed him one of her shoes. Then she showed him, unhesitatingly at his request, her naked foot, small but undeformed.

But it took much urging to get her to call him Chlallie instead of Mlister Bleamis, and she frequently forgot. He was disturbed by this greater readiness to bare a covered part of her body than to violate a deference. He asked her if she had ever been intimate with a white man. When she said no, he was infinitely relieved, as if her Chinese experiences were less offensive, more forgivable, easier to forget —like a widow's past. But she let him know that many of the Canton girls—many of the six thousand brought to America—slaked Caucasian as well as Mongolian lust, but hardly ever did the same girl provide for both, because the Chinese objected, not the whites. Many Chinese girls were sick; made many whites sick. But she was well.

He wanted her to tell him how she had decided to come to San Francisco; he was almost afraid to hear her answer. Some of the slave girls were sold by their parents; some were lured by false promises; some were shanghaied, and she was one of the latter. Agents of the Hip Ye Tong Company drugged her and carried her aboard ship.

"The goddam sonsabitches!" exclaimed the saloonkeeper in elegant indignation.

His eye healed and he got to feeling pretty much his old self again, and he could have dispensed with Polly a full

week before he did, but during that surplus week he decided he would never dispense with her.

He summoned Shun Wo.

"I want Polly," he said.

"You bluy?" inquired Shun Wo blandly.

"I want to marry her."

"You bluy alleesame."

The Chinese owner, with answers as oblique as his eyes
but wholly understandable, pointed out that when one
bought a girl through the great Hip Ye Tong Company,
the company guaranteed a clear title to her—against American authorities, against rival slave companies, against any
lover. The Hip Ye Tong Company was velly blig and velly
stlong.

A few months later the two were married, and Ah Toy
became Polly Beamis. Then she wore her hair at the back of
her head in rings and coils, ribboned and shiningly waxed
and held by gold bodkins which Charlie Beamis bought.
The people of Warren had to admit that they were the hap-
piest couple in town.

But the people did not quite know how to treat them.
The prostitute had become a magdalene and then a wife,
and this matter did not seem to trouble the community any
more. The problem was whether to behave toward Charlie
Beamis as if he had married a Nez Perce woman. It was
Charlie who settled the question.

He said to several of the men one evening in the saloon:
"You goddam bastards better not try to treat me like a
squaw man. China is about the oldest civilized nation in the
world, and Idaho compared with it is a goddam wilderness,
and women from there ain't squaws."

Later the Beamis' moved to a farm on the South Fork
of Salmon River, where they lived for thirty years. There
is no record of any children. After a third of a century of
happiness together, Charlie died. His Polly remained on the

farm, with occasional trips to Warren, an old Chinese woman revisiting a town as much decayed as herself. She also went at times to the churchyard mound that held her husband, and made a few journeys to Boise to visit Chinese families there, whose language she had by then almost completely forgotten.

While Polly Beamis was living in Idaho, a national law was passed imposing a $2000 fine upon anyone bringing a woman like her from China. So the traffic practically ceased. But six thousand had already come; and these, without hope of descendants, were doomed to occupy alien graveyards until Resurrection Day.

This white man's widow, however, had plenty of money and could have solaced herself with a sepulchre in her homeland. But during her final illness she specified that she should be buried near her husband, and in 1923, in her late seventies, she was laid in a grave companionably beside him.

A MORTUARY MATTER

Dan La Follett was a gambler in a Central Oregon mining camp. To this place hardened gold-diggers had come from California, among them Black Dan, with nimble hands, soft and white withal. He was never short of dust in his clean buckskin poke, but his hands bore no callouses from getting it.

He was tall and handsome, in accordance with the gambler pattern, and it is the nature of a democracy that the rough men looked up to him all the more because he was believed to have come from an excellent family in the East. He was thirty years old, a creditable age for a gambler to achieve.

One man in particular in the new camp considered this life span sufficient. He had lost heavily to the gambler. At the time he showed no more emotion in losing his all than the very polite Black Dan did in taking it. But before another night of activity arrived it became apparent that the loser had harbored passions dark enough. It was a beautiful summer evening near sundown, and Black Dan was standing in front of Marchand's Saloon. There was a pistol shot. Black Dan fell to the earth, his neat clothes at once terribly soiled with dust and blood.

He wasn't dead, but he was wounded beyond recovery. He was hospitalized on a table in the saloon, where, according to the sober chronicle of a veracious historian who had it from an eyewitness, the few short hours left to him were spent as follows: 'To beguile the last weary moments of his earthly pilgrimage he had the women of his acquaintance called in, and they sang songs and poured whisky down his and their own throats until the spark of his unprofitable life was quite extinguished.'

Black Dan's professional associates chipped in with enough dust to hire one Dick Norby to go out to the boothill cemetery and dig a grave in those lonesome precincts under the moon and stars. Norby dug conscientiously deep, and, being used to handling a pick and shovel, got through about an hour after midnight, even though it was hard ground of gravel and earth cemented together through centuries.

Norby didn't go back to the saloon to report. A full day on the gold bars, plus this overtime, had made him tired and sleepy, and he turned in.

But activity was still going on in the saloon, and near the closing hour another man was killed, an amateur gambler this time. Other amateurs made up a purse and hired a certain Sailor Jack to go out and dig this one's grave, ready also for a morning funeral.

The period between two A.M. and dawn, with the moon now dipping close to the horizon and the camp asleep, made the cemetery lonesomer than ever. While he still had the moon, Sailor Jack prospected about to find as soft digging as possible in the hard earth. He saw the mound of fresh dirt, stepped up, and looked down into the rectangular depths which Dick Norby had quitted an hour before.

He hurried down the hill to the cabin of the spokesman for his employers, roused him out of the blankets, announced that the sepulchre was ready, and made the practical suggestion that the corpse be placed therein at once.

The spokesman wanted to know what kind of shenanigans Sailor Jack was trying to pull. He couldn't possibly have dug a grave so soon. It would take him till daylight, and he'd have to put muscle into it to finish by then.

"I'm tellin' you the grave is ready," declared Sailor Jack. "Get your man up there and I'll guarantee a place for him."

So the amateurs carried their comrade up and put him in.

The next morning, at sunup, the professional gambler pallbearers ascended boothill with their comrade. The women who had assisted in the dead gambler's expiring gaities walked behind, with countenances set suitably in grief. After them tramped the whole camp.

At the mound of fresh earth the pallbearers set the corpse down in astonished discomfiture, for though life is a gamble, a receptacle of lifeless clay never had been before.

Black Dan's grave had been jumped.

THE CHICKEN DISPUTE

The Fire Underwriters Association of the Pacific describe how in 1897, in the good days of McKinley & Hanna, Al Overton was issued policy No. 41,144 by the Farmers' Mutual Insurance Company at its Gold Hill agency in the Rogue River valley of southern Oregon.

The policy was in the sum of $100, covering 'hens and roosters, plucked or unplucked, in coop, field, hen-house, or crate, while situated about the insured's ranch of forty acres, more or less, lying in a southerly direction three miles from Gold Hill.' In event of loss, the company was not to be liable for mixed breeds in a proportion exceeding $1 for three hens, or roosters, as the case might be; and for Plymouth Rocks, not exceeding $1 for two fowls of that strain. Early in 1898 Mr. Overton's hen-house burned down from causes unknown. George Foote, special adjuster came at once from the home office.

"Mr. Overton," he said, "it appears that you lost by this fire 120 hens and roosters of mixed breeds, and 120 Plymouth Rocks."

"That's right," said Mr. Overton.

"Do you or do you not consider it significant that the exact number lost in each case was 120?"

The bereft poultryman lifted his eyes from the ground that was still littered roundabout with scorched feathers, and answered, "Oh, it just happened to come that way."

"Well, we'll call it a coincidence. Our contract is to pay you at the rate of $1 for each three of the mixed chickens, and $1 for each two of the Plymouth Rocks."

"That's what the policy says," remarked Mr. Overton.

"Now $1 for three and $1 for two are equal to $2 for five, are they not?"

The insured, after slowly doing some mental arithmetic, admitted that this computation was correct.

"Then," continued the adjuster, "at the rate of $2 for five chickens, a hundred chickens would be $40, wouldn't they?"

"Yes, that's correct."

"Then," went on Mr. Foote, "two hundred would come to $80, and forty more would be $16, making a total of $96."

"Well, I reckon that's right," acknowledged Mr. Overton hesitantly and disappointedly; "but when I figured it in the house I made it $100, and so did the children and the schoolmaster who boards with us."

Mr. Foote gave him a check for $96, took a receipt, gathered in the policy, and left.

When Mr. Overton went into the house, Mrs. Overton looked at the check questioningly. Johnny, aged thirteen, and Martha, aged eleven, looked at it disapprovingly. The schoolmaster, regarded in the neighborhood as a mathematical prodigy, looked at it the longest and most severely.

"But let us not be precipitate in considering it in error," he said. Whereupon, at the kitchen table, he began to figure. Johnny on one side of him and Martha on the other, leaned over the red-framed slate. They added, subtracted, multiplied, divided. They calculated it in all kinds of ways. They finally took time out for supper, and Mr. Overton did the chores, simple now in the absence of the chickens. As soon as the dishes were washed and the table cleared, the three cipherers returned to their calculations by the light of a kerosene lamp (for the California Light & Power Company had not yet brought a switch-on brightness to the Rogue River valley, magically manufactured by the swift Rogue River itself).

Mr. Overton, ingloriously ignored in the figuring, sat and looked at the mathematicians, waiting in suspense for the decision. When the schoolmaster's brow wrinkled, and shallow creases appeared above Johnny's eyes and upon Martha's arrogant little forehead, he had hopes that $96 was going to turn out to be correct. But at midnight the schoolmaster declared that the right amount was unmistakably, demonstrably, incontrovertibly $100.

During the next few days, Mr. Overton's family and the schoolmaster made Mr. Overton seem very witless and simple and mathematically incompetent. They told the neighbors and the neighbors joked Mr. Overton. They joked him so much that he got mad and brought suit against the Farmer's Mutual Insurance Company for $4 and costs, alleging fraud.

The case was tried in the courthouse in Jacksonville. Since the whole southern part of the county was divided into two mathematical camps, the crowd was large. Mr. Overton's derisive neighbors were there, and his unsympathetic family, and the schoolmaster, who expected to be called as a mathematical expert, and also Mr. Foote, formal and aloof.

Mr. Overton felt very much alone. He wished with all his heart he would lose. In that way he would win—win back his self-respect.

The judge decided not to call up any witnesses or to ask for expert testimony (whereat the schoolmaster's face fell), but he explained that he had gone over all the evidence and had given it hours of the most judicial analysis. He believed he had decided the matter justly, and his decision was as follows:

"The case appears to be resolved into one main question: Did the loss of said fowls by the assured constitute a legal claim against said insurance company to the full amount of $100? That is quite easily demonstrated, to-wit, namely: 120 divided by 3 equals 40 multiplied by $1 equals $40. 120 divided by 2 equals 60 multiplied by $1 equals $60. $40 plus $60 equals $100, total loss.

"Defendant claims that $96 is the loss, which, if figures cannot lie, appears to be correct: $1 for three and $1 for two equals $2 for five. Two-fifths of 240 equals $96.

"It is clear that there is a difference of $4, but where it comes in is not so apparent. Still it must be remembered that courts are not schools of higher mathematics. After carefully weighing the evidence, judgment is given against the defendant in the sum of $4, while the costs, which we assess nominally in a like sum, will be paid by the plaintiff."

The decision, of course, confirmed Mr. Overton's simplicity. He made up his mind to sell out, move across the Siskiyous into Shasta Valley, and once more hold his head high. So in time the Rogue River valley lost an upright citizen.

29

CALL IT FOLKLORE

IT'S THE CLIMATE

Lest you think the following piece on the subject of earthly immortality is inspired by one of two well-known books, please be advised that the substance of it was printed in the *National Magazine* for October, 1855, and that H. Rider Haggard's *She* was not published until 1886 and James Hilton's *Lost Horizon* not until 1933. The hero, furthermore, did not find his strange experience in a land of mystery, but fell victim to the lifegiving power of the California climate.

He was a Spaniard, Manuel Lombardo by name, with a hacienda in the Sacramento Valley about halfway between the Buttes and Mt. Shasta. He was too far away to see the former, but the latter was in constant view in good weather, and the weather was mostly good, that being the mischievous cause of Lombardo's mounting and ever-mounting years.

This Spanish gentleman had an heir, an adopted son Felipe. Lombardo had got in on the ground floor of about everything in northern California, for at this time, 1855, he was two hundred fifty years old, and since a very little money put out at compound interest in his early days would of course have increased tremendously during the interval, there was a great deal for Felipe to wait for. But the waiting was unconscionably long, and held no promise of ending. Senor Lombardo, notwithstanding his venerable years, seemed to be practically indestructible. The northern California climate had kept him in perfect health. He was as supple as a boy.

Lombardo felt all right physically, but in spirit he was tired of life. Early friends, upon whom the Sacramento climate had not had so life-prolonging an effect, were gone. He was so enormously advanced in years that all the superannuated oldsters referred to him as grandpa. If they hadn't known he was two hundred fifty years of age he could have passed for being as young or even younger than some of them. But they did know it, particularly since Felipe, on his birthday, had ordered up a vast cake with almost as many little candles on it as quills upon the fretful porcupine.

Senor Lombardo was lonely, companionless in any true sense; without human sympathy. If he referred to something that happened a hundred and fifty years before, his auditors looked blank. So the greater portion of his rich existence had to be kept suppressed. He lived, as it were, upon the latter surface of his years.

He wanted to die. But there seemed no chance in a natural way. He thought of suicide, but the padres told him that was sinful. He was nominally a good Christian, so he banished that idea from his mind.

At last Felipe suggested he try the effect of another climate.

"Where?" asked Lombardo.

"China," answered Felipe.

He went over his will with his lawyer, the latter assuring him that it was in good order and Felipe would get everything promptly.

"He's had to wait so long already, I don't want him to be delayed by the courts."

"Felipe will get the property at once," the lawyer assured him.

It was a happy Felipe who saw his adopted father off on the boat. Lombardo was no less happy. It was committing suicide, if you came right down to it, but in a way which the padres said was not sinful.

In China that soon happened which he devoutly wished and which everybody expected.

Now, when a Chinaman dies in America, his strongest wish is to be shipped dead to China. In reverse, Lombardo desired above all things to be returned to northern California, and to be sepulchered near the old Sacramento Valley hacienda. He had stipulated in the will that his corpse should be brought back for burial. The penalty for Felipe's not doing so would be disinheritance.

So Senor Lombardo was shipped home and interred with due ceremony in the family cemetery. The padres prayed for his soul, which they supposed to be on its way to heaven, for a person can do an immense amount of good in two hundred fifty years. Felipe was happy, for on Friday all the money, all the mortgages that were held, all the land, all the compound interest—everything would be turned over to him.

But no sooner was Lombardo enclosed in the soil of northern California, with the Sacramento zephyrs blowing over his grave, than he came to life. And it didn't take him until Friday to do so, either. He arose on Wednesday. Being endowed with herculean strength, he burst through the precincts of the tomb, and made his living appearance before the chopfallen heir in the hacienda. Felipe wanted to believe at first that he was only a ghost, but was convinced soon enough to the contrary.

The old man, finding himself unable even to *stay dead* in northern California, quietly submitted to his fate.

SAZERAC LYING CLUB

Uncle John Gibbons in the 'sixties was the stage driver between Belmont, near the southern end of the Toquma range, and Austin, near the northern end of the Toiyabe range—two high, narrow Nevada mountain ridges lying close alongside each other one hundred seventy-five miles east of Reno, appearing upon a large map almost as if the middle and index finger of a man's hand were traced there. In the trough between them is the Great Smoky Valley, and about two-thirds of the way toward Austin is a big salt marsh.

Belmont—once county seat of Nye County, where a sixth of a billion dollars in precious ores was mined—has now passed away like a tale that is told. Austin, now on Route 50 and containing five hundred souls, once had ten thousand, including five preachers, twelve doctors, and thirty-three lawyers.

In Austin, Uncle John Gibbons was a prominent member of the Sazerac Lying Club, named in honor of the Sazerac Saloon. The town's editor, Fred H. Hart (said to have been Bret Harte's cousin), took down the things Uncle John and the other members related, and printed them in his paper, the *Reese River Reveille*. Still later he gathered the chronicles into a book which he had published in San Francisco in 1878.

Ordinarily, Uncle John brought the stage into Austin right on the dot when it was due. One day he was very late. When he finally arrived, he dumped off the mailsacks and express packages—not having any passengers that trip—and drove on to the barn without vouchsafing an explanation of why he was a good three hours behind time.

He kept silent until the evening the Sazerac Lying Club met. Then he explained in full.

In the Great Smoky Valley, several miles after changing horses at the halfway stage station and a short distance after leaving the salt marsh, he saw ahead of him what he first thought was a dark, heavy bank of clouds descending athwart the road into the valley. But, as the stage approached nearer, imagine his astonishment when he perceived unmistakably that the thick, roily volume of vapor was actually a great mass of living creatures. In minute detail he described it to his fellow Sazeracs—and the rest of the account follows in Uncle John's exact words:

"The team was gittin' kind of scary, but I held 'em level, and as I kept gittin' nearer I saw the thing warn't nothin' but a flock of sage-hen; so I jest threw the silk at the leaders, and yelled fire and brimstone at the wheelers, calk'latin' to slash the team squar through the flock without any trouble.

"But, boys, thar was more sage-hen obstructin' of that road than I had reckoned on: and when the leaders struck into them sage-hen, they was throwed back on their haunches jest as if they had butted clean up agin a stun wall. As far as you could see thar warn't nothin' but sage-hen; you could about see the top of the pile of 'em.

"Thar I was, banked up by a lot of insignificant sage-hen, and the United States mail detained in the road by feathers —as you might remark. Wal, to make a long story short, I unhitched one of the wheelers and straddled him and rode back to the station for help. A prospectin' feller was sittin' by the fire. I stated the situation. The hostler and the cook they saddled up some of the stage stock and got a couple of axes, intendin' to go back with me and chop a road through the sage-hen. But this here prospector he spoke up and says he:

" 'See here, boys,' says he, 'don't you think we could blast 'em out quicker'n we could chop through 'em?'

"And the hostler and the cook spoke up and said they thought so too.

"And then this here prospector got his blastin' apparatus, and then the whole raft of us started back for the place where the stage was; and when we got thar—wal, I wish I may be runned over if thar was a sage-hen in sight as far's a man could see with a spy-glass."

Members of the Sazerac Lying Club had to take their turns. Nobody could hog all the telling. Uncle John had no wish to do so; he enjoyed the recitals that came to his ears almost as much as those that went out of his mouth. He heard about the smoke that was so thick in a choked chimney that it had to be dug out with a pickax, and about the mean mining boss and his faithful gunpowder man—the latter, while ramming a blasting hole, was blown skyhigh, came down in the same place and continued ramming, but was niggardly docked the sixteen minutes he was in the air.

In advance of Uncle John's regular turn one evening there was an inquiry about the salt marsh which he had to pass on each stage trip coming and going. At one time nine camels had been employed to haul the salt to the quartz mill at Austin—part of the official herd bought for desert use by Jefferson Davis when he was Secretary of War. Auctioned off by the government to one of the keepers, these nine had successfully plodded back and forth with their heavy loads through the Great Smoky Valley, justifying in one instance, at least, the wisdom of their original purchaser, who was then spending troubled days in Richmond as president of the Confederate States of America.

When asked how the salt works were coming on, Uncle John replied:

"Bad, rather bad, that is, bad for the salt company which is losin' considerable salt, but good for the ranchers and some other people."

"How's that, Uncle John?"

"Wal, you see, the pipe leaks."

"What of that?"

Uncle John explained to him and other Sazeracs:

"The salt water that runs through the leak evaporates soon as it strikes the air, and the wind, which is always blowin' in the valley, ketches up the salt and carries it over the valley in clouds. For a mile each way from the marsh the air's so thick with salt that half the time I can't see the stage team, and it jest keeps rainin' salt all the time. When the ranchers in the valley want salt, they jest set an open sack out in front of the house, and in less than twenty minutes it's filled chock up to the mouth with the finest kind of cookin' salt."

NEVADA TELEVISION IN THE 'SEVENTIES

In mountainous countries, owing to the rarefaction of the atmosphere, the range of human vision is very wide. There are high places in Nevada plainly discernible at a distance of over two hundred miles. The extent of Nevada vision was the subject at one meeting of the Sazerac Lying Club.

"Mr. Old Reliable," said the Chair, "let's hear your little lie."

This member spoke as follows, soberly and without interruption:

"I'd hear tell so much about the light air in this country, and how a man could see a deer on top of a mountain a hundred mile off, that I made up my mind to try somethin'.

"The other mornin' I climbed up onto the summit of Mount Promethus to take a peep and see what I could see. The mornin' was clear, not a cloud bein' in the sky, and when I began to look over west, the fust thing I seed was Virginny City, strung out along the side of old Mount Davidson jest natural as life.

"I thought at fust it was a mirage, cause Virginny is a hundred and eighty miles from here in a air line; but I soon seed that the thing was as real and honest as the Methodist Church steeple, which was a pretty considerable distance off, as you may know, but it didn't seem more'n twenty foot away from me.

"Wal, I got to lookin' around to see what was goin' on in Virginny. I seed the quartz wagons goin' through the streets, and the minin' superintenders drivin' around with their spang-up teams, and all the population bowin' and scrapin' to 'em; and I seed a couple of fellows havin' a shootin' scrape on C Street, and the ladies steppin' across the street and holdin' up their dresses and most of 'em had on striped stockings.

"I couldn't hear the steam whistles on the histin' works at the mines, but I could see when they tooted 'em, and I could see 'em changin' shifts at some of the mines, and the night shift comin' up on the cage and the day shift goin' down.

"But the most important thing I seed was in the courthouse. I looked into the county jail, and I seed a feller what was in for stealin' a bronco horse, sittin' in cell Number Four filin' off his irons. He was red-headed, had a wart on his nose and checkered pants and a Californy gray shirt. I came down as quick as I could, and told the sheriff up here at the courthouse, and he sent a telegraph to the sheriff over at Virginny, tellin' of him to look out for cell Number Four.

"Pretty soon he got a answer, and the Virginny sheriff said that cell Number Four held a awful criminal who had jest escaped by blowin' up the courthouse with nitro-glycerine, and he was goin' out in a couple of days—soon as a reward was offered—to hunt up that feller what had escaped from Number Four."

A ROLLING STONE

Marial is a backwoods post office in Curry County, the southwestern corner of Oregon. It remained especially remote up nearly to the time of the Second World War. From Marial the mail went sixteen miles by pack mule to Illahee on the Rogue, eight by truck down that rushing stream to Agness, on down the river thirty-two miles by motorboat to the Gold Beach boat landing, by truck six miles to Gold Beach, then by motor stage one hundred and thirty-two miles by way of Crescent City to Grants Pass. A letter mailed at Marial on Tuesday would get to Portland the following Monday. Much, very much like old times!

The man who handled the pack-train part of the postal service was Hathaway Jones. Forty years he had been carrying the United States mail in the Coast range mountains.

"Mr. Jones," said a visitor, "in all that time you must have seen some pretty queer things?"

"Sure have," he agreed, "more'n most people, I guess. Queerest thing I ever saw, though, didn't happen while I was carryin' mail. Want to hear about it?"

"Go ahead."

So, without further interruption, Hathaway Jones, veteran pack-mule man of Curry County, gave the following account of what he personally saw along a wild, canyoned tributary of the Rogue River where it dashes through the Coast range:

"I was out huntin'. About twenty years ago, I guess it was. In October. Was comin' down a long ridge, it was gettin' along late in the day, and I was about tuckered out from all the uphill walkin'. I come to a big boulder, shady and cool on the side away from the sun. I set down to rest, with my gun across my knees, and then leaned back—and, instead of the dern thing being solid, I thought it moved with my weight, big as it was.

"I turned around and pushed on it with my hand. I could move it as easy as anythin'. It was about twelve feet through itself, but it was balanced on a little rock not a foot through.

"I thought to myself, it would sure be fun to roll it down

into the canyon. Its size would sure make it go a-tearin'.

"I give it a good hard push and it kind of rocked a little. Pretty soon I got it to teeterin' good and then away she went. The canyon was about two thousand feet to the bottom and it was awful steep.

"Well, you know, it just plowed a furrow right down through the trees, and you could look down and see it tearin' along. It went down to the bottom, and—get me—instead of stoppin' it went right up the other side, pretty near to the top. Fact I thought it was goin' right over.

"It got just about to the top, like I say, and then back down it come, right down the same track. And—get me— when it got to the bottom, it didn't stop either, but come right back up toward me. It was comin' fast, too.

"I got scared, thinkin' it might knock a tree down on me. So I got a good long ways off. But it didn't. It got right near to the place I'd pushed it off from, and stopped, and down she went again.

"I had all the rock-rollin' I wanted that day. So I went on home.

"Well, it was near two years later, about the same time of the year, too, in another October, I come walkin' up this same canyon. But I just didn't think about it bein' the same one right then.

"I come along, not thinkin' about the year before, and then I looked and there seemed to be quite an open spot, a kind of cleared right-of-way, in the trees just ahead. Then I heard the queerest rattlin' sound, like no animal ever made. I got up to the open place, and—get me—there was a strip of bare ground kind of like a ditch and fifteen feet wide, runnin' way up to near the top on both sides of that canyon.

"And, you know, about that time I heard the queer rattlin' sound again, and here, down in the bottom of the ditch, come a little rock about the size of a little marble, rollin' like everything. It kept a-comin' and a-comin' till it got near to where I was and then got slower and stopped. Right away it went down again, and went way out of sight in the bottom of the canyon and up the other side. Pretty soon it come back again, and that went on all the time I stood there and watched it.

"And—get me—that big rock I pushed over two years before must have been a-rollin' all that time, till it was wore down, as I say, no bigger'n a marble, and was still a-rollin' and I reckon' gettin' smaller. Anyhow, when I come along there the next year I couldn't see nothin' or hear that rattlin' sound in the faintest way, and bushes was growin' up in the bare strip."

LAVA POSTSCRIPT

The lava region of today is not to be thought of as forbidding, bleak, and desolate. Some of its human associations have here been recorded, yet these but touch upon man's total enterprise, which has made, and each year is making, the ancient Circle of Fire into an agreeable place to live and an especially attractive place to visit. It is now an area of fifty-odd counties, prosperous towns and cities, watercourses and thoroughfares, forests, fields, and pastures, manufactories and great construction works.

In terms of supporting a population, it is rich with an inexhaustible richness. One of its counties raises five million bushels of potatoes a year; another is the non-redwoods lumber capital of the world. Its thriving communities are uncrowded, with such little concentration that Boise, Reno, and Klamath Falls, three hundred miles away from one another, are the biggest centers.

It is even a dispensation that in this land all the fire has not even yet gone out of the lava. In Klamath Falls eight hundred homes and buildings, besides a section of highway, are heated by the underlying natural hot water. A property owner, to tap this warmth, merely has to sink a well 125 to 800 feet deep and lower a pipe coil into it. He gets water with a temperature varying from 165° to 210°F.

A land of extraordinary wealth. If a desert, how dominated by oases.

And how immune to exploitation, for the supreme wreckage by the molten rocks contradictorily stored up resources that will never give out, as represented by its soil. The period of fire has produced a supply of compost beyond the capacity of a million fertilizer plants. The lava has crumbled into an impalpable powder and been mixed with long accumulations of decaying vegetation. The great cliffs and basaltic heaps contain nearly all the elements to feed vegetable life, and since basaltic rock is fragile and short-lived, its pulverization into soil is continually going on, producing loam through mechanical breaking-down, water erosion, and chemical decomposition. In this manner fertile acres are constantly being built up. The soils of volcanic origin are the most productive and most lasting of all soils. As you look at piles of basaltic rock from a motor car, they might give you the impression of a poor country; in reality it is one of the richest in the world.

Yet it is not an expanse of tame shires. It is still a bold and striking land. This is so because it is an oasis land. The taking of abundance from the rich areas does not injure the setting, which continues in a vastness of peaks and buttes and ridges and rimrocks and black volcanic plains.

Here man is seen at his best. There are no evidences of his spoliation, only evidences of his building-up, hand in hand with penitent nature which is also immensely active in rebuilding. Lava inhabitants perforce have to work to erase and restore; and where the toiler is, not driven but of himself eager, there also is the dreamer.

INDEX

INDEX

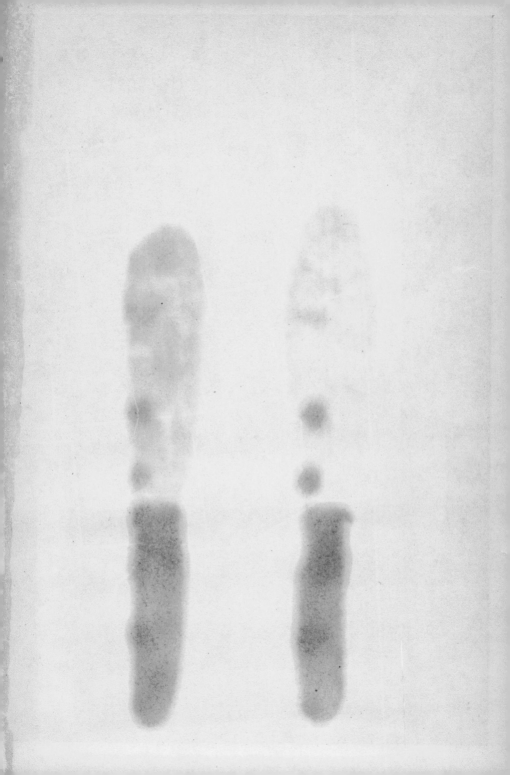

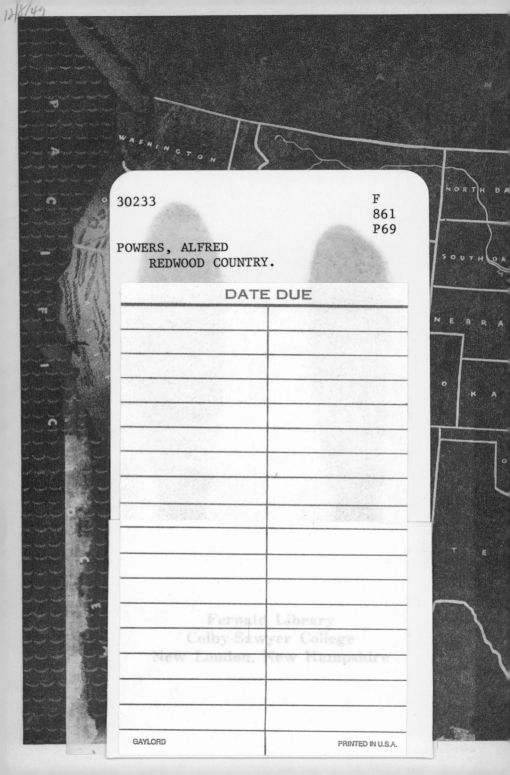